The Music Story Series

EDITED BY
FREDERICK J. CROWEST.

THE STORY OF MINSTRELSY

The Music Story Series.

3/6 net per Volume.

Already published in this Series.

THE STORY OF ORATORIO. By ANNIE PATTERSON, B.A., Mus. Doc. With Illustrations.

THE STORY OF NOTATION. By C. F. ABDY WILLIAMS, B.A., Mus. Bac. With Illustrations.

THE STORY OF THE ORGAN. By C. F. ABDY WILLIAMS, M.A., Mus. Bac. With Illustrations.

THE STORY OF CHAMBER MUSIC. By N. KILBURN, Mus. Bac. With Illustrations.

THE STORY OF THE VIOLIN. By PAUL STOEVING. With Illustrations.

THE STORY OF THE HARP. By W. H. GRATTAN FLOOD, Mus. Doc. With Illustrations.

THE STORY OF ORGAN MUSIC. By C. F. ABDY WILLIAMS, M.A., Mus. Bac. With Illustrations.

THE STORY OF ENGLISH MUSIC (1604-1904)—MUSICIANS' COMPANY LECTURES.

This Series, in superior leather bindings, may be had on application to the Publishers.

English "Six men's" Song. 13th Century.

Sumer is icumen in.

This composition, attributed to John Fornsete, monk of Reading, establishes England's musical pre-eminence in the 13th century. In the original parchment the stave lines are coloured red. En

The Story of Minstrelsy

BY

EDMONDSTOUNE DUNCAN

London
The Walter Scott Publishing Co., Ltd.
New York: Charles Scribner's Sons
1907

MADE AND PRINTED
IN GREAT BRITAIN.

"To pretend to frame a history, or anything resembling one, from the scanty gleanings it is possible to collect upon the subject of our ancient songs and vulgar music, would be vain and ridiculous. To bring under one view the little fragments and slight notices which casually offer themselves in the course of extensive reading, and sometimes when they are least likely to occur, may possibly serve to gratify a sympathetic curiosity, which is all here aimed at, and when so little is professed, there can scarcely be reason to complain of disappointment."

RITSON'S "DISSERTATION."

Preface.

An inquiry into the origin of Minstrelsy would necessitate a consideration of the earliest beginnings of Folk-song, the invention of which, if not anterior to, is in all likelihood coeval with the origin of Speech. But men may have sung before speech was vouchsafed them. The animal world gives the thought a curious impulse:

> "Hark! hark! the lark at Heaven's gate sings."

Man's highest Te Deum can do little more.

The curious may discover some pleasure in tracing the faint—almost illegible—characters which stand for the first records of music. Such an enterprise, however interesting, is not within the scope of our book. "Language," says Max Müller, "begins where interjections end. There is as much difference between a real word, such as *to laugh* and the interjection *ha! ha!*

between *I suffer* and *oh!* as there is between the involuntary act and noise of sneezing and the verb *to sneeze*. We sneeze and cough, and scream and laugh, in the same manner as animals; but if Epicurus tells us that we speak in the same manner as dogs bark, moved by nature, our own experience will tell us that this is not the case." That scream and laugh is possibly the first hint at emotional expression—apart from speech. One can further picture the cries of rage and pain, of defiance and warning, which primitive man must have uttered, in a language not that of speech, but rather a musical foreshadowing of the battle-cry, the hunting song, the funeral chant; for the struggle for existence would explain the two first, while the third should be as old as the human race.

We must, of course, look to the East for the original attempts at a systematized music. It is the privilege of ancient history to mix facts with fables, or where the first is wanting, to supply the second. Thus, we read that music was invented by the Emperor Fu Hsi (B.C. 2852). If so, the effort must have exhausted the musical energy of China, which to this day has got no farther than single sounds; and, if we are to believe

Preface

Van Aalst, these are delivered without any expression. There is a painting on one of the tombs in the Pyramids which represents a group of eight flute-players engaged in concert, the date of which (according to Lepsius) is prior to 2000 B.C. An instrument probably older than the flute was discovered at Dordogne (France)—a kind of whistle formed by boring a sound-hole in the hollow bone of an animal (some two inches in length). It is presumed (by M. Lartet) to have been

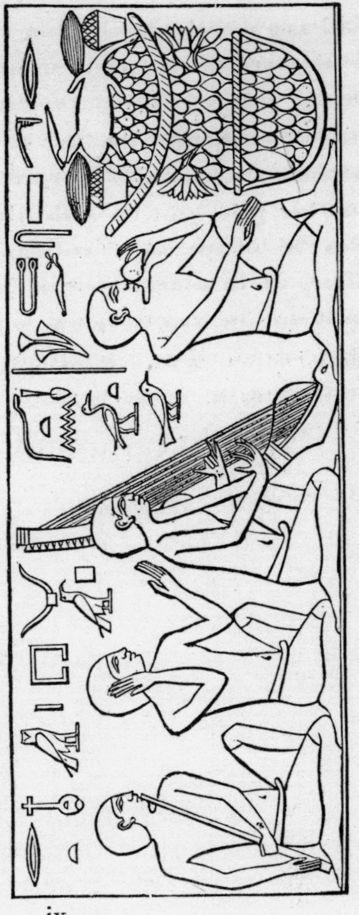

FIG. 1.—AN EGYPTIAN CONCERT.

used as a whistle when hunting animals. Hardly more reliable are the accounts which fix the origin of the Druids' orders in Britain as dating from 1013 B.C., or the introduction of the harp into Ireland by Heber and Heremon, 1000 B.C. Those who would have history cast her pale light on such dark times must be glad even of scraps such as these. But the only real history which concerns music is that contained in the fossil remains, sculpture, and painting of ancient times, which needs more elucidation than it has hitherto received, to be of any popular use.

EDMONDSTOUNE DUNCAN.

October, 1907.

Contents.

CHAPTER VI.

CHAPTER VII.

CHAPTER VIII.

CHAPTER IX.

Contents

Story of Minstrelsy

CHAPTER XV.

OF SONGS.

CHAPTER XVI.

APPENDIX A.

APPENDIX B.

APPENDIX C.

List of Illustrations.

The Story of Minstrelsy.

CHAPTER I.

Definition of Minstrelsy—Druids—Pytheas—*Saxon Chronicle*—Thor and Wodin—Vortigern—Wassail—Caxton's *Chronicle*—Scalds—Romans—King Arthur—Gleemen—Bede—Alfred the Great—Anlaf the Dane—Cnut—The Horn—Chanson Roland.

MINSTRELSY scarcely needs a set definition; for, though it originally applied to the art of a particular class of musician, the word has grown with the times, and, without violence to its derivation, has come to mean much more. In our pages it stands for the whole body of secular song which is not too new to be unproved by Time, and which possesses sufficient breadth to be ranked as National. The chief merit of such a definition is its convenience. Thus "Lilliburlero" and "Rule Britannia" may be discussed, no less than "Chevy Chase" or the "Agincourt Song"; not, indeed, that we erroneously imagine Purcell or Arne to be minstrels, but because their work so sufficiently reproduces the true spirit of national song as to make any representative collection absurd lacking them. The use of the word *minstrel* in the Old Testament seems to have been in the sense of an instrumental musician. "But now bring me a minstrel," commanded the prophet Elisha. "And it came to pass, when the minstrel played, that the hand of the Lord came upon him." In the description of the raising of Jairus's daughter (Matt. ix. 23, 24), we read that when our Saviour "came into the ruler's house, and saw the minstrels and the people making a noise, He said unto them, Give place: for the maid is not dead, but sleepeth."

Dr. Percy's famous definition of the minstrels as "an order of men in the Middle Ages, who subsisted by the arts of poetry and music, and sang to the harp verses composed by themselves, or others," fitted very well the Provençal joglar, who was both poet and musician, and travelled from court to court; but when it came to be employed in connection with the English joglar, the class had so changed that minstrel meant mountebank, travelling showman, tavern singer.

Stafford Smith no doubt had this in mind when he wrote that "great confusion is observable in the writings of most of those who have professed to give any account of the minstrels; in which term they seem to have included, without distinction, the three classes of men which ought to have been kept separate—the Common Harpers, the Minstrels, and the Provençal Poets." A clear definition of the minstrel class is given by Riemann as follows:—"Minstrels (*Ménestrels; Ménétriers*) was the special name of the musicians in the service of the Troubadours (*Trouvères*); they developed the songs devised by the troubadours (with viol, and probably also hurdy-gurdy accompaniment). But those poets and singers who were not born of noble blood were also termed minstrels (*Troveori bastarti*); the name troubadour was only given to knights. Finally, the term minstrel acquired the general meaning of musician, especially fiddler (performer on the viol)."

Druids

Caius, the historian, gives the date 1013 B.C. as the period when the Druids' orders originated in Britain. That it should be some nine years before the accredited date of the Creation and Fall of Man appears to have been no drawback. Certain it is that for many centuries, whatever of music was fostered in our islands among the rude and barbarous inhabitants of those remote times, the Druids were the only class of men likely to have cultivated and developed its capabilities. The entire culture of the nation—such as it was—appears to have been in the hands of this powerful priesthood. The three chief orders were the Druids (proper), the Vates, and the Bards. Nothing could be done without the direct advice and influence of the Druid chiefs; indeed, originally, with the Aryan and other races, the chief was priest as well as king. The Celts gradually established a distinct order of priesthood, whose principal duties lay in invoking the unknown deities to succour their friends and frustrate their foes; divination—by a study of the stars, clouds, wind, smoke, the flight of birds—sacrifices, human and otherwise. The Bards, it is understood, were poets and musicians. Marcellinus (who, with Strabo, may be considered an ancient authority on the matter) tells us that the Bards were accustomed to sing in heroic verse the brave deeds and illustrious acts of their countrymen, accompanied on the lyre. The dress of the order was a kind of long habit, which, in the case of an officiating priest, would be covered with a white surplice. In Ireland, the bards' graduate wore six colours in their robes, said to be the striped *braccæ* of the Gauls, still worn by the Highlanders. From the Bardic MSS. it is further seen that kings wore seven colours, lords and ladies five, governors of fortresses four, officers and gentlemen three, soldiers two, and the people but one colour.

Bards

Strabo relates that the special office of the Bards, or Hymners (as he calls them), was to celebrate in verse the praises of their national gods and heroes. The epic poems thus brought into circulation, handed down traditionally, would further contain much of native history. These poetical pieces were recited with an accompaniment of the lyre. Doubtless, the bard also had a place in the high ritual of the mystic ceremonial celebrated in the oaken groves—in the sacrifice to the sun, or the culling, with golden sickle, of the sacred mistletoe. Incantation may have had its accompaniment. Plutarch records a vile use to which music was put when he states that the cries of the victims in the human sacrifices of the Druids were drowned by the sound of songs and musical instruments.[1] As the tide of Latin and Teutonic influence swept the southern and eastern shores of England, the Druid bards were driven west and north—to Ireland, Wales, and North Scotland. Long after the name of the order had perished the practices survived, particularly in Ireland, where they obtained until the fifth century, when St. Patrick put an end to the system. In Wales, too, the bardic orders were definitely instituted with a legal standing. To this day—when not set aside by religious revivals—the Eisteddfodau is a popular survival of gatherings which in earlier days English kings were wont to summon. Beyond a small interchange of melodic property, Wales, Ireland, and Scotland do not seem to have had a really marked influence upon English Minstrelsy, if one is permitted to judge from surviving folk-song. No reliable bardic airs of real antiquity have come down to us,[2] though there are many traces of Druidism surviving even to this day, such as the ceremonies of All-Hallowmas and the bonfires of May-day and

[1] The "Holy Inquisition" put music to the same abuse.

[2] It is not unlikely that some of the Irish airs have an origin in the times which are alluded to above, but conjecture is quite vain in such matters, and of historical guidance there appears to be none. With regard to the Welsh claims, there seems no reason for doubting that some of the airs date from the tenth century, and that the harmony is not, as Burney imagined, spurious, though so late a date as the tenth century is outside the period above considered.

Midsummer-eve, which hint at the grim ritual of pre-Christian days.

Commenting upon a passage in Shakespeare, Dr. Burney remarks (*Hist.* iii. p. 335): "Poker and tongs, marrow-bones and cleavers, salt-box, hurdy-gurdy, etc., are the old national instruments of music on our island." The hurdy-gurdy, a stringed instrument of great antiquity, is known to have been in use before the Norman Conquest; while to the other instruments mentioned by the learned doctor, if not so respectable, a still remoter use may be allowed.

Pytheas

When Pytheas, the Greek navigator and geographer (384-322 B.C.), visited the Cornish shores he observed the custom, peculiar to the natives, of carrying horns, which, judging from early specimens, were capable of being employed alike for musical purposes and for those of drinking. It is difficult to estimate what effect the Roman invasion can have had upon music. No doubt for many years the martial tones of the battle-trumpet would be all that the Saxon heard of his polished invader's art. Yet in the armed camps and settlements many an ancient lay must have helped to charm away the tedious winter hours. The entry in the *Saxon Chronicle* is characteristic of the sparseness of historic material which helps us in our sketch of these times:—

"Sixty winters ere that Christ was born,[1] Caius Julius, Emperor of the Romans, with eighty ships sought Britain.

[1] The true dates are 54 and 55 B.C.

There he was first beaten in a dreadful fight, and lost a great part of his army. Then he let his army bide with the Scots,[1] and went south into Gaul. There he gathered six hundred, with which he went back into Britain. When they first rushed together, Cæsar's tribune, whose name was Labienus, was slain. Then took the Welsh sharp piles, and drove them with great clubs into the water, at a certain ford in the river called Thames. When the Romans found that, they would not go over the ford. Then fled the Britons to the fastnesses of the woods; and Cæsar, having after much fighting gained many of the chief towns, went back into Gaul."

There is extant a curious form of oath, which was imposed on the Saxon of the eighth century when abjuring Paganism: "I renounce the devil and all his works and words, Thunaer [Thor], Wodan, and Saxon Odin, and all such sorcerers their familiars." Although Odin had come to be regarded as a mythological personage, even to the extent of idolatry, there seems to be good ground for believing him to have been a real historical character.[2] This warlike prince, powerfully aided by a regular order of minstrels, seers, and priests, succeeded in reviving the old mythology and mysteries of the North. Odin not only gave to the world all the materials of a great epic, he also founded a kingdom. All literature and music

[1] An error arising from the MSS. of Orosius and Bede containing the words *in Hiberniam* for *in hiberna.* The text should therefore read "in winter quarters."

[2] "I am inclined," says Schlegel in *The History of Literature*, "to adopt the opinion of those who regard Odin as an historical personage of the third century."

are permeated with the heroic bravery of Walhalla and its tremendous catastrophes of gods and men. With the advent of Charlemagne, Odin and his kingdom sank into obscurity. The poetry, however, lives on, fragments of it being discoverable in the "Nibelungenlied." The oath above given is understood also to point to the fact that Odin is a person quite distinct from Woden (or Wodan), from whom, according to the *Saxon Chronicle,* "arose all our royal kindred,[1] and that of the Southumbrians also."

Vortigern

In the year 449 A.D. Vortigern (or Wurtgern), king of the Britons, invited Hengist and Horsa—descendants of Odin—to come to his assistance against the Picts and Scots. A large number of Saxons were brought over by these two famous leaders, who, finding Vortigern's battles were easily won, bethought them of striking a blow on their own behalf. So they despatched messengers for reinforcements, describing the worthlessness of the Britons and the richness of the land. "Then," says the *Saxon Chronicle*, "came the men from three powers of Germany—the old Saxons, the Angles, and the Jutes." Various battles were fought between 455—when the brothers faced King Vortigern—and 473, when Hengist (says the same authority) "fought with the Welsh and took immense booty, and the Welsh fled from the English like fire." If in place of Welsh and English we read *Celts* and *Saxons*, the passage becomes clearer.

[1] All "our royal kindred" in general, and Alfred the Great in particular.

"Drink heil"

No doubt that at least as early as the third century the coast settlement of the Saxons in Flanders must have sent us occasional travellers, but their principal foothold in England (and the first reason for Britain being called England) was secured at the date above given.

It has been remarked that the two very first Saxon words which we know from historical evidence to have been pronounced in this country were "Was heil hla, ond cyning!" (Be of health, lord king!); to which the king replied, "Drink heil" (Drink health). This pleasant interchange of greetings took place between King Vortigern and Rowena, the daughter of Hengist, at Hengist's then newly-built castle of Sydingbourn, Kent. It is further recorded that King Vortigern was so charmed with the young Saxon beauty that he afterwards obtained her in marriage—divorcing his first wife—and granted the whole of Kent to Hengist. The same story appears in Robert de Brunne's metrical *Chronicle of England*,[1] which tells us the name of the

[1] The incident appears thus in *Chronicles of England* (Westminster, Caxton, 1482):—

"Of Ronewen that was Engist's doughter / and how the kyng Vortiger espowsed her for her bewte.

"So whan this castell was made / and full well arayed / Engist pryvely dide sende by letter to the countree where he came fro / after an hundred shyppes fylled with men that were stronge and bolde, and also well fightinge in all batailles / And that they shold also bring with them Ronewen his doughter / that was the fayrest creature that a man might se. And whan those people were come that he had sent after / he toke them in the castel with moche joye. And himself uppon

Latimer, or interpreter, who acted between the British king and the Saxon lady; this, it appears, was a Breton knight, one Breg, who, according to Warton, held the position of "King's Domestic Secretary."

With Hengist's victory over King Vortigern, much of Britain fell under Danish rule, which now could

a daye / went unto the kynge / and prayed him there worthily that he wold come and se his newe Maneer[1] that he had made in the place that he had compassyd wyth a thwonge of the skynne. The kyng anone graunted hym freely / And wyth hym wente thyther / and was well apayed with the castell / and wyth the fayr werke. And togyder they ete and dranke with moche joy / and whan nyghte came / that this kyng Vortiger sholde goo into hys chabre / to take there his nyghtes rest. Ronewen that was Engistis doughter came wyth a cuppe of golde in her honde / and knelyd before the kyng / and sayde to him 'Wassaylle,' and the kynge knewe not what it was for to meane / ne what he shold answere. for as moche as hymself / ne none of hys Brytons / cowde noo englysshe speke ne understonde it / but spake in the same langage that Brytons doon yet. Nevertheles a latyner tolde the kyng the full understondyng thereof 'Wassaill' And that other shold drynk 'haill.' And that was the fyrste tyme that 'Washaill' and 'drynhaill' came up in this lond. The kyng Vortiger sawe the fayrnesse of Ronewen. and his armes layde abowte her necke and thryes swetly kyste her. And anone ryght he was enamoured upon her / that he desyred to have her to wyf / and askyd of Engist her fader. And Engist grauntyd hym upon this covenaunt / that the kyng shold gave hym all the countree of Kent / that he there myghte dwelle in and his people. The kyng him graunted pryvely wyth a good wyll. And anone he spowsyd the damoysell / and that was moche confusyon to hymselfe. And therefore all the Brytons became so wroth / for by cause he spowsid a woman mysbyleve[2] / wherefore they went all from hym / and no thynge to hym toke kepe / ne halpe hym in thynge that he had doon."

---

[1] Maner, Manor; *i.e.*, house.

[2] Without permission.

further boast a territory including not only Denmark, but also the southern Swedish provinces of Halland, Skene, Blekinge, the whole of Schleswig, and a part of Normandy. In the train of the conquerors came a body of men who were the constant attendants of the Kings of Denmark, Norway, and Sweden. These were the Scalds—the ancient Scandinavian poets or bards, whose duty it was in peace or in war to sing the events which befell their lords. Nor were their songs merely for diversion at the great solemn state-banquets, for the scalds were necessary also on the battle-field, where they encouraged the hero in the fight, or lulled him as he lay a-dying. Much of the history of the people of those early times is found in the numerous sagas and eddas still extant. Hailing originally from Iceland—the University of the North—the Scalds soon made their influence felt in England, where before the Celtic bards had reigned supreme. Not a trace of their music can now be distinguished, but their poetry shows a wonderful distinction and nobility of idea. A brief example may be cited in the *Bragi Edda*, from which we learn that the Bragi cup at guilds and feasts necessitated the dedication of a vow, which was afterwards to be held sacred and inviolable, that he who pledged would perform some deed worthy of a Scald's song; so great was the incentive to chivalrous acts. Men of rank and of good blood were not ashamed of the exercise of the poet's art, though how much of their eddalays were chanted to music it is now quite vain to inquire.

Scalds

Probably the early Icelandic bards were content with the mere recitation of their works. Four or five centuries were covered by the labours of these pioneers in the Gothic minstrelsy of Europe.

We have considered one great event which the fifth century brought forth—namely, the successful invasion of England by the Saxons; but there remains a second which could not but powerfully stir the hearts of the people. This was no less than the complete withdrawal of the Romans from this country, an event which occurred somewhat earlier in the century. The *Saxon Chronicle* refers to it as follows, under so late a date as 435 A.D.[1]:—

> "A. D. 435. This year the Goths sacked the city of Rome; and never since have the Romans reigned in Britain. This was about eleven hundred and ten winters after it was built. They reigned altogether in Britain four hundred and seventy winters since Caius Julius first sought that land."

"What subjects could have given to poetry more energy and importance than these incidents?" exclaims Sharon Turner, in his *History of the Anglo-Saxons*; "the Bardic genius must not only have burnt with new zeal and inspiration, but the chiefs must have more liberally encouraged and the people more enthusiastically applauded it." Such was the motive for native song. Dr. Percy proves that "the Anglo-Saxon harpers and gleemen were the immediate successors and imitators of the Scandinavian Scalds, who were the

[1] 407 would perhaps be nearer the accepted date.

great promoters of Pagan superstition, and fomented that spirit of cruelty and outrage in their countrymen, the Danes, which fell with such peculiar severity on the religious and their convents."

Rescue of Colgrin

The hint of ecclesiastical opposition given in the above quotation suggests the inquiry, What had the Church so far achieved?—a consideration which must be reserved for a further occasion. It is related by Geoffrey of Monmouth that Ella, who succeeded Hengist as King of the Saxons, had a son named Colgrin, who was shut up in York, and closely besieged by Arthur and his knights. In order to gain access to Colgrin, his brother Baldulph shaved his head and beard, and assuming the dress and manner of a Scald, was thus enabled to approach the trenches before the city wall without suspicion. In this disguise he gradually advanced, playing on his harp the while, until within reach of his friends, and under cover of darkness he was drawn up by a rope, and entering the city accomplished his purpose. Rapin gives the date of the incident as 495, though it must be admitted that the authentic history of King Arthur scarcely begins so soon. The character of the story is, however, confirmed by others of the same class. The true Arthur—a chieftain, and possibly the son of Uther—has been somewhat obscured by the fabulous king of romance. There is an anecdote furnished by Caradoc of Llancarvon which gives an account of the seizure of King Arthur's wife by Melva, a Somerset prince, who carried off the lady to Glastonbury. The outraged chief retaliated by summoning his knights and hastening to the rescue of his queen. The monks then interposed, and Melva surrendered his fair captive. The tale ends happily with substantial rewards for the monks and a joyful return of the knight and his lady. This Arthur is understood to have first assisted the Saxons, while afterwards, in opposition to Cerdic, he did his utmost to check them. Contemporary history shows that there were several kings in Britain at this period, but the paramount sovereign was Pendragon, a name borne by Arthur and by his father before him. Into the romance itself, however fascinating the study, it is no part of our duty to go. More to our purpose—as casting some light upon the history of the Gleemen—is

"Traveller's Song"

the Anglo-Saxon poem contained in the Exeter codex, entitled, "The Traveller's Song"—the earliest specimen of its kind. In this unique work—understood to have originated in Germany before our Saxon ancestry were thoroughly settled in their new domain of England—an account is given of one Widsith, a travelling gleeman, who recounts his adventures and travels in foreign countries. This wandering poet is of the Myrging tribe, dwelling near the Eider. His song celebrates the praises of those princes who treated him with generosity—paying them a right bardic tribute.

During the gradual development of the Anglo-Saxon rule, and onwards to its consolidation under Egbert in the ninth century, the Gleemen played an important part, leading a thoroughly cosmopolitan life. They went from court to court, and everywhere were treated as honoured guests. Gifts of great price were theirs; and a successful member of the craft was looked upon as a poet laureate. Of the verses they sang, it is not unreasonable to infer they often had composed a fair proportion. As non-combatants, they possessed many peculiar privileges, and while their person was under the protection of particular patrons, it was none the less safeguarded by the great respect in which the order was universally held.

FIG. 2.—PSALTERY OF THE NINTH CENTURY.

Such songs as were sung by these men were learned by heart and communicated orally; for it must be borne in mind that Guido's notation did not come into use until the eleventh century. We need not speculate upon the question of harmony—certainly not until the tenth century, although the instruments employed would admit of, if not suggest it. For the Anglo-Saxons had instruments of chords, as well as wind-instruments, as is witnessed by illustrations from old MSS. exhibiting the horn, trumpet, flute, harp, and a four-stringed lyre, all of which—it may be presumed—were in popular use. Bede mentions a rarer instrument when he expresses a desire for "a player upon the cithara—or that which we call rotae."[1]

In Bede's *Ecclesiastical History* there is a passage which seems to show that it was customary at a banquet or festival to send round the harp, so that each guest in turn might contribute a song. The following is a modernized version (from King Alfred's Saxon translation) of this celebrated passage, which refers to the poet Cædmon :—

"He never could compose any trivial or vain songs, but only such as belonged to a serious and sacred vein of thought, when his pious tongue was soon unloosed. He had lived and moved in the worldly state until late in life, and he was not practised in the art of verse. So, oft, in an entertainment, where for sake of merriment it had been agreed that each in turn should sing and harp, as the (dreaded) instrument was seen approaching, he arose in shame[2] from the supper-table and went home to his house."

---

[1] The instruments in the early days—until the sixth century—used by the Romans under Cassiodorus, were of three kinds: the Percussionalia, the Tensibilia, and the Inflatila. "The percussionalia," says Sharon Turner, "were silver or brazen dishes, or such things as when struck with force yielded a sweet ringing. The *tensibilia* consisted of chords tied with art, which on being struck with a plectrum soothed the air with a delightful sound, as the various kinds of cytharae. The *inflatila* were wind-instruments, as tubae, calami, organa, panduria, and such like." (Quoted from Cassiodorus, op. ii. p. 507.)

[2] King Alfred was fond of paraphrasing; the words *for shame* do not occur in Bede, whose text is as follows :—"Ille ubi appropinquare sibi citharum cernebat, surgebat à mediâ cœnâ, et egressus, ad suam domum repedabat." But the royal addition is of importance as it shows what was expected of a guest. Being found wanting, Cædmon, in the king's phrase, *aras he for sceome*.

In Hawkins' *History* (bk. v., c. xlii.) the story is much amplified. Cædmon, upon his return, has a vision, in which an angel asks him to sing, and even suggests the subject in the following words, "Sing the beginning of creatures." Now was Cædmon's tongue untied, and he sang a heavenly song, which when the vision had passed was still in his mind. Thus Cædmon became a poet.

Alfred the Great

Alfred the Great is well known to have studied music and poetry at an early age. While yet in his teens he had twice been to Rome, and sojourned in Paris, as well as paid a visit to Ireland. A contemporary writer bears witness to the prince's industry in mastering the Saxon language—an accomplishment which was afterwards to be put to such excellent account. "Saxonica poemata," says Asserius, "die noctuque audiens memoriter retinebat." Now, in the year 878, Alfred found himself dispossessed of power and authority, and practically a fugitive from the Danes; and he bethought him to match craft against force, and to oppose skill and courage to the sheer weight of numbers which the Danes could boast. He therefore took his life in his hand, and assuming the garb of a gleeman, and armed with nothing more formidable than a harp, entered the Danish encampment at Bratton-hill, Eddendun. The royal minstrel was admitted without suspicion to the king's table, where his songs won him an attentive audience. Alfred having picked up whatever knowledge seemed useful, retired in due course, having made a careful study of the nature of the ground and the disposition of troops. This exploit enabled him to call together his men, reassure them, and in a sudden onslaught which came as a surprise to the Danes, he so turned the scale of battle that the victory at Ethandune led to his immediate restoration. Not the least interesting feature of the episode is the fact that Alfred sang lays to the Danes which they could understand as well as appreciate.[1]

Clergy turn Minstrels

Though we are scarcely yet directly interested in the doings of our neighbours the French, it is none the less of importance to note that in the year 923 (according to Dufresne) many of the regular clergy and monks took up the profession of minstrelsy. Such a fact points to the great popularity of this strolling class of poet-musician, for it is not to be presumed that well-educated men would desert their calling—the penalty of which was an instant deprivation of the clerical tonsure—unless there had been some prospect of compensation or gain on the other side. But we shall shortly return to this matter. Even our own monks were not wholly antagonistic to the native representative of secular song; for we find

[1] "It is an indisputable fact that the Saxons of North Germany spoke the same dialect as those of England; the Franks likewise originally used it, since it was common to the whole of the Germanic North. The Romans could employ the services of a Frank interpreter in England, the Saxon Briton needed none in Sweden, and when Alfred entered the Danish camp in minstrel's disguise, he sang no foreign lays, but had merely to modify his pronunciation slightly." (Schlegel's *History of Literature.*)

St. Dunstan (born 925) as a student much attracted by songs and histories, which he read with delight, to the grave scandal of his pious superiors. The volumes which fell under his eye were the property of some Irish ecclesiastics who had visited Glastonbury, and left the worldly treasures exposed. St. Dunstan was no doubt duly punished for this lapse of discipline, and we read that "he was arraigned for studying the vain songs of his Pagan ancestors, and the frivolous charms of histories"—a statement which proves that the graduate saint had gone somewhat deeply into the subject.

To the year 934 may be attributed the adventure of the Danish king, Anlaf, who entered the Humber with a fleet of 615 ships. The weak opposition which he met with in landing was soon overcome; then, in order to gain time, King Athelstan sent messengers to treat with the Danish sovereign, whom they found retired for the night. Anlaf rose from his couch, and having hastily summoned a council of war, decided to pay a secret visit to the English camp. He therefore, like King Alfred before him, disguised himself as a harper, and singing as he went, easily gained access to the king's tent. Here his dancing and music so pleased Athelstan that the supposed harper was handsomely rewarded. Anlaf then took his leave; but whether through pride or some superstitious scruple, he proceeded to bury Athelstan's gift in the sand. While so engaged, one of the king's soldiers, a Dane, recognized Anlaf, and reported the affair to his chief. Athelstan thereupon demanded of him why he had not seized the royal spy; to which the soldier replied, "O king, the oath which I have lately taken to you, I once gave to Anlaf. If I had broken it to him, I might have been faithless to you; but deign to hear a servant's counsel, and remove your tent to another quarter." This advice was acted upon, and in place of King Athelstan, the newly-arrived Bishop of Sherborne and his men occupied the royal tent. Anlaf's surprise attack immediately followed, and the poor Churchman fell a victim to its shock. The *Saxon Chronicle* does not mention Anlaf's escapade, though Athelstan's final victory over the Danes, in 938, is specially celebrated in all the glory of verse. Here is a brief specimen :—

"A.D. 938. Here
Athelstan King,
Of earls the lord,
Rewarder of heroes,
And his brother eke,
Edmund Atheling,
Elder of ancient race,
Slew in the fight,
With the edge of their swords,
The foe at Brumby!
The sons of Edward
Their board-walls clove,
And hewed their banners,
With the wrecks of their hammers.
So were they taught
By kindred zeal,
That they at camp oft

> 'Gainst any robber
> Their land should defend,
> Their hoards and homes."

The victory referred to raised Athelstan in the estimation of all Europe, while it excited wild rejoicings on the part of the Anglo-Saxons, who turned it into the song which we have quoted, and sang it until it became popular—finally taking its place as a record of English history.[1]

As we approach the end of the tenth century, strange portents and ominous signs are recorded by writers of the period, who could not escape the general, or at least widespread belief that the world would end in 1000 A.D. Thus, the *Chronicle* just cited mentions, under date 979—"This same year was seen a bloody welkin ofttimes in the likeness of fire; and this was most apparent at midnight, and so in misty beams was shown; but when it began to dawn, then it glided away." The single line devoted to the year 995 is still more eloquent, as it also brings us nearer to the dreaded date—"This year appeared the comet-star."

Yet the affairs of the country went forward much the same as before. The Danes ravaged the country; the English quarrelled among themselves; and the music most like to be heard during such troublous times was that of the scald and gleeman, before camp-fires at the close of day. "It is hard not to look kindly at the

[1] Compare Sharon Turner's remarks, *History of the Anglo-Saxons*, vol. ii. p. 188, ed. 1836.

FIG. 3.—BAS-RELIEF OF ELEVENTH CENTURY.

gleeman," says Dr. Green, "for he no doubt did much to preserve the older poetry which even now was ebbing away. When Christianity brought with it not only a new vehicle of writing in the Roman characters, but the habit of writing itself, it dealt a fatal blow at the mass of early poetry which had been handed down by oral tradition. Among the Franks, Charles the Great vainly strove to save the old national songs from perishing, by ordering them to be written down. In England, Alfred did what he could to save them, by teaching them in his court. We see them, indeed, lingering in men's memories till the time of St. Dunstan. But the heathen character of the bulk of them must have hindered their preservation by transfer to writing; and custom hindered it yet more, for men could not believe that songs and annals handed down for ages by memory could be lost for want of memory. And no doubt the memory of the gleeman handed on this

FIG. 3.—BAS-RELIEF OF ELEVENTH CENTURY.

precious store of early verse long after the statelier poems of Cædmon or Cynewulf had been set down in writing. But useful as their work may have been, and popular as were both gleeman and tumbler, the character of the class seems to have been low, and that of their stories is marked by the repeated prohibition addressed to the clergy to listen to harpers or music, or permit any jesting or playing in their presence."

Hock Tuesday

Saint Brice's Eve, November 13, 1002—still celebrated in 1734, according to Bevil Higgons—gave birth to the first Mystery, or attempt at religious drama. The subject of this ancient play—afterwards known as the "Coventry Mystery of Hock Tuesday," is discovered in the massacre of the Danes, which took place early in the eleventh century. "The matter [of the play]," says an old writer, "mentioneth how valiantly our English women for the love of their country behaved themselves." In its first state, it is probable that the play was in dumb show, with skirmishes and encounters between Danes and English, many of the former being led captive by the "valiant" English women.

The year 1016 saw Cnut with his Danish army advancing unopposed, by Lincoln and York upon London, which, for a brief period, held out valiantly against its sturdy foe. When the issue of Assandun had befallen, and Cnut's rule (after some merciless preliminaries) had begun to establish itself in righteousness, naturally enough the scalds were not forgotten; and if not accorded first place in the court festivities, they were at least greatly encouraged by the king's keen appreciation and unprecedented generosity. Not only among his own people but even with strangers and foreigners the royal bounty scarce knew any bounds. This is well seen during his journey from Flanders to Rome (in 1031), when even the common wayfarers—of whom there must have been a goodly number on the road to Rome—were succoured and fed without so much as the need of asking it.

It would seem that this king was not only a patron of art, he was himself able to compose verses on occasion. Bentham quotes, in his *History of Ely*, a pleasing story of Cnut and his queen proceeding by water to the convent on the Isle of Ely, where a solemn banquet was to be held. As the royal barge drew near, the monks were heard chanting the *hours*, a circumstance which so

Cnut as a Poet

delighted the king that he was moved to extemporize the following verses:—

"The monks of Ely sweetly sung
Whilst Cnut the king there row'd along;
Row near the land, knights (quoth the king),
And let us hear the song they sing."

Ritson observes that from this little piece it may be conjectured that rhyme had been introduced by the Danes; and that no rhymed poetry of the earlier Saxons is discoverable. Sharon Turner, however, mentions a rhymed version of the Gospels, written in the ninth century by Otfrid in "Franco-theotisc," and some Latin rhyme of 622. The first piece of this kind in the *Saxon Chronicle* is under date 1011, though the poem of 959 contains irregular rhyme. Schlegel, speaking of the same matter, remarks that "it need not surprise us to find all German dialects adopting it, in the earliest stages of development."

It is said that the true character even of so exalted a person as a king may be best seen in small private acts which arise on the spur of the moment, and have nothing to do with a previously laid plan. The reader may judge if the following anecdote falls within such a consideration. One of Cnut's most favoured minstrels—Thorarin by name[1]—had composed a short poem extolling his patron's courage and nobility of

[1] The names of the famous scalds of Cnut's court are given by Snorre as follows:—Sighvatr, Ottar the Swarthy, Thordr Kolbeinson, and Thorarin Loftunga.

character, and the poet immediately repaired to the royal presence in order to recite his panegyric. Cnut was still at the banquet-table, at the close of a repast, with many courtiers and petitioners about him. The minstrel, growing impatient of delay, attempted to gain his sovereign's ear by suddenly exclaiming, "Sire, let me beg of you to listen to my song, which is very short." Cnut resented this unmannerly interruption, and replied with some sternness, "Have you no shame in daring to appear before me with a short poem on my greatness? Now, unless by this hour to-morrow you can offer me full thirty strophes, your head shall be forfeit for your impudence." Thorarin was a quick inventor, and had no difficulty in invoking a sudden muse, though his pride had been deeply hurt. When the appointed hour came, he stood before Cnut, humbled, but ready with a work which in point of length was all that his master could desire; and it may also have served to keep its author in mind that the king had shown him a way how to enlarge both his patience and his poem. Thus Thorarin kept his head.

It need not be a matter of surprise that so ancient an instrument as the Horn has been fabled by poets and writers from early times. Warton speaks of the Arabian books abounding with the most incredible fictions concerning Alexander the Great, fictions borrowed and improved from the Persians. He continues—"They call him Escander. If I recollect right, one of the miracles of this romance is our hero's horn. It is said that Alexander gave the signal to his whole army by a wonderful horn of immense magnitude, which might be heard at the distance of sixty miles, and that it was blown or sounded by sixty men at once. This is the horn Orlando won from the giant Jatmud, and which, as Turpin and Islandic bards report, was endued with magical powers, and might be heard at the distance of twenty miles. Cervantes says that it was bigger than a massy beam. Boyardo Berni and Ariosto have all such a horn; and the fiction is here traced to its original source." (*History of Poetry*, sect. iii.)

Pusey Horn

A curious custom obtained with the Danish kings of conveying landed property by means of a token; of this the Pusey estate in Berkshire is an example. Cnut granted the lands in question to an officer who, adopting the favourite ruse of those times, penetrated into the Saxon camp disguised as a minstrel, and brought back valuable information which enabled the Danes to avoid a surprise attack. For this piece of good service he was rewarded with the broad lands of Pusey, and an ox-horn,[1] some two feet long, was the token by which the estate was conveyed and held. This curious instrument—which tradition holds was the gift of Cnut—like the horn of the early Briton, could sound a right merry note, or hold a brimming cup of mead, accordingly as the screw-stopper at the mouthpiece was manipulated.

[1] Another use to which the horn was put is mentioned in Wilkins' *Leg. Sax.*, p. 12. A stranger leaving the main road for byways and woods was required by law to blow a horn, or at least shout, under penalty of being treated as a thief.

A richly-carved and ornamented horn was a valued gift of the period. On festival days at the monasteries such vessels would be brought forth for the elder monks to drink a solemn pledge to the departed donor.

Thirty years after Cnut's death, we meet with an important historical incident which is related by William of Malmsbury, and shows the stimulating effect which the minstrel art could bring to bear even upon the issues of battle. Before the Battle of Hastings, William of Normandy harangued his men, reminding them of their ancestors and the valorous Rollo, their founder. He had scarcely finished speaking when his men advanced to the attack, led by Taillefer, loudly chanting songs of Roland and Charlemagne. It is said that the intrepid soldier-minstrel, outstripping his friends, struck the first blow in this memorable fight. Down went an English ensign-bearer, quickly followed by a second victim; but ere the Norman could recover himself to strike a third blow he was himself biting the dust. The opposing ranks then joined battle. "When Taillefer rode into the battle at Hastings," says Stopford Brooke, "singing songs of Roland and Charlemagne, he sang more than the triumph of the Norman over the English; he sang the victory, for a time, of French romance over Old-English poetry." The event is referred to in the following lines from the "Roman de Rou":—

"Taillefer qui mult bien chantout
Sur un cheval qui tost alout,

Roncevals

Devant le Duc alout chantant
De Karlemaigne, et de Rollant,
Et d'Oliver, et des vassals
Qui morurent en Rencevals."

"Telfair, who well could sing a strain,
Upon a horse that went amain,
Before the Duke rode singing loud
Of Charlemagne and Rowland good,
Of Oliver, and those vassals
Who lost their life at Roncevals."

(*Translation by Ritson.*)

CHAPTER II.

First Christian Church—Saint Cæcilia—Organum hydraulicum—"Aeterna Christi munera"—Antiphons—Neumes—Dunstan—Boys in monasteries—Benedictines—Cloveshoe—Church minstrels.

The Church

HAVING reached the period of the Norman Conquest, we may usefully look back a moment and consider what the Church had been doing all this time. Music would quite naturally find a place in the ceremonials of the first Christian Church, since the Founder himself sanctioned its use at the Last Supper.[1]

Whether the old Hebrew melodies were employed, or, as is more likely, the new spiritual birth called into being newly inspired airs, it is impossible to decide. Nor is it known with certainty who brought the Good News to England. Tradition variously ascribes it to St. Paul, and to Joseph of Arimathea. It is certain, however, that by the third century there were many converts to the Faith in these islands. Rome had already martyred Cæcilia (during the reign of Marcus Aurelius, 177 A.D.); the Emperor's long arm was now

[1] "Et hymno dicto, exierunt in montem Oliveti." (Matt. xxvi. 30.)

employed to check the growth of the Church in England. Thus, we read that Constantine, Governor of Britain early in the fourth century, was instructed to pull down the churches. But persecution merely purges a good cause, and the spiritual teaching took firm and lasting root.

The Organ

The Organ, whether the invention of Saint Cæcilia or not, made its appearance during the second century, its immediate predecessors being the bag-pipes and pan-pipes. These primitive organs had a species of keyboard acting upon a set of eight or fifteen pipes, and were fitted with bellows or air-pumps.[1]

It is unlikely that the organ was employed in England until the seventh or eighth centuries. Aldhelm (or Ealdhelm) of Malmsbury speaks of "listening to the greatest organs with a thousand blasts, the ear is soothed by the windy bellows, while the rest shines in the gilt chests."[2] Aldhelm died in 709; but before his time, mention of a musical instrument called "organ" may be met with in the writings of Cassiodorus and Fortunatus. Wulstan the deacon (A.D. 963 *obiit*) gives an account of an instrument erected at Winchester, which required the services of "seventy strong men labouring with their arms to drive the wind up with

[1] Another variety known as the *Organum hydraulicum*, invented by Ctesibus (*circa* 170 B.C.), and described by Hawkins as "an instrument that produced music by the compression of water on the air," had no doubt been long in existence.

[2] "Maxima millenis auscultans organa flabris Mulceat auditum ventosis follibus iste Quamlibet auratis fulgescant caetera capsis."

all its strength, that the full-bosomed box may speak with its four hundred pipes which the hand of the organist governs." This remarkable organ was governed by four hands, however, for the deacon continues—"Two brethren [religious] of concordant spirit sit at the instrument, and each manages his own alphabet."[1]

Nor was the organ the only musical instrument which the Anglo-Saxons employed during worship. "When," says Wulstan, "the choral brethren unite, each chaunts your prayers by the peculiar art whereof he is master; the sound of instruments of pulsation is mixed with the sharp voices of reeds, and by various apparatus the concert proceeds sweetly." From ancient MSS. it is seen that the horn, trumpet, flute, and harp, and a four-stringed lyre were among the instruments in popular use.[2] The earliest Christian compositions of which we have any record are the "Hymns and Antiphons of the Office," which may be attributed to the end of the fourth century. St. Ambrose (333-397) was the principal, if not the only composer, and some ten of his melodies are still extant. Two of these are given by

[1] Wackerbarth's *Music of the Anglo-Saxons*.

[2] "In the MSS. which exhibit David and three musicians playing together, David has a harp of eleven strings, which he holds with his left hand while he plays with his right fingers; another is playing on a violin or guitar of four strings with a bow; another blows a short trumpet, supported in the middle by a pole, while another blows a curved horn. This was probably the representation of an Anglo-Saxon concert."—SHARON TURNER, iii. p. 455.

way of illustration.[1] During the fourth century St. Sylvester founded a *Schola Cantorum* at Rome, where boys and men were taught to render the church hymns in a uniform manner.

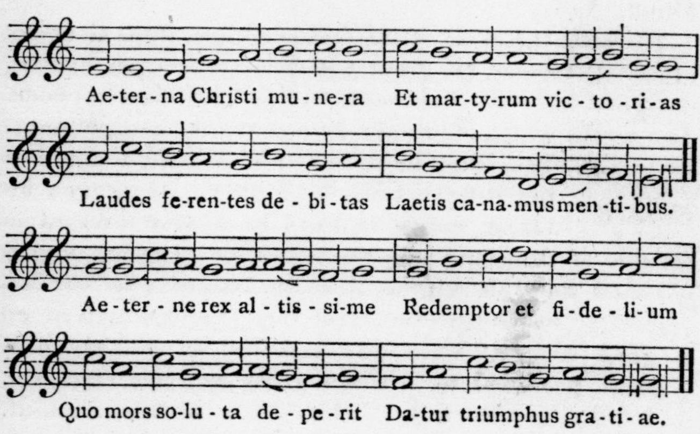
Ae-ter-na Christi mu-ne-ra Et mar-ty-rum vic-to-ri-as
Laudes fe-ren-tes de-bi-tas Laetis ca-na-mus men-ti-bus.
Ae-ter-ne rex al-tis-si-me Redemptor et fi-de-li-um
Quo mors so-lu-ta de-pe-rit Da-tur triumphus gra-ti-ae.

Notation, in our sense of the word, did not come into existence until the beginning of the eleventh century; but crude attempts by the aid of neumatic notation were in progress about 555. Into the Greek musical

[1] "How were these Ambrosian hymns handed down?" asks Mr. Abdy Williams. "We hear and read little of them, for the Roman or Gregorian church music has overshadowed the Ambrosian, which is practically confined to Milan." Following Gevaert, the same writer adds, "After his (Ambrosius') time, composition fell into the hands of priests and monks and inferior poets, who continued all through the Middle Ages to compose more or less correct Ambrosian tunes." (*Story of Notation*, pp. 42-43.)

system, which is said to have had a vogue of about a thousand years, it is not necessary to go,[1] beyond remarking that Boethius' obsolete theory of the Greeks was studied by the monks during the whole of the Middle Ages.

Towards the close of the sixth century, Pope Gregory (550-604) formed his great collection of church hymns, designed to be used throughout the ecclesiastical year. The work, which is practically a universal antiphonary, was probably written in *neumes,* and is still a canon of the Roman Catholic liturgy. Gregory's interest seems to have been first aroused in favour of England by the sight of English slaves exposed for sale in the Roman market. In 597 his emissary, St. Augustine, and forty monks arrived on English soil. "They advanced in an orderly procession, preceded by a silver cross as their standard, and carrying also a painted portrait of our Saviour, and chanting their litany as they approached."[2] We can but briefly note the arrival of this great man, and the impulse thus given to ecclesiastical music, which was now and hereafter to be Gregorian. Most of the history of succeeding events is due to the Venerable Bede. From him we learn that Theodore and Adrian introduced ecclesiastical chanting first into Kent in the year 669. A few years later, one John of Rome visited this country, bearing the Pope's special mandate to

Neumes

[1] The reader is referred to Mr. Abdy Williams' *Story of Notation* ("Music Story Series"), pp. 1-49, where this matter is fully discussed.

[2] Sharon Turner, iii. 339.

impart the Roman methods of church-singing; first to the particular monastery where he came, and afterwards to the rest of the clergy. It is said that under this John's successful tuition, ecclesiastical singing became a popular study with the Anglo-Saxon monks. Another famous prelate who bore a distinguished part in advancing the music of the Church was Dunstan, Abbot of Glastonbury: one who

Dunstan

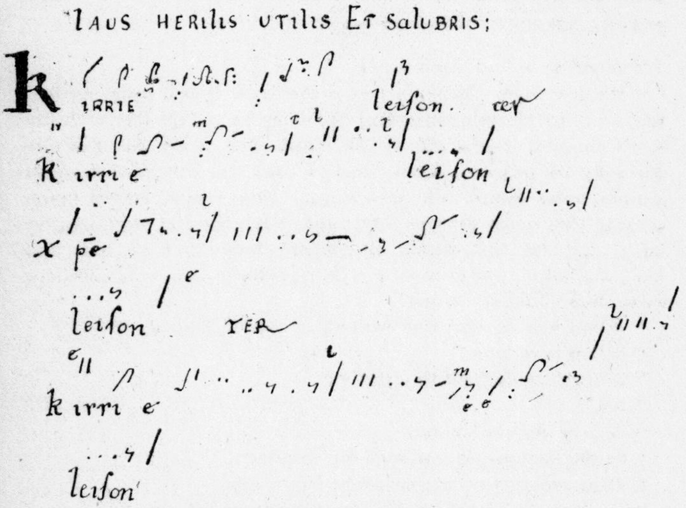

FIG. 4.—KYRIE BY ST. DUNSTAN.

Example of the neumatic notation of the "Winchester Troper." The MS., dating from the early part of the eleventh century, is preserved in the Library of Corpus Christi College, Cambridge.

could sing and harp with any minstrel. It is singular that his should be the very period when the monks in France were to be found quitting the cloister for the open-air life of the minstrel.

"Minstrels and monks between them," says Stafford Smith, "were the only teachers of music in Europe for some centuries." It is known that boys were admitted to the monasteries, as the following quotation from an account of their employments serves to show. It is put in catechetical form:—

"What have you done to-day?"

"Many things. When I heard the knell I rose from my bed and went to church and sang the song for before-day with the brethren, and afterwards of All Saints, and at the dawn of day the song of praise. After these, I said the first and seventh psalms, with litany and first mass. Afterwards, before noon, we did the mass for the day; and after this, at mid-day, we sang, and ate, and drank, and slept; and again we rose and sang the noon, and now we are here before thee, ready to hear what thou shalt say to us."

"When will ye sing the evening or the night-song?"

"When it is time."

"Wert thou flogged to-day?"

"No."

"Where do you sleep?"

"In the sleeping-room with the brethren."

"Who rouses you to the song before day?"

"Sometimes I hear the knell and rise; sometimes my master wakes me sternly with his rod."

In these schools, the origin of which were those of Rome, followed in after-times by those of Charlemagne, the elements of music, theoretical and practical, together with the rudiments of grammar and poetry, were systematically studied. The importance of such work, which was apparently confined to a few of the best monasteries, becomes more striking if the general ignorance of the clergy is considered. In the time of King Alfred, for example, "there were very few," says that monarch, "who could understand their daily prayers in English, or translate any letter from the Latin."[1] Alfred's own influence tended to encourage a widely different state of things. The monasteries had suffered not only from the depredations of the Danes, but also at the hands of the regular clergy.

Cloveshoe

The discipline of the early Benedictines had soon given way to more easy-going methods. As early as 747 the Council of Cloveshoe had forbidden the monks to admit the "sportive arts; that is, of poets, harpers, musicians, and buffoons." In the train of the histriones and gleemen, who were in the habit of visiting the monasteries, came dice, dancing, and singing; which it was complained were indulged even until the middle of the night. As a consequence, a priest was forbidden to be "an eala-scop or an ale-poet, or to any wise gliwege, or play the gleeman with

[1] Such ignorance still prevailed in Henry VIII.'s day, when an old priest was admonished for reading (in his *Portasse*) *Mumpismus Domine* for *Sumpsimus*. He protested that he had used *Mumpsimus* for thirty years and would not leave his old *Mumpsimus* for their new *Sumpsimus*. Henry VIII. often remarked that some were too stiff in their old *mumpsimus*, others too busy and curious in their new *sumpsimus*.

himself or with others." Severe as such measures might appear, severer had been known; for in Rome, during the fourth century, actors and mountebanks (descriptions which would doubtless include the secular musician) were excluded from the benefits of the Christian Sacraments, while excommunication awaited those who so much as visited the theatres on Sundays and Holy-days. Yet in spite of all such restraints a *Mima* acquired so much celebrity in the sixth century that she was raised to the imperial throne. The same ups and downs attended the progress of Christian music in England. At the time of the Cloveshoe Council it was in a flourishing state, just as was the Church itself. Dunstan, as we have seen, restored it to much of its former distinction; if not, indeed, to a more important position than before. Finally, the old Benedictines were superseded by the Cistercians in 1128, who soon established some thirty monasteries, and succeeded in placing their order on a footing that no longer admitted of interference from episcopal authority. "The libraries of the monasteries were full of romances," says Warton, "and it is reasonable to suppose that many of our ancient tales in verse containing fictitious adventures were written, although not invented, in the religious houses. Minstrels sometimes assisted at divine service, as appears from the record of the 9th of Edward IV., quoted above (page 107), by which Haliday and others are erected into a perpetual guild (Gild), etc. (See the original in Rymer, xi. 642.) By part of this record it is recited to be their duty "to pray [*exorare ;* which it is presumed they did by assisting in the chant and musical accompaniment, etc.] in the King's chapel, and particularly for the departed souls of the king and queen when they shall die," etc.

Some of them dressed in a clerical manner, with the head "rounded tonster-wise [tonsure-wise], his beard smugly shaven."

The strict clergy discountenanced these men. Their writings abound with complaints that princes and nobles should offer them so much encouragement. Some of the monasteries went so far as to forbid the minstrels so much as to enter their gates. This is in curious contrast to the proof of the regard which the order was held in at Beverley, where a pillar made by the minstrels (in St. Mary's Church) bears lasting evidence to this better condition of things.[1]

It would be absurd to suppose, as some writers have asserted, that "all our ancient melodies sprang from descant,"[2] which can hardly be said to have originated until the early part of the eleventh century; but it is certainly reasonable to admit an interchange of ideas, secular and sacred, the analogy for which is seen in the poetry preserved. Unfortunately, the melodies of these times are too scarce to allow of any very accurate conclusions being formed. It is not, however, unreasonable—though we cannot trace their history—to believe that, in addition to the few well-authenticated pieces, many an old scrap of music must have been handed down and incorporated in the compositions of times

[1] See *Story of Notation*, p. 148. [2] Stafford Smith.

not entirely beyond our reach. Having shown the relations which the monks and minstrels maintained towards one another—a mutual condition which finds its culmination in the founding of the Minstrels' Priory in 1102—we shall turn to a consideration of the Troubadours, who come into prominence during the eleventh century.

CHAPTER III.

Chivalry and Romance—Lais—Normandy—Troubadours—Joglars—Tournaments—Duke Guinne—The "gay science"—Anselm Faiditt—Feats of agility.

Troubadours

CHIVALRY and Romance were the underlying forces which brought about the birth of Provençal song. Latin had long decayed. Originally the language of France, established by the continual residence of the Romans, it became corrupted by Tudesque, the jargon of the Franks and other Gothic barbarians. From this intermixture of tongues the Romanse rustique, or rustic Latin, resulted. The most ancient of the French songs were called Lais. At an early period (eighth century) songs were widely employed for the usual purposes—the celebration of remarkable events, heroism, and the marvellous in history. Charlemagne got by heart many of these ancient and barbarous pieces, which he assiduously collected. The "Chanson Roland" is in French rhyme. Normandy took the lead in giving a fresh impulse to the development of poetry and music in Europe, which was everywhere awakening to the period of activity created by the Crusades. But if Normandy was the first in the field, the most celebrated songs came from

Provence. The Troubadours (called also Trouvères in the North of France) were the inventors or originators of the poems which the Chantères sang. A far more numerous though altogether inferior class was that of the Jongleurs (Joglars or Joculatores), who commonly acted as instrumental accompanists, though they could themselves usually both sing and play. The three groups of men—which together formed a large body that, as time went by, could boast of emperors, kings, and noblemen amongst their numbers—were classed generally as "La Jonglerie."

"Dans les premiers temps," says Coussemaker, "les trouvères chantaient eux-mêmes leurs compositions, en s'accompagnant de la harpe, de la vièle, ou de quelque autre instrument. Plus tard, ils abandonnèrent ce soin aux jongleurs et aux ménestrels pour se livrer exclusivement à la composition de la poésie et de la musique."[1] The correctness of this view is proved by the surviving compositions. All the early pieces are single melodies, written on a four-lined stave in the square notation of the Church. Whatever accompaniment was added would probably be extemporized. A glance at our chapter on Harmony[2] will serve to show what combinations of notes were being used in these early centuries. It is difficult to understand what was done with the bands of performers. Did they play in two or three parts, or in unison? With the later troubadours, such as Adam de la Hâle and William de

[1] *L'Art Harmonique aux XIIe et XIIIe Siècles*, p. 180.

[2] Page 219.

Machault, there is more definite record to guide us in forming an opinion. The subject is more fully considered under the chapter on Harmony, where a three-part rondel by Adam de la Hâle is quoted by way of example.

The presence of the troubadours at tournaments and feasts was everywhere welcomed, and they were great travellers, going from court to court at home and abroad. Their principal theme was the praise of an adored mistress, real or imaginary. Lays of the Virgin, tales in verse, and especially the achievements of princely patrons and sovereigns, proved further fruitful sources of inspiration. The love-songs were called *canzonets* or *chansons,* the evening song was a *serenade*, and the day song *aubade. Roundelays* ended with the same refrain. Songs in praise of princes, like those extolling or decrying any public event, were termed *servantes*. The dance-songs were also numerous, especially those sung and played to the round dance. Quarrelsome or contentious songs were known as *Tenzone,* while the Arcadian or idyllic came under the general description *pastourelle*. Many of the earlier troubadours accepted no reward for their services, contenting themselves with the applause of fair ladies. Princely sums and estates were accepted by others. William, Duke of Guinne, who died in 1126, joined in the first Crusade. Count William of Poitiers (1087-1127) was another early troubadour. Numbers of their chansons are still extant. The oldest are by Châtelain de Coucy, an example of which we quote. Bertran de

Born excelled in the composition of servantes. Helen, sister of Richard Cœur de Lion, was praised by this troubadour. Songs by the King of Navarre (*circa* 1235) are quoted by Stafford Smith, Burney, and Hawkins. They possess a definite melodic outline, but they are highly monotonous to modern ears. Other distinguished members of this brilliant company were Pierre Rogier, Bernart de Ventadour, Thomas Erars Coronèe, Jehan Erars, Gaces Brulez, Perrin Dangecort, Thiebaut de Blason, and Messieurs Tierres.

Our example is understood to be of the end of the twelfth century. The subject of the poem may be seen from the following translation:—

"Spring's new beauties, full display'd
In all their splendour, prompt my song;
But my heart a lovely maid,
As her captive, drags along.
In such deep distress, I'm told,
If the cause of all my pain
Within my arms I once enfold,
Boundless bliss I should obtain."

CHANSON.
Chastelins de Couci (12th Century).
Le nou-veau tems et Mais et vi - o - let - - te, Les
Et mon fin cœur m'a fait d'une a- mour - et - - te Un
ro - sig - naux me mo - nent de chan - ter.
doux pre - sent Que je n'ose re - fu - ser.

Toulouse

Or me l'on dit en tel en - nu - y ment Que si je
ou j'ai cure et mon pen - se Ti - en - ne u - ne
fois en-tre mes bras nud te Ains re - jou - isse outre - ment.

Some among their number achieved fame of a durable kind as musicians; such were Raoul de Coucy, King Thibaut IV. of Navarre, Adam de la Hâle, and Guillaume de Machault. Our own Richard I. was a troubadour. His servant, Blondel, on the other hand, was a minstrel in the true sense of the word; for, as was explained at the outset, the original meaning of the word minstrel applied to the musicians in the service of the troubadours. Accepting the first Crusade (in 1095) as the starting-point of the history of the troubadours, little more than a hundred and thirty years elapsed before the beginning of their decline. This, however, was not immediate, for as late as 1320 a troubadour academy was founded at Toulouse.[1] The movement, though it declined in France, lingered on in Spain until the fifteenth century. A fine collection of late Spanish Minstrelsy issued in 1890 by the Academy

[1] This institution was named "The Seven Maintainers of the Gay Science," and was visited, soon after its formation, by Petrarch.

of Madrid under the title *Cancionero Musical de los Siglos, XV. and XVI.*, shows that the florid contrapuntal accompaniments of Lopez of Mendoza (1398-1458), Enriquez, and several anonymous troubadours possess remarkable freedom of style, fully equalled, however, if not excelled, by the great musicians of the period, Dunstable, Dufay, and Binchois, and by the organists Paumann and Hofhaymer. It is curious also to note that the "gay science" was taken up by ladies of the first rank, who not only imitated the men in the composition of verse, but they further established a "Court of Love," where was determined any question of gallantry which might arise from the delicate code of honour practised by all who aspired to the ranks of chivalry. The stories of these times abound in the marvellous. Burney gives an account of a celebrated troubadour named Anselm Faiditt, married to a beautiful *nun,* who followed her lord from court to court, singing his songs as she went. Many of the troubadours attended their patrons through the hardships of war; and as a whole, the reputation won by members of this distinguished class of men helped not a little to place the arts of poetry and music

FIG. 5.—FOURTEENTH CENTURY FIDDLE.

(From the Cathedral of Aix-la-Chapelle.)

in a more respectable light than had previously been known in the history of mankind.

The Italian poetry, which arose as the Provençal declined, is under great obligations to the troubadours. Both Boccaccio and Dante studied at Paris, and were familiar with the songs of Thibaut, King of Navarre, Gaces Brules, Châtelain de Coucy, and others. The latter poet, indeed, is said to be directly indebted to Raoul de Houdane, a Provençal bard living about 1180. Petrarch is further understood to have benefited by the works of Anselm Fayditt and Arnaud Daniel,[1] "the most eloquent of the troubadours." The very word "sonnet" came to Italy by way of Provence; witness such a verse as the following, which occurs in the *Roman de la Rose*:—

"Lais d'amour et *sonnets* courtois."

The Provençal joglar played, sang, and recited, as we have already seen, but he also knew something of juggling and conjuring. To the Bufos was relegated the exhibition of learned dogs and goats, feats of agility and strength, in conjunction with a humble display of the common strolling minstrel's art. If we compare the English joglar, his character appears more akin to the bufo than the true joglar; and when the title "minstrel" came to be applied to him, he had become a veritable mountebank. Some of these men, says Du Fresne (art. "Ministelli"), "occasionally per-

[1] Arnaud Daniel visited Henry IV.'s court in England.

formed feats of agility, like the man on the back of a horse, who danced on a rope in the air." He continues in a strain which would have been the admiration of the accurate Ritson and the despair of the amiable Percy, "From these men, in fact, sprang all the varieties of poetical and musical compositions, whether they comprised truth or fiction, invective or encomium, subjects of pity or terror, reverence or detestation; and whether they were conducted in an uninterrupted historical narration and sung by one person, or broken into a number of parts in the form of a dialogue and recited or sung by as many persons."

CHAPTER IV.

The Conquest—King's Minstrel—Minstrel's Priory—Ebor the Organ-builder—Rudel—Two-part music—Pierre de Corbain.

FROM the brief sketch given of the Provençal minstrel, it may be inferred that his English *confrère* could scarcely vie with him either in ability or magnificence. Indeed, all things native to the soil—especially speech itself—were held in some contempt, not only at the time of the Conquest but long prior to it. "Even before the Conquest," writes Warton, "the Saxon language began to fall into contempt, and the French, or Frankish, to be substituted in its stead; a circumstance which at once facilitated and foretold the Norman accession. In the year 652 it was the common practice of the Anglo-Saxons to send their youth to the monasteries of France for education; and not only the language, but the manners of the French were esteemed the most polite accomplishments. In the reign of Edward the Confessor, the resort of Normans to the English court was so frequent that the affectation of imitating the Frankish customs became almost universal; and the nobility were ambitious of catching the Frankish idiom." The same author shrewdly observes that "it

The Conquest

was no difficult task for the Norman lords to banish that language of which the natives began to be absurdly ashamed." In the eclipse of language—temporary though it was—no wonder that native music went down before the brilliant and successful men who came to this country in the train of the Conqueror.

The Normans had cultivated the minstrel art before it reached Provence. They were a late colony from Norway and Denmark,[1] and in the time of Rollo (778 *circa*), it is only reasonable to suppose, many Scalds must have settled in their midst. Taillefer is always referred to as a troubadour, and it is quite possible that the Provençal troubadour and Norman rymour were already in constant association. During the reign of William the Conqueror one little fact comes to light which concerns Minstrelsy—and that is, the entry in the great Doomsday Book as follows:—

"Glowecesterscire.
Fol. 162, Col. 1. Berdic Joculator Regis habet iii villas, et ibi v car. nil redd."

We thus see that the Joculator Regis, or King's Minstrel, had house and land assigned him in Gloucestershire. It will now appear that such records as we have to offer relate to Norman and French minstrelsy rather than to native, which cannot be distinguished again until perhaps the middle of the thirteenth century, when the English language itself was struggling into birth.

[1] Percy's *Reliques.*

William Rufus

The only music (apart from the Church) which would receive encouragement during William's reign would be that of the Conqueror's own minstrels. Our own gleemen sang in a tongue foreign to the Court, while many of the Saxon nobles had, as we have shown, for years been cultivating French arts and manners, in addition to the language itself. "In the first ages," according to Dr. Percy, "after the Conquest no other songs would be listened to by the great nobility but such as were composed in their own Norman French; yet as the great mass of the original inhabitants were not extirpated, these could only understand their own native gleemen or minstrels, who must still be allowed to exist unless it can be proved that they were all proscribed and massacred, as it is said the Welsh were afterwards by the severe policy of Edward I."[1] The learned essayist mentions *The Horn Child*, an old metrical romance, in support of his contention. This, it appears, is a translation of an older French poem,[2] of which the following couplet is a fair specimen:—

> "Horne sett hi abenche, his harpe he gan clenche;
> He made Rymenild a lay and he seide weilaway."

William II.'s reign does not furnish any incident of importance to our subject; but early in that of his successor an exceptional event occurs which may be noticed: this was the foundation of the Priory and

[1] A popular error.

[2] Sir F. Madden regards the English as the original and the translation French.

Hospital of St. Bartholomew, by Royer (Raherus) the King's Minstrel, in the third year of the reign of Henry I. (1102). The priory—a religious establishment which in those times ranked second to an abbey—was situate in Smithfield, London—a spot afterwards to become famous for its fairs and executions, and, finally, its markets.

Henry I.

Stow mentions "Rahere" as a pleasant, witty gentleman, a description which is supplemented by Dugdale, who says that this Rahere (or Royer) "was born of mean parentage, and that when he attained to the flower of his youth he frequented the houses of the nobles and princes; but not content herewith, would often repair to the court and spend the whole day in sights, banquets, and other trifles, where by sport and flattery he would wheedle the hearts of the great lords to him, and sometimes would thrust himself into the presence of the king, where he would be very officious to obtain his royal favour; and that by these artifices he gained the manor of Aiot in Hertfordshire, with which he endowed his hospital. He is said to have been a great musician, and Hawkins adds that he kept a company of minstrels—*i.e.*, fiddlers, who played with silver bows. A well-preserved monument of this interesting personage is still to be seen in the Church of St. Bartholomew, Smithfield. Henry I. was a great builder of castles and churches. The *Saxon Chronicle* notes that "every one built a castle who was able." Before the death of Stephen eleven hundred and fifteen might be counted. Some of the churches of this reign may be added, including Rochester (1077), Hereford (1079), Gloucester (1088), Chichester (1091), Norwich, Durham (1093), Peterborough (1107), and Oxford (1120) Cathedrals. Portions of Ely, Exeter, Winchester, and Canterbury Cathedrals are also of this period.

The wife of Henry I. ("Good Queen Maud") did much to encourage the founding of monasteries; indeed, so many labourers became bricklayers and carpenters, for this precise purpose, that great discontent was occasioned. A piece of extraordinary barbarity is attributed to Henry I., who had suffered some annoyance at the hands of a Norman minstrel named Luke de Barre. The minstrel's fault is stated by the king himself. "Luke de Barre," said he, "has never done me homage, but he has fought against me. He has composed facetiously indecent songs upon me; he has sung them openly to my prejudice, and often raised the horse-laughs of my malignant enemies against me." The horrible punishment thereupon meted out to this luckless minstrel was that of having his eyes torn out. When freed from his torturers, Luke de Barre finished their ghastly work himself—by dashing his brains against the wall.

Fitzstephen gives an account of Thomas à Becket's journey to Paris, to conduct negotiations for the marriage of Henry II.'s daughter to Louis VII. The great English prelate entered the French towns "preceded by 250 boys, on foot, in groups of six, ten, or more together, singing English songs, according to the custom of their country."

Thomas, the first Archbishop of York after the Conquest, devoted much of his time to "making organs and in teaching his clergy to make them, and to set hymns both in prose and verse to music." William of Malmesbury states that this prelate adapted any secular tune which pleased him to ecclesiastical use, making what alterations appeared necessary.[1] It seems as if the Church at this time was endeavouring to keep pace with secular music, and we find John of Salisbury complaining that the church-singers "endeavour to melt the hearts of the admiring multitude with their effeminate notes and quavers, and with a certain wanton luxuriancy of voice."

A famous Provençal troubadour, Jeffrey Rudel, flourished about 1161. It is related of this impetuous minstrel that one fine day in the company of Geoffrey, brother of Richard I., he heard (from pilgrims returning from Palestine) of a certain celebrated and beautiful countess of Tripoli. So greatly did the charms of the lady work upon the imagination of the susceptible Jeffrey that he forthwith made a pilgrimage to the shrine of his living saint. But the slow progress of the ship did not suit the lover's ardour. He became deadly sick, and ere he could land was well-nigh dead. The countess, much affected by a recital of the story of his coming, hastened on board. The poet at her touch awakened, and regarding her with affection, assured

[1] "If he heard any of the secular minstrels sing a tune which pleased him, he adopted and formed it for the use of the Church, by some necessary variations."

her that his object was accomplished and that he could die in peace, having seen her wondrous beauty. "He died of love," say the chroniclers, and the lady seems to have been of the same opinion, for she erected a splendid tomb of porphyry, bearing an Arabic inscription, and herself took the veil. One of Rudel's poems, written (it is said by Rymer[1]) during his romantic voyage, is still extant.

Warton mentions "a splendid carousal after the manner of the Normans," given by a Welsh prince in 1176. Rhees ap Gryffyth, King of South Wales, gave this great feast on the occasion of Christmas. It was proclaimed throughout all Britain. Every poet in Wales attended. Contests were arranged for the bards, with "great rewards and rich gifts for the overcomers." Just about this time occurred an incident concerning which there remain a few verses, that in the scantiness of available material become correspondingly valuable. Robert, Earl of Leicester, after the spoiling of his town, got together an army of Flemings and Normans from over the seas. With this rabble he made a descent upon the coast, and marched towards Bury St. Edmund's. On the way a halt was called, and the gallants spent the time in dancing on the heath and singing in anticipation of their easy victory (as they befooled themselves into imagining):—

"Hoppe Wylikin, hoppe Wyllykin,
Ingland is thyne and myne."

---

[1] *Short View*, p. 71.

But while engaged in this idle pastime the king's army fell upon them, and those who were not killed or drowned were made prisoners. Another poetic effusion, equally short, may further be cited as belonging to the time of Henry II. Hugh Bigood, Earl of Norfolk, was wont to boast of the impregnable strength of his castle of Bungey, as follows:—

> "Here I in my castle of Bungey,
> Upon the river of Waveney,
> I would ne care for the king of Cockeney."

The boast was nevertheless a vain one, and the owner of the castle had to pay Henry II. a heavy sum to save his vaunted stronghold from destruction. These two rhymes, according to Ritson, are the earliest specimens of the English language, not being pure Saxon. An interesting item is preserved of the year 1180, when Jeffrey the harper received a corrody or annuity from the Benedictine Abbey of Hide, near Winchester, "on condition," says Warton, "that he should serve the monks in the profession of a harper on public occasions." The abbeys of Conway and Stratflur in Wales respectively maintained a bard; and the Welsh monasteries in general were the grand repositories of the poetry of the British bards. Percy goes further, and discovers that the corrody or annuity was for his music and his songs. He further concludes that the songs, to be of any entertainment to our English monks, would be in the vernacular. An amusing story is told by Wood of two itinerant priests coming one evening to a Benedictine retreat near Oxford. Supposing them to have been *mimes*, or minstrels, the cellarer, sacrist, and others of the brethren welcomed them in their midst, A.D. 1224 expecting to derive some substantial entertainment by their *pesticulatoriis ludierisque artibus*. But when the wanderers were discovered to be nothing more than two poor ecclesiastics, they were turned adrift into the night without ceremony, and given a good whipping into the bargain.

A famous passage from Giraldus Cambrensis applies to the vulgar music of the time of Henry II., as follows:—"In general there is not the least uniformity in musical modulation. Every man sings his own song, and in a crowd of singers, as is the custom here, so many songs and various voices will you hear. In the northern parts of Britain, beyond the Humber and on the borders of Yorkshire, the people there inhabiting make use of a kind of symphoniac harmony in singing, but with only two differences or varieties of tones or voices. In this kind of modulation one person sings the under part in a low voice, while another sings the upper in a voice equally soft and pleasing. This they do, not so much by heart as by a habit, which long practice has rendered almost natural; and this method of singing is become so prevalent amongst these people,[1] that hardly any melody is accustomed

[1] Fitzstephen, a monk of Canterbury, writing about 1160, mentions, among the sports and pastimes of the day, that the maidens were fond of dancing by moonlight. He further observes that "after dinner, all

to be uttered simply, or otherwise than variously, or in this twofold manner." The question of harmony being employed in some crude form is thus decided. The earlier troubadours wrote down their melodies (in the old square notes used by the Church), but do not seem to have indicated the accompaniments, which were in all probability added extempore. That harmony existed long before the period of which we are writing will be seen in a separate chapter. The later troubadours, such as Adam de la Hâle and Guillaume de Macchault, practised harmony in three or four parts. Two-part music was written down in England during the tenth century; but whether by monks or minstrels there is no evidence to show. We find one Pierre de Corbain, a troubadour of this period, or perhaps a little later, boasting that he is skilled in the plain chant, in singing to the lute, in making canzonets and pastorals and in dancing—so the art of the monk and minstrel could not have admitted of any precise demarcation.

Harmony

the young men of the city go out into the fields to play football." Miracle-plays are also mentioned.

CHAPTER V.

Richard I. and Blondel—Dürrenstein Castle—A king's ransom—Talbot—A love-song—Chester Fair—Magna Charta—A soothsayer and minstrel—"Sumer is icumen in"—Middle Ages—Last of the Crusades—Fabled massacre of Welsh bards—Minstrels and heralds.

"King Richard is the beste
That is found in any geste."

RICHARD I., himself a troubadour of notable skill, was also a magnificent patron of the minstrels, many of whom he invited over from France. The names of three of the most celebrated have come down to us. There was Fouquet of Marseilles, a poet, musician, and singer of singular personal attraction, a favoured guest at the courts of Richard, and of Raymond Count of Thoulouse, and Beral de Baulx. Fouquet closed a remarkable career as minstrel by becoming "absolved of the sin of poetry" and entering a monastery, where his religious progress in course of time led to his being created Archbishop of Thoulouse. Anselme Fayditt also had a distinguished career. Many of his poems still survive, and not the least esteemed is that portion of his work which Petrarch borrowed for his *Triumfo di Amore*, and duly acknowledged in a panegyric. The third of Richard's French minstrels was Blondel de

Nesle, of widely popular fame due to the romance of the following anecdote:—Richard I. returning from the disastrous Crusade of 1193, found himself suddenly taken prisoner by Leopold, Duke of Austria, whose enmity he had incurred during a former Crusade, and by whom he was cast into the dungeon of the castle Dürrenstein, near Vienna. "A whole year elapsed," says Fauchet, "before the English knew where their monarch was imprisoned. Blondel de Nesle, Richard's favourite minstrel, resolved to find out his master; and after travelling many days without success, at last came to the castle where Richard lay confined. Here he discovered the name of the castle and its owner, also that it held a royal captive. Suspecting that the prisoner was none other than his master, he found opportunity to approach beneath the window of the king's chamber. Here he began to sing a French chanson, which Richard and Blondel had formerly written together. When the song reached the king's hearing, he instantly guessed who was the singer; and as the minstrel paused at the first half of the chanson, Richard took it up and finished it. Then were the minstrel's suspicions confirmed. He returned at once to England, and informed the king's barons of the place of their sovereign's confinement. By this means Richard was soon released." Much doubt has been cast on this story, which, however, has taken firm hold upon the popular imagination. It is confirmed in several details by history; and some writers go so far as to claim that the actual verses sung by Blondel can be produced. Percy (following Burney) offers the following lines in this connection:—

BLONDEL.

Donna vostra beutas	*Your beauty, lady fair,*
Elas bellas faissos	*None views without delight;*
Els bels oils amoros	*But still so cold an air*
Els gens cors ben taillats	*No passion can excite;*
Don sieu empresenats	*Yet this I patient see*
De vostra amor que mi lia	*While all are shunn'd like me.*

RICHARD.

Si bel trop affansia	*No nymph my heart can wound*
Ja de vos non portrai	*If favour she divide,*
Que major honorai	*And smiles on all around*
Sol en votre deman	*Unwilling to decide;*
Que sautra des beisan	*I'd rather hatred bear*
Tot can de vos volria.	*Then love with others share.*[1]

It is known that Richard whiled away a part of the time he was in captivity by composing songs, a specimen of which may be seen in Ellis's *History of the Troubadours.* The ransom demanded was 100,000 marks of pure silver, a sum which caused widespread distress in the raising. The plate of the churches and monasteries was taken to convert into marks; the Cistercians, lacking plate, surrendered their wool;

[1] Another song credited to the same occasion is given in *The Story of British Music* (Crowest), p. 221, beginning—"Fierce in me the fever burning," where it is quoted from Fauchet's *Recueil de l'origine de la Langue et Poesie Françoise.*

besides which the clergy and laity were forced to contribute a fourth part of their yearly incomes, and every knight had to provide at least twenty shillings.[1]

The reign of Richard I. affords another story which illustrates the chivalrous opportunities of those times. The young heiress of D'Evreux Earl of Salisbury, had been conveyed in secret to France, where she was kept in hiding by her Norman relatives. A certain knight named Talbot took up the quest of her discovery and restoration to her English friends. For full two years he pursued his search; first in the guise of a pilgrim, afterwards in the character of a harper. His skill in the romance stories and "gests of the ancients," as they were termed, gained him an easy access to the lady's household, when once he had discovered it. He then availed himself of the opportunity to carry off the missing heiress, whom he afterwards succeeded in bestowing in marriage on his natural brother, William Longspec (son of "Fair Rosamond"), who afterwards, by virtue of his marriage, became Earl of Salisbury.

Throughout Richard's reign the minstrelsy of England and France was drawn closer together, and the adventures, characters, and stories which figure in the literature of the two countries were for the time being

[1] *English Chronicle*, 1483, St. Alban's (Caxton):—"And afterwarde he was delyverd for an huge raunson, that is for to say an hudred thousande pounde. And for the whyche rauson to be paid, eche other chalyce of Englonde was molten and made into money. And alle the monkes of the ordre of the Cisteaux [the Cistercians] gave all ther boks thrugh out all Englond, for to doo them to sell and the raunson for to paye."

so much common property. France, with her splendid castles and gorgeous barons, her schools of chivalry and highly-trained minstrels, led the way; and our earliest romances prove that England was no tardy follower in the paths of poetry thus newly opened up to her.

If Warton is right in assuming the following little love-song to be of "before or about the year 1200," he goes far to prove that English was then beginning to assert itself as an individual language.

Blow northerne wynd, send
Thou me my swetynge; blow
Northerne wynd, blou, blou, blou.
Ich wot a burde in bowre bryht
That fully semly is on sight,
Menskful [graceful] maiden of might,
Faire and free to fonde, &c.[1]

Chester Fair

A curious tale of the minstrels frequenting Chester Fair comes down to us from the time of King John (1212). Hugh, first Earl of Chester, in his charter of the foundation of St. Werburg's Abbey, had granted an exemption from arrest to all who attended the city fair, providing they committed no crime during fair-time. It so fell out that Randle Blundevil, sixth Earl of Chester, was closely besieged by the Welsh, who forced him to fall back on his Castle of Rothelent (Rhuydland), in Flintshire. A message was thence despatched to Roger Lacy, Constable of Chester, commanding him to come

[1] This song is contained in the Harleian MSS. 2253, which Ritson, who quotes the song in its entirety (*Ancient Songs*, p. 26), dates as of the time of Edward II.

with all speed to the earl's relief. This despatch reached Randle in the midst of fair-time, and he bethought him to increase his slender forces by recruiting from the miscellaneous attendants which the fair had gathered together. "Roger," says Sir Peter Leycester's *Historical Antiquities*, "having got together a tumultuous rout of fiddlers, players, cobblers, debauched persons, both men and women out of the city, marched immediately towards the earl." This proved too much for the Welsh, who perceiving, as they thought, a great army advancing upon them, incontinently turned and fled, without waiting for a nearer view of the harmless rabble. For this singular piece of service, the earl granted to constable De Lacy a charter of patronage and authority "over all the fiddlers and shoemakers in Chester." The constable kept to himself the "authority and donation of the shoemakers," conferring on his steward power over the fiddlers and players. Ritson makes merry with this story,[1] and quotes Dr. Percy's definition of the minstrels—"an order of men who subsisted by the arts of poetry and music, and sang to the harp verses composed by themselves"—picturing them as "most miserably twanging and scraping in the booths of Chester Fair." Whatever the class to which these men belonged, certain it is that the charter was duly executed, and held good for many a long year, as may be seen from Blount's *Ancient Tenures* (1679), where it is mentioned that Lawrence Dutton, in the fourteenth year of Henry VII.,

[1] *Ancient Songs*, p. vi.

claimed that all minstrels in the County and City of Chester should appear before him annually on the feast of St. John Baptist, when each had to contribute four flagons of wine, one lance, together with the sum of fourpence-halfpenny. It appears also that these minstrels had to play on their instruments as Lord Dutton, or his steward, attended divine service on the first day of the fair. Licences were also granted to the minstrels on the same occasion, which carried privileges by which these vagrant performers were unmolested, at a time when the minstrels in other parts of the country were being punished as "rogues, vagabonds, and sturdy beggars." Thus, the exploit of the Chester minstrel-rabble was of some benefit to their successors, in the exercise of their humble calling.

"England," says Macaulay, "which since the Battle of Hastings had been ruled generally by wise statesmen, always by brave soldiers, fell under the dominion of a trifler and a coward. From that moment her prospects brightened. John was driven from Normandy. The Norman nobles were compelled to make their election between the island and the continent. Shut up by the sea with the people whom they had hitherto oppressed and despised, they gradually came to regard England as their country, and the English as their countrymen. The two races, so long hostile, soon found that they had common interests and common enemies. Both were alike aggrieved by the tyranny of a bad king. Both were alike indignant at the favour shown by the court to the

A.D. 1215

natives of Poitou and Aquitaine. The great grandsons of those who had fought under William and the great grandsons of those who had fought under Harold began to draw near to each other in friendship; and the first pledge of their reconciliation was the Great Charter, won by their united exertions, and framed for their common benefit." (*History of England*, chap. i.)

One John of Raumpayne (of this same reign) became celebrated as "a sothsayer, jocular, and minstrelle." The age seems to have encouraged superstitious arts, and even Roger Bacon lent his name to the mysteries and secrets of the alchemist and the philosopher's two stones. Raumpayne's services were wanted in the cause of a quarrel which had thus originated. One day, at a game of chess, Sir Fulco Guarine so incensed the Prince of Wales (afterwards King John) that the latter, in the words of the chronicler, "brake Fulco's head with the chest borde." After this polite intimation that the royal loser was wroth with his opponent, Sir Fulco returned the blow with such interest that it had almost occasioned a change in the succession of English sovereigns, for (as the chronicle saith) "he had almost killid hym." The scene of the quarrel then changed to Whitington Castle (Shropshire), which together with its original heiress had been won in open tournament by Sir Fulco's ancestor. After the accession of King John, this castle was seized by the Prince of Wales, who placed in possession his retainer, one Morice. An appeal of the Guarines to the king was treated with contempt, so they fled into Bretagne for a space. Anon returning to the recovery of their castle, they set John of Raumpayne, the minstrel above-named, as a spy upon Morice, the usurper of their rights. The minstrel contrived that they should lie in wait for Morice, whom they succeeded in wounding; while a knight named Sir Bracy went so far as "to cut off Morice's hedde," an act of intrepidity which soon afterwards led to his arrest. The vengeance of the king was averted by the occult aid of Raumpayne; for "he founde the meanes to cast them that kepte Bracy into a deadly slepe; and so," concludes our chronicle, "he and Bracy cam to Fulco at Whitington," which, now that Morice was got rid of, was allowed to return to the rightful owner.

"Sumer is icumen in"

Musicians have been much puzzled by the wonderful perfection of the work "Sumer is icumen in," as compared with existing examples of the same period. Many such another composition must have been conceived ere this could be set down; for masterpieces are never produced without calling into existence a series of efforts leading up to the crowning work. The fine air and large degree of contrapuntal mastery which this "six-men's song" contains cannot therefore be regarded as accidental, and it is not unreasonable to believe that "it must have been preceded by hundreds of similar compositions, or it could not have reached so high a degree of development."[1] Ritson, "our great poetical antiquary in this sort of thing," was the first to fix upon the thirteenth century as the true date of the MS. containing this

[1] *Story of Notation* (Abdy Williams), p. 112.

A Six Men's Song.[1] (13th Century).

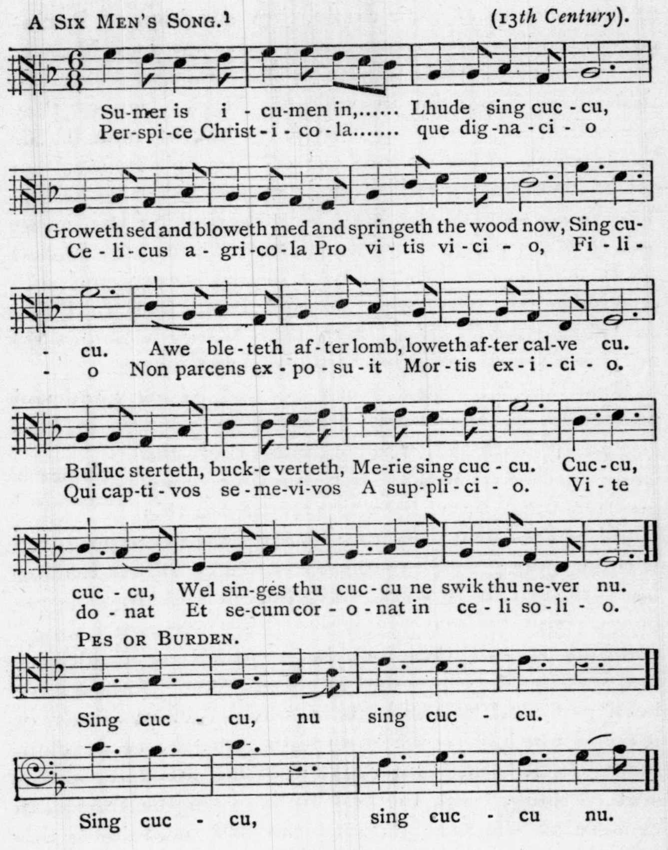
Su-mer is i - cu-men in,...... Lhude sing cuc - cu,
Per-spi-ce Christ - i - co - la....... que dig-na - ci - o
Groweth sed and bloweth med and springeth the wood now, Sing cu-
Ce - li - cus a - gri - co - la Pro vi - tis vi - ci - o, Fi - li -
- cu. Awe ble - teth af - ter lomb, loweth af - ter cal - ve cu.
- o Non parcens ex - po - su - it Mor - tis ex - i - ci - o.
Bulluc sterteth, buck - e verteth, Me - rie sing cuc - cu. Cuc - cu,
Qui cap - ti - vos se - me - vi - vos A sup - pli - ci - o. Vi - te
cuc - cu, Wel sin - ges thu cuc - cu ne swik thu ne - ver nu.
do - nat Et se - cum cor - o - nat in ce - li so - li - o.
Pes or Burden.
Sing cuc - cu, nu sing cuc - cu.
Sing cuc - cu, sing cuc - cu nu.

[1] See Frontispiece.

piece, which Hawkins, Burney, and Warton regarded as of two centuries later, and in regard to which Wanley hesitated to fix any date."[1]

Ritson remarks—"This curious piece, which was for long thought to be the most ancient English song, with or without the musical notes, any where extant," is preserved in a manuscript of the Harleian Library in the Museum (No. 978). It has been already published by Sir John Hawkins, in his very instructive and entertaining *History of Music*, vol. ii. p. 93; and on page 96 of the same volume it is reduced into the scale of modern composition. The ingenious author remarks that Mr. Wanley has not ventured precisely to ascertain the antiquity of this venerably musical relic, but adds the following observation will go near to fix it about the middle of the fifteenth century; a conjecture in which he is doubtless greatly mistaken, as the MS. is evidently of much higher antiquity, and may with the utmost probability be referred to as early a period (at least) as the year 1250. So good a judge of ancient MSS. as Mr. Wanley was could never have been restrained by fear, from giving his opinion of their age; that consideration, however,

Henry III.'s Reign

[1] In Naumann's *History of Music*, vol. i. p. 221 (Cassell), there is the following egregious blunder:—"It has been reserved for Mr. William Chappell to prove the real antiquity of this celebrated composition." Coussemaker makes an equally mistaken note in *L'Art Harmonique*, p. 72 (Paris, 1865). His words are—"M. William Chappell a demontré, dans son savant ouvrage sur les chants populaires de l'Angleterre, que l'écriture de la partie du manuscrit qui contient ce canon est du xiiie siècle."

might have had its weight both with the learned historian and those who have adopted his opinion."[1]

Under the words here given are those of a Latin hymn, to which Sir John Hawkins, on the authority of Du Cange, thinks the term *rota* alone refers, an opinion for which there does not appear sufficient reason; the word implying no more than our *round*. And, hence, perhaps a passage in Shakespeare may receive some illustration. In *Hamlet*, Ophelia, speaking of a ballad of the false steward who stole his master's daughter, exclaims—

> "O how the wheel becomes it,"

evidently meaning the burden or return of the stanza.

A *rote* was likewise an ancient musical instrument, as we may learn from Chaucer—

> "Wel coude he sing and playen on a *rote*."

The thirteenth century is admittedly "one of the most memorable in the history of mankind," and he who would understand the Middle Ages must make it his especial study, as one of the landmarks between the ancient and modern world. With the larger issues of such an age we are not concerned. But music, it must be allowed, invariably reflects the spirit of the time; and though it may not be possible to trace the influence of direct events—such as the first meeting of an English Parliament (1265), the creation of a first Poet Laureate,

[1] Dr. Burney and T. Warton.

or the conquest of Wales (1283)—whatever tended to give a quickened impulse to the life of the people would contribute no less powerfully to the gradual awakening of music, in common with the whole of the arts. To the minstrel of the meanest orders opportunities were there in abundance, for, as most of the trade of the country was transacted at public fairs, song and dance were in constant requisition. English was gradually emerging into currency, as the song in praise of the cuckoo (just considered) well shows. Yet in the revival of learning Latin held a foremost place, as even the current *musical* treatises sufficiently prove. The court poet, "Master Henry the Versifier," was a Frenchman named Henry de Avranches, who in 1251 received one hundred shillings, which Warton supposes to have been for the year's stipend. There is mention also of a harper at the court of Henry III., who is stated to have received forty shillings and a pipe of wine, an additional pipe of the same commodity being given to the harper's wife. The writer mentioned exclaims, "But why this gratuity of a pipe of wine should also be made to his wife, as well as to the husband, who from his profession was a genial character, appears problematical according to our present ideas."

In the last of the Crusades, Prince Edward (afterwards Edward I.) was accompanied by a harper, or minstrel, of whom a curiously brief glimpse is obtained in the following anecdote:—The prince, after his temporary occupation of Nazareth, had fallen back on Acre. An attempt was then made by the

A.D. 1271

Emir of Jaffa to assassinate him. As a letter was handed to the prince, the emir's messenger drew a sudden dagger and aimed a blow at his heart. The royal crusader was sufficiently alert to ward off the blow and strike down his assailant, whom he quickly despatched. Attracted by the noise of the scuffle, out rushed the prince's harper, who, with a valiance which vied with Falstaff's of a later day, beat out the brains of the already defunct assassin with a tripod.[1] For this piece of useless service the prince administered a severe rebuke.

"Ruin seize thee, ruthless king"

The fabled massacre of the Welsh bards is, as is well known, a poetical injustice to Edward I.'s memory. Fierce and relentless he certainly was in battle, and those of the Cymric minstrels who tempted the arbitrament of war would meet with scant mercy. History, however, offers no hint of anything more than what may be termed fair and free fight. The massacre of the bards is bad history, and Gray's fine ode exists in spite of it.[2]

At the marriage of two of Queen Eleanor's daughters, during the year 1290, the minstrels were present in great force. The first ceremony (that of Joan Acre) brought together the English and Scottish "kings of the minstrels," Gray and Caupenny, and the chief harper of the Mareschal of Champagne, together

[1] "Apprehendit unus eorum tripodem, scilicet Cithareda Suus, et percussit eum in capite, et effundit cerebrum ejus."

[2] Gray is understood to have drawn his material from Carte's *History*, who in his turn had been misled by Sir John Wynn's memoirs.

with their trains. At the second nuptial-feast (that of Margaret) there were present no less than 426 minstrels, some of whom are stated to have been English. Amongst this goodly number of musicians, the king's harper, Walter de Storton, distributed £100 (equivalent to not less than £1,500 in modern currency), gift of the bridegroom.

A Knight's Vigil

Towards the close of Edward I.'s reign a still more important concourse of minstrels is to be noted. The company was summoned by proclamation, the occasion being the Prince of Wales undergoing the ordeal of knighthood. On the eve of the Feast of Pentecost (May 22, 1306) some 270 noble youths assembled at Westminster, with their pages and retinue, to watch through the night, in accordance with the rules of chivalry—some in the Temple Church, others in the Gardens, and the prince himself with a favoured few at Westminster Abbey, where the final ceremony took place in the morning. Then a great feast was held, where were served two swans, covered with nets of gold, and brought to table by the minstrels. Nor must we forget to add that, in conformity with the highest traditions of chivalry, the prince took a solemn vow—namely, to avenge the death of Comyn, and to punish the Scottish rebels. Some of the names of the minstrels are recorded as follows:—Le Roy Champaigne, Caupenny, Boisecue, Marchis, and Le Roy Robert, each of whom received the equivalent of £50 of our money, while one Le Roy Druet got no more than £30. These were the chiefs, but mention is made of many others, such as Robert de Colecestria, John de Salopia, and Robert de Scardeburghe. The Bishop of Durham and the Abbot of Abyndon brought their harpers; while such names as these represent the rank and file:—Guillaume sans Manière, Reginald le Menteur, Makejoye, Perle in the Eghe, Northfolke, Haleford, Carletone, Adam de Werintone, Grimmeshawe, Fayrfax, Merlin, with others too numerous to give. The total expended on this assemblage of minstrels was equal to £3000 of our money.

Minstrels now appear to have been treated much the same as heralds. King-at-arms and the king of the minstrels were regular officers, receiving similar salaries at home and abroad;[1] and mention of one King Robert, a minstrel, occurs in this reign. During that of Edward II., William de Morlee (Roy de North) received a grant of some houses which had previously belonged to John le Boteler, another king of the minstrels. In 1387, Richard II. granted permission to travel abroad, and introductory letters, to John Caumz, also a king of minstrelsy. This view is proved to be

[1] In France and Germany there were the *Rex Juglatorum*, *Roy des Violins*, and *Roy des Menestriers*. As early as 1321 the Menestriers of France became a regular corporation, comprising thirty-seven jongleurs and jongleresses. The head, and afterwards the whole body, took the title of *Roi des ménétriers*. They founded the Hospital of St. Julien in 1331. Admission by examination was instituted in 1407, to the exclusion of mere mountebanks and tumblers. The order lingered on until the second half of the seventeenth century, and in its latter days included the famous twenty-four *violons* of Louis XIV.

correct by Froissart's *Chronicles*, where we read—"The same day th' Erle of Foix gave to heralds and minstrels the sum of five hundred francs; and gave to the Duke of Tourayn's minstrels gowns of cloth of gold furred with ermin, valued at two hundred francs." The origin of the Masques may be referred to this reign; while the polished manners and extravagance which they encouraged found a climax in Henry VIII.'s reign, and an anti-climax with the Stuarts. Many things now conduced to stimulate the love of display: French manners, dress, and furniture were being rapidly imported; commercial intercourse with India was re-established. The time was thus ripe for the Masque.

CHAPTER VI.

Monks and Minstrels—Pentecost—Proclamations—Robin Hood—"Ensi va"—*Piers Plowman*—Morris Dance—Gests—Ritson's MS.—Theorists—Tutbury Court—Henry V.—Agincourt—Lydgate—Minstrels' pay—Nowell—"Row the boat, Norman"—Miracle-plays—Musicians' charter—Waites—Music-printing—Sir John Howard—"Chevy Chase" and "John Dory."

THE intercourse with the monks which the minstrels enjoyed is much insisted upon by Warton in his *History of Poetry*. It is well known that most of the monasteries had become more or less influenced by the invasion or wholesale importation of French ecclesiastics; although, while allowing for such a fact, a large number of English monks must still have remained at their posts. What influence such men might have in providing a sympathetic audience for the small minority of English minstrels still in existence can only be conjectured. "The monks," says our authority, "who very naturally sought all opportunities of amusement in their retired and confined situations, were fond of admitting the minstrels to their festivals; and were hence familiarized to romantic stories." At

Date 1309

the feast of the installation of Ralph, Abbot of St. Augustin's, Canterbury, harpers and singers were engaged to assist in entertaining the 6000 guests present at the Abbey Hall—the sum of seventy shillings being mentioned as payment made. An unusual item of information is given in connection with the Bishop of Winchester's visit to St. Swithin's Priory (in 1338), when the "Song of Colbrond" was sung by one Herbert, a minstrel, who further recited (or sung) the "Tale of Queen Emma delivered from the Trial by Fire." So rarely does such information occur, that the entry in the priory register deserves attention:—"Et cantabar Joculator quidam nomine Herebertus Canticum Colbrondi, necnon Gestum Emme regine a judicio ignis liberate in aula prioris."

In a poem of about 1312, Adam Davie has the following distich:—

"Merry it is in halle to here the harpe,
The Minstrelles synge, the Jogelours carpe."

A remarkable anecdote is given by Stow (in his *Survey of London*, 1633), who states that when Edward II. this year (1316) did solemnize the Feast of Pentecost at Westminster, in the great hall, whilst sitting at table in royal state, with his peers about him, there entered a woman habited like a minstrel, riding a great horse trapped as minstrels use. Riding about the tables "showing pastime," she at length approached the king and presented a letter; then turning her horse about, she saluted the company and retired. The contents of this letter formed a remonstrance against the king's favouring his minions to the neglect of his knights and faithful servants. Upon its nature becoming known, the king rebuked the doorkeepers, who promptly replied that minstrels were always admitted, especially during high solemnities and feast-days. The story has been ridiculed by Ritson, who assumes that the lady appeared in the character of a tumbler or tomblestere. There is, however, some ground for believing that women sometimes entered the minstrel profession. In private many ladies could harp and sing, as is well seen from the numerous references made by Chaucer to their accomplishments in this direction. If others did not exist in a public capacity, it seems difficult to explain the existence of such words as the following, quoted by Du Cange:—Gligmeden (glee-maiden), Jengleresse, Joculatrix, Ministralissa, Femina Ministerialis, etc.

Proclamation of Edward II.

Proclamations, or royal edicts, were only effectual in as far as they were supported by existing law; and though a later king (Henry VIII.) sought to give them the virtue of Parliamentary acts, and for a time succeeded, such virtue was eventually categorically denied in the presence of James I. Proclamations concerning the minstrels appear to have been invariably repressive. As an example, witness the following which was put forth in 1316 by Edward II.:—

"Edward by the grace of God, . . . to Sheriffes . . . greeting. Forasmuch as many idle persons, under colour of Minstrelsie, and going in messages and other feigned business, have been and yet be received in other men's houses to meat and drink, and be not therewith contented if they be not largely considered with gifts of the lords of the houses. . . . We willing to restrain such outrageous enterprises and idleness, have ordained that to the houses of prelates, earls, and barons, none resort to meat and drink, unless he be a minstrel; and of these minstrels that there come none, except it be three or four minstrels of honour, at the most in one day, unless he be desired by the lord of the house. And to the houses of meaner men that none come—unless he be desired; and that such as shall so come, hold themselves contented with meat and drink, and with such courtesy as the master of the house will show unto them of his own goodwill, without their asking of anything. And if any one do against this Ordinance, at the first time he is to lose his Minstrelsy, and at the second time to forswear his craft, and never to be received for a minstrel in any house. . . . Given at Langley, the vi. day of August, in the ix. year of our reign."

The abuses which this edict was intended to put down were real enough. That it did not succeed is more than probable, for the same class of offence constantly crops up in the records of the minstrels. A few further proclamations of this class will be found later in these pages.[1]

The proclamation just referred to would scarcely affect the best class of minstrels, who were sufficiently distinguished by the phrase "minstrels of honour" which it contains. Such a view is supported by a passage in Stowe, referring to a gathering of minstrels on the Sunday before Candlemas 1377, when an entertainment was provided by the young aristocracy for the amusement of Prince Richard, son of the Black Prince. The passage is as follows:—

[1] See Edward IV. and Queen Elizabeth.

"On the Sunday before Candlemas, in the night, one hundred and thirty citizens, disguised and well horsed, in a Mummery, with sound of trumpets, sackbuts, cornets, shalmes, and other minstrels, and innumerable torchlights of waxe, rode from Newgate through Cheape, over the Bridge through Southwarke, and so to Kennington besides Lambeth, where the young Prince remained with his mother, and the Duke of Lancaster, his uncle, the Earles of Cambridge, Hertford, Warwicke, and Suffolke, with divers other lords."[1]

Historians of the period recorded even the laughter of kings. Thus, in a roll of some private expenses of Edward II. there is an entry relating to a payment of fifty shillings to a person who danced on the table before the king. The chronicler adds, "Et lui fist tresgrandement rire." Of another, who rode (and often *fell* from) his horse, a circumstance that caused his majesty to laugh heartily ("de quex roi rya grantement"), it is related that the tumbler was awarded twenty shillings—no small pay for such a performance.

Robin Hood appears to have flourished about this period, for in 1324 a person named "Robyn Hode" received wages as one of nineteen persons in the service of Edward II. If we are to believe the ballads, he was pardoned and taken into the king's household, as "vadlet" or porter of the chamber. It seems likely that the hero of the greenwood flourished about the time named, since the Court Rolls of the Manor of Wakefield show that before the rebellion of Earl Lancaster a person of no small distinction bearing this name lived at Wake-

[1] Stow's *Survey of London*, p. 148, ed. 1618.

field, not far from Barnsdale. The interested reader is referred to Ritson's *Robin Hood Garland;* or if he prefer the ballad-story itself, to Wynken de Worde's "Lytel Geste."

Edward III.'s long reign (1327-57) does not help us much with our story, though some useful details concerning music—directly or indirectly—will be chronicled. The music of the king's band was supplied by "5 trompetters, 1 cyteler, 5 pypers, 1 tabrete, 1 mabrer, 2 clarions, 1 fedeler, and 3 wayghtes." A song preserved in the Bodleian Library, Oxford, is of this reign; but, unfortunately for our purpose, it is of French origin. It is taken from an epic poem, copied (it is understood) at Bruges, the date being 1338.

Date of MS. 1338.

En - si va qui a - mours demaine à
son com-mant. A qui que soit do - lours,
en - si va qui a - mours, As mau-vais
est lan - gours nos biens, mais non por-quant
En - si va qui a-mours demaine à son commant.

The author of *Piers Plowman,* Robert (or William) Langland, priest and fellow of Oriel College, Oxford, flourished about this period. His references to minstrelsy[1] are more curious than illuminative:—

> "Not to fare as a fideler, or frier to seke feastes,
> Homely at other mens houses, and haten their own.
> . . . .
> And myrth and minstrelsy amongst men is nought.
> . . . .
> And gladder than the gleman that golde hath to gyfte."

The priests are described as—

> "Chief chanteurs at the nale."

The alehouses, more respectable in olden days than now, were places of common resort for the poets and musicians of those early times:—

> "And then saten some and songe at the nale."

Chaucer, who was born either in 1328 or 1340 (authorities are conflicting), is considered in another chapter; so here we pass him by. An act of supreme importance in history—though not directly concerning music—was that of 1362, which provided that "all pleas in the court of the king, or of any other lord, shall be pleaded and adjudged in the English tongue." Jousts, tournaments, dances, and carols, says an old

[1] Langland writes of himself:—

> "Ich can nat tabre, ne trompe, ne telle faire gestes
> Ne fithelyn, at festes, ne harpen;
> Japen ne jagelyn, ne gentilliche pipe;
> Nother sailen, ne sautrien, ne singe with the giterne."

chronicle, were the recreations of the court. It appears, too, there is some ground for believing the Morris Dance to have been first introduced during Edward III.'s reign. The dance was of Moorish origin, and came to be associated with the English May games, and afterwards formed a part of all the common pageants. In Cheshire the following tune is still danced:—

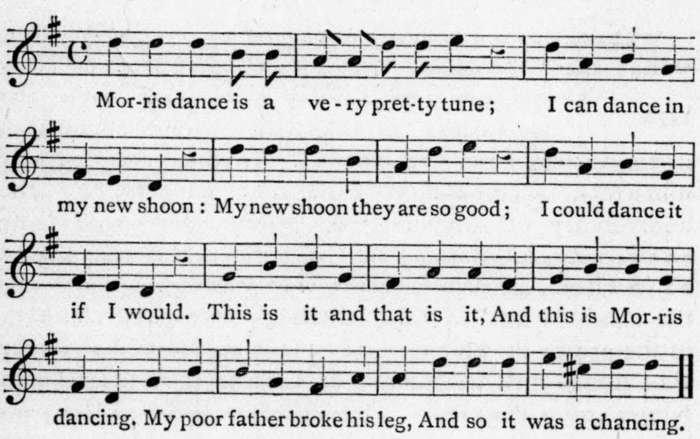

Mor-ris dance is a ve-ry pret-ty tune; I can dance in
my new shoon: My new shoon they are so good; I could dance it
if I would. This is it and that is it, And this is Mor-ris
dancing. My poor father broke his leg, And so it was a chancing.

It is not to be supposed that this Cheshire tune is anything more than a late survival of the old dance which John of Gaunt is said to have introduced to the court of Edward III. In its earliest form the Morris was danced in fancy dress, with bells round the ankles, knees, or wrists, accompanied with much stamping and knocking of heels, which (it is said) was found to give the dancers the gout. In the pageants, a hobbyhorse, a dragon with whifflers, and marshals formed part of the Morris troupe. Its popularity was at its height in Henry VIII.'s day, and though revived at the Restoration, it never regained its ancient prestige. Shakespeare wrote the epitaph of at least a part of such shows in the line—

"For O, for O, the hobbyhorse is forgot."

"I take this opportunity of remarking," says Warton, "that the 'minstrels,' who in this prologue of Nassyngton are named separately from the
1374 'gestours,' or tale-tellers, were sometimes
distinguished from the harpers. In the year 1374 six minstrels, accompanied with four harpers, on the anniversary of Alwyne the Bishop, *performed* their *minstrelsies,* at dinner, in the hall of the convent of St. Swithin, at Winchester; and during supper sung the same 'gest,' or tale, in the great arched chamber of the prior; on which solemn occasion the said chamber was hung with the arras, or tapestry, of the 'Three Kings of Cologne.' These minstrels and harpers belonged partly to the royal household in Winchester Castle, and partly to the Bishop of Winchester. There was an annual mass at the shrine or tomb of Bishop Alwyne in the church, which was regularly followed by a feast in the convent. It is probable that the 'gest' here specified was some poetical legend of the prelate to whose memory this yearly festival was instituted, and who was a Saxon Bishop of Winchester about the year 1040. Although songs of chivalry were

equally common, and I believe more welcome to the monks at these solemnities." The same writer finds a parallel instance under the year 1432. On this occasion the treasurer disbursed four shillings to six minstrels from Buckingham for singing in the refectory a legend called the "Martyrdom of the Seven Sleepers," on the Feast of the Epiphany.[1]

The liberality of Richard II. to his musicians is well seen from a Harleian manuscript (No. 433), where annuities and rewards are exceptionally generous. The "impression" of boys for the Chapel Royal seems to have been first begun in this reign. One John Melynek was empowered "to take and seize for the king all such singing-men expert in the science of music as he could find and think able to do the king's service, within all places of the realm, as well as cathedral churches, colleges, chapels, houses of religion, and all other franchised or exempt places, or elsewhere." Other kings and queens, as will later appear, "took and seized" youths for the royal services, but the above authority is unique as regards the pressing of men for ecclesiastical service.

In a duodecimo MS. of about 1377 contained in the British Museum, a few examples of vulgar music occur, specimens of which may be seen in Ritson's *Ancient*

[1] The Greek version of the legend was never printed. But Warton found a Norman poem (in Saxon character) in the British Museum, which he thinks was afterwards put in English rhyme. The legend is of "the seven" being enclosed in a cave at Ephesus by the Emperor Decius; they were found sleeping (but alive) 372 years afterwards.

Songs. There are six pieces in the MS., with the following titles:—

"Lullay, my childe, and wepe no more" - -	fol. 1.
"Now has Mary born a flour" - - - -	„ 2.
"I have loved so many a day" - - - -	„ 2*b.*
"Lullay, lullow, lullay, my barne, slepe softly now"	„ 3*b.*
"I saw a swete semly syght" - - - -	„ 4.
"Puer natus in Betlehem" - - - - -	„ 6*b.*

Unfortunately, the MS. is fragmentary and extremely fragile. It belonged at one time to Ritson, who states that it was written (partly at least) in the times of Richard II. and Henry IV. He adds that it "contains perhaps the oldest specimens of vulgar music that can be produced." The handwriting is said to be that of "the famous John Brakley, frier minor of Norwich."

I haue loved ſo many a day, ligthly ſpedde bot bett' I may

Yis end' day wen me was wo vnd' a bugh, y' I lay,
Naghc gale to mene me to

On the following page is a picture of the "Virgin Mother" rocking her cradle.

I ſaw a ſwete sēlȳ ſyght a blisful birde
A maydín mod^{s} mek & myld in c^{e}díl kep

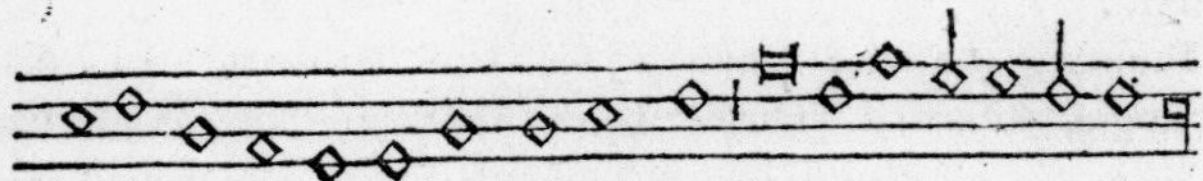

a bloſsū bright y^{t} m̃nȳg made and mirgh of māge
a knaue child y^{t} ſoftly ſlepe ſcho ſat and sāge

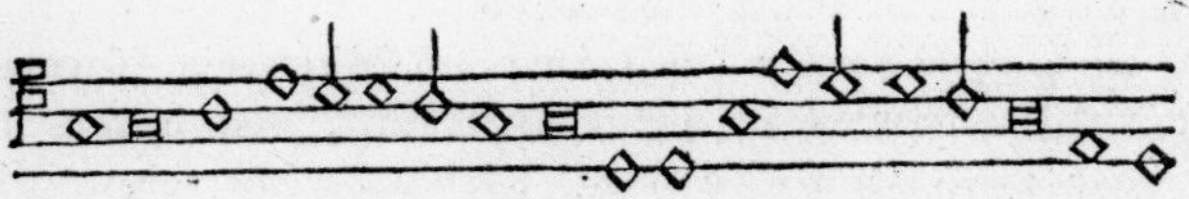

I ſaw a ſwete sēlȳ ſight a bloſsū bright a bliſ-
A maydín mod^{s} mek and mild ī c^{e}díl kepe a knaue

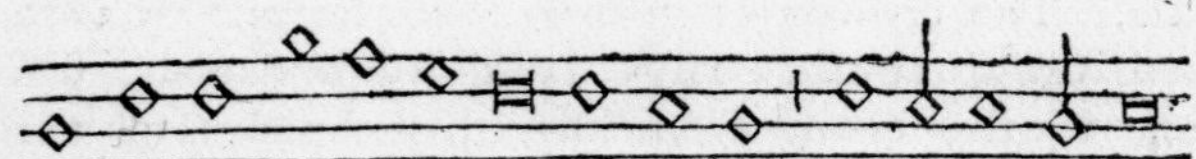

ful bird yt m̃nȳg made and mrthe of m [ange].
child y^{t} ſoftly ſlepe ſcho ſate and ſange.

Many theorists flourished during the reign of Edward III. Such were Simon Tunsted of Norwich, the two De Muris, Torksey, Thomas of Tukesbury, Robert Handlo, Lionel Power, Chilston, and Theinred the Monk. Some of their treatises have been printed by

Coussemaker, who reproduced no less than forty of those written between 1300 and 1400. Readers are referred to the *Story of Notation* ("Music Story Series") for an account of these old writers, whose labours were invaluable in the development of the art of music.

A.D. 1380

Passing to the year 1380, the Statutes of New College, Oxford, show that William of Wykeham enjoined his scholars to sing songs in hall, both before and after supper, on all festal days. Such a direction given by the founder would seem to indicate that singing, probably in parts, was to be expected of educated people.

Minstrels' Court at Tutbury (Staffs.)

A curious record of a Court of Minstrels, formed under the auspices of John of Gaunt, also refers to the year 1380—the fourth of Richard II.'s reign. It appears that in ancient times the Dukes of Lancaster, usually of royal stock, kept great house at Tutbury Castle. The crowds of visitors, here hospitably entertained, drew together large bands of minstrels, who, owing to the common incidental jealousies of their profession, were found somewhat difficult to keep in due order. A code of rules was therefore drawn for their observance. A King of Minstrels (*Roy des Ministraulx*) was chosen, and a Court legally empowered to take and arrest all disobedient members of the craft. Hawkins quotes at some length (*History of Music,* bk. v., chap. xlii.) from Dr. Plot's account of this Minstrels' Court-leet, or Court-baron. Without entering into the minute details of this institution, the following are some of the principal provisions:—

Those who refused their services, or failed in their discharge, were liable to instant arrest. Power was assigned to "our well-beloved" King of Minstrels to execute judgment. The "king" was to summon a court of his fellow-minstrels, to hear plaints and determine controversies.

Dr. Plot distinguishes between the ancient and contemporary procedures at these annual meetings. He describes the procession of minstrels to church, where they go "two and two together, playing their music, with the 'king' for the year marching between steward and bailiff, each with a white wand in hand." Every attendant was expected to contribute one penny to the vicar of the parish church on these occasions. After church a roll was called, and twenty-four of "the sufficientest" among them chosen to form juries, of twelve for Staffordshire and twelve for the other counties. The foremen, after selection, gave a charge, commending to their brethren the consideration of the origin of all music, wind and string; also the antiquity and excellence of both. Such charges were illustrated by quotations from holy writ, and an appeal to the minstrels' own experience. The proceedings terminated with presentations of the various officers, "a noise (*i.e.*, company) of musicians" playing the while, and the circling of the wine-cup in their honour.

The business of the court being over, the minstrels proceeded to a "plentiful dinner," which was followed by a "bull-running." This barbarous performance meant that a bull, with his horns and ears cropped, his tail docked, and his nose filled with pepper, "to make him mad," was then turned loose for the minstrels to pursue during a whole day. He was considered captured if so much as a wisp of hair was torn from him. Finally, after some further cruelties, such as baiting the bull with dogs, the carcase was handed over for the pleasure or profit of the whole body of minstrels, as they thought fit. There is a reference to this ancient barbarity in a Robin Hood ballad of early date:—

Bull-running

"This battle was fought near Tutbury town,
When the bagpipes baited the bull,
I'm King of the Fidlers, and swear 'tis a truth,
And call him that doubts it a gull.
For I saw them fighting, and fiddled the while.
And Clorinda sung Hey derry down;
The bumpkins are beaten, put up thy sword, Bob;
And now let's dance into the town.
Before we came to it we heard a great shouting,
And all that were in it look'd madly;
For some were a bull-back, some dancing a morrice,
And some singing Arthur a Bradley."

The only Act of Henry IV. which survives in connection with minstrelsy is set forth in a statute (dated 1402) which applied to the Welsh bards. The curious hybrid wording alone merits quotation:—

Henry IV. (1399-1413)

"Item, pur eschuir plusieurs diseases et mischiefs qont advenuz devaunt ces heures en la terre de Gales par plusieurs Westours Rymours Minstralx et autres Vacabondes, ordeignez est et establiz qe nul Westour, Rymour Ministral ne Vacabond soit aucunement sustenuz en la terre de Gales pur faire kymorthas ou coillage sur la commune people illoeques."

The severity with which the statute treats the bards—once the companions of kings—not only indicates that they had lost caste; it was aimed at checking the particular mischief which the bards' songs incited—liberty, from their point of view; rebellion, as the statute regarded it. The privilege which these men possessed, it is said, had led to spying and the carrying of secret intelligence, which the strenuous measures of the dominant country sought to put down.

The reign of Henry V. supplies us with several incidents which serve to illustrate our subject. "The coronation of Henry V.," says Warton, "was celebrated in Westminister Hall with a solemnity proportioned to the lustre of those great achievements which afterwards distinguished the annals of that victorious monarch. By way of preserving order, and to add to the splendour of the spectacle, many of the nobility were ranged along the sides of the tables on large war-horses, at this stately festival; which, says my chronicle, was a second feast of Ahasuerus. But I mention this ceremony to introduce a circumstance very pertinent to our purpose; which is, that the number of harpers in the hall was innumerable, who undoubtedly accompanied their instuments with

Henry V.

heroic rhymes. The king, however, was no great encourager of the popular minstrelsy, which seems at this time to have flourished in the highest degree of perfection." Another writer observes that the number of harpers was exceedingly great, and that the sweet strings of their harps "soothed the souls of the guests by their soft melody." It would almost seem that minstrelsy was dying harder in England than abroad, where the Provençals had already ceased writing. When preparing to visit France in 1415, Henry expressly summoned his minstrels to attend him.[1] A French writer speaks of the English camp, on the day before Agincourt, as "resounding with national music." Immediately before battle, however, a strict silence was enjoined.

> "Agincourt, Agincourt, know ye not Agincourt?
> Where the English slew or hurt
> All the French foemen."

The king returned in triumph to London, where the gates were hung with tapestry showing the old heroic battles. Children were placed in artificial turrets, singing verses in honour of the occasion. Henry would not countenance their music, which he not only forbade, but commanded that for the future "no ditties should be made and sung by minstrels or others" in praise of

[1] Eighteen of these men are mentioned as receiving "12d. per diem," a sum equal to about 15 shillings in our values.

the battle, and that the thanks should be rendered to God alone.[1]

A song inspired of this great event is happily preserved to us in the so-called "Agincourt Song."

Song on the Victory at Agincourt (1415).

[1] Holingshed's *Chronicle* says, "He would not suffer any Dities to be made and sung by Minstrels, of his glorious victorie; for that he would wholly have the praise and thankes altogether given to God."

grace and might of chi - val - ry, There God for
him wrought marv' - lous - ly Where - fore Eng - land may
call and cry, De - o................ gra - ti - as.
CHORUS. ALTO.
TENOR.
De - o gra - ti - as An - - gli-
BASS.

Stafford Smith appears to have brought it to light, by his publication of a facsimile in his *Collection of English Songs* (1779). Burney also included the music in his *History* (vol. 2), in 1782.[1] Mention should further be made of the copy which Percy included in his *Reliques*—unfortunately, an inaccurate one. The MS. from which these versions were taken was in the Pepysian Library, Cambridge, from whence it has been since lost. Fortunately, Trinity College possessed a manuscript roll of thirteen pieces, the "Agincourt Song" being one. As this roll is now printed, a description is unnecessary. It may, however, be pointed out that this "Agincourt Song" is modelled almost precisely on the lines of the Carols of the fifteenth century, twelve of which form the rest of the contents of the MS. roll. The authorship has been attributed to John Dunstable, with a high degree of probability. Another

Agincourt

[1] Burney remarks that "Specimens of musical compositions at such an early period are so scarce, and this in particular seems so much to belong to my subject, that a history of English music would be deficient without it." (*History*, ii. 383.)

MS. of this battle-song is preserved in the Bodleian. It is seen, on comparison, that there are important variations in the three versions. That we quote is the Trinity College MS. It may have been this "ditty" that Henry V. forbade being sung by the children in the artificial turrets, but it must be confessed that there is no evidence forthcoming. So great an occasion as that of Agincourt could not but call forth a large number of poetical and musical compositions, one of which ("among many others") is referred to by Warton as the "Seyge of Harfleet and the Battallye of Agynkourte," written in 1417—that is, two years after the battle.

Henry's humility was not assumed when he imposed his *Non nobis*, as is seen from the fact that, contrary to custom, he would not allow his helmet to be publicly exposed to the people's gaze, "that they might behold the dintes and cuttes whiche appeared in the same, of such blowes and stripes as he received the daye of the battell."[1]

Then we discover that in the year following Agincourt he duly celebrated the Feast of Pentecost, having for his guests the Emperor, and the Duke of Holland; while sixteen minstrels—one of whom, Thomas Chatterton, is mentioned by name—were retained for their amusement. Their rewards are stated to have been "rich gowns." In the early days of the Plantagenets such rewards were not uncommonly in the shape of arms, clothes, horses, and gifts in kind. But we have

[1] Holingshed.

already seen that substantial sums of money, and even houses and land were sometimes the guerdon of the best class of minstrel. It is, therefore, with no surprise that we find King Henry V. granting, at death, an annuity of one hundred shillings to each of his minstrels, a legacy duly executed by his successor, in 1423.

"The reign of Henry VI.," says Ritson, "is an era of great consequence in the poetical annals of this country; not so much, indeed, from the excellence, as from the magnitude and multiplicity of its metrical productions. The works of Lydgate, monk of Bury, alone, are nearly sufficient to load a waggon."

A.D. 1422

After his coronation at Paris, Henry VI. made a triumphal entry into London, where a series of allegorical spectacles were represented; some of the figures being a giant, representing religious fortitude, Enoch, Eli, the Trinity, two judges, eight sergeants of the coife, Dame Clennesse, Mercy, Truth, and others of a like nature. One of Lydgate's songs has for its subject this very event. It runs thus:—

"Rejoice! ye Reames of englond and of ffraunce,
A braunche that sprang oute of the floure de lys,
Blode of Seint Edward and Seint lowys,
God hath this day sent in governaunce.
God of nature hath yoven him suffisaunce
Likely to atteyne to grete honoure and pris.
O hevenly blossome, O budde of all plesaunce,
God graunt the grace for to ben als wise
As was thi fader by circumspect advise,
Stable in v'tue withoute variaunce."

At the coronation feast of this king, some curious dishes were served up, if their devices mean anything. In the first course a subtlety ("sotiltie") was contrived showing St. Edward and St. Lewis, in coat-of-mail, "holding between them a figure like King Henry, similarly armed, and standing *with a ballad under his feet.*" In the second course a device of Emperor Sigismund and Henry V., arrayed in mantles of garter, and a figure like Henry VI., kneeling before them with a *ballad against the Lollards.* The third course offered a presentment of Our Lady, with a child in her lap and a crown in her hand, with St. George and St. Denis upon either side presenting to her King Henry, *with a ballad in his hand.* It is said that these so-called subtleties were devised by the clergy, who desired to turn attention from their own misdemeanours to those of the Lollards or Wickliffites. The latter certainly gave the churchmen occasion for a grudge, for we find an ecclesiastic complaining that "the people laugh at us, and make us their songs all the day long."

If the clergy were bitter against the ballad-writers, they had good reason to be also jealous of the minstrels
A.D. 1430 proper, who at this time were better paid than were they, as may be learned from Hearne's note as follows:—"The fraternity of the Holy Crosse in Abingdon, in Henry VI.'s time, being there where now the hospital is, did every year keep a feast, and then they used to have twelve priests to sing a dirige, for which they had given them fourpence a-piece. They had also twelve minstrels, some from Coventry

and some from Maidenhead, who had two shillings and threepence a-piece, besides their diet and horse-meat." The chronicler adds, "Observe that in those dayes they payd there mynstrells better than theyre preistes." The reason, of course, was that the people of those days, as in more enlightened times, loved better to be pleased than instructed.[1]

Another historical instance may be quoted from 1441, when eight priests were hired from Coventry to assist in celebrating a yearly obit at Maxtoke Priory Church. Hither also came six of Lord Clinton's Mimi, or minstrels, to sing, harp, and play in the monastery hall, while the monks enjoyed a special anniversary refection. For their respective services the priests received two shillings to the minstrels' four; moreover, the latter supped in *camera picta*—that is, in the painted chamber of the convent, with the sub-prior, by the light of "eight massy tapers of wax." In dismissing this part of the minstrels' history, it may be added that during the same year, the Maxtoke prior gave the sum of sixpence (not less than five shillings of our present money) to a Doctor Praedicans, an itinerant preacher, in pay for his sermon.[2]

As a specimen of the music of these times, quotation is made of a Christmas carol which is understood to date from 1460. Originally the music had two sets of words—sacred and secular, an arrangement which

[1] Warton's *History of Poetry*.

[2] In Elizabeth's time (1560), a record of the Stationers' Company has the following:—"Item, payd to the preacher, 6s. 2d. Item, payd to the minstrell, 12s."

seems to have been common during the Middle Ages. The MS. which disappeared while in the hands of the printer, was, fortunately, already in type, being edited for the Percy Society by T. Wright. We give a copy of the music, with the first verse of the carol exactly as they appear in the Percy Society's volume:—

> "Nowell, nowell, nowell, nowell!
> This is the salutation of the angel Gabriel.
>
> Tidings true there be come new, sent from the Trinity,
> By Gabriel to Nazareth, city of Galilee.
> A clean maiden and pure virgin,
> Through her humility
> Hath conceived the person second in Deity."

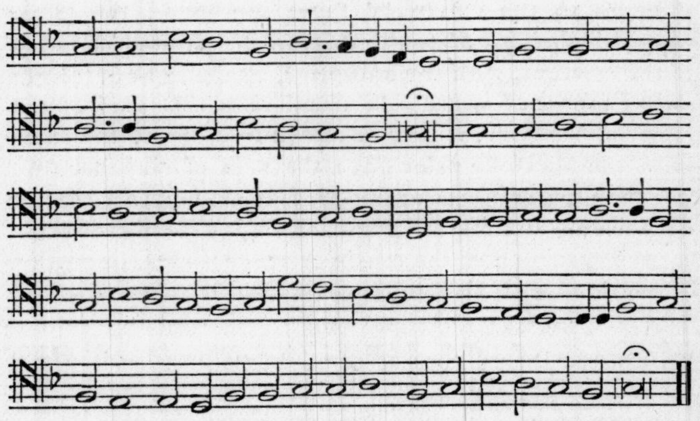

The editor of the MS. quoted remarks that "the great variations in the different copies of the same song show that they were taken down from oral recitation, and had often been preserved by memory among minstrels who were not unskilful at composing; and who were not only in the habit of voluntarily or involuntarily modifying the songs as they passed through their hands, but of adding or omitting stanzas from the different compositions which were imprinted on their memories." The MS., which contains drinking songs and satires on the fair sex, was in all probability originally the property of a country minstrel, who would sing at fairs and rural gatherings. The value of these songs was thus appraised by Dr. Johnson: "The merriment is very gross, and the sentiments very worthless."

A fragment of a popular song is mentioned by the poet Skelton in the "Bowge of Court"—his best serious poem—introduced by Haruy Hafter, one of the characters, as follows:—

"His throat was clear, and lustily could feign
And ever he sang, sith I am nothing plain,
To keep him from piking it was a great pain.
Hold up the helm, look up, and let God steer;
I would be merry what wind that ever blow,
Heave and ho! rumbelow, row the boat, Norman row.'

Heave and ho, rum-below, Row the boat, Norman, row, Row to the ha-ven.

For three equal voices; the second entering two bars after the first, and the third voice two bars after the second.

Hilton's "Catch that Catch can" (1652) preserves the music we have quoted. Playford afterwards substituted "Whittington" for "Norman." This Norman was Mayor of London in the thirty-second year of Henry VI.'s reign. The Thames watermen are credited with the authorship of the song; for Norman, instead of proceeding through the streets to Westminster, was rowed thither by water, and thus earned their thanks and a song. D'Israeli notes in his *Curiosities of Literature* (1785), "Our sailors at Newcastle, in heaving their anchors, have their 'Heave and ho! rum below,'" which serves to show the singular vitality this *occasional* song possessed. In the poem which preserves the song, Skelton has other references to the music of his time, which may be briefly quoted. Here is a pupil (the same Haruy Hafter) desirous of learning prick-song:—

"Princes of youghte, can ye sing by rote,
Or shall I sail with you a fellowship essay,
For on the book I cannot sing a note;
Would to God, it would please you some day,
A ballad book before me for to lay,
And learn me to sing (Re mi fa sol),
And when I fail, bob me on the noll."

Of another character (viz., Ryot) it is said—

"Counter he coude (O lux) upon a pot."

"O Lux beata Trinitas," so unceremoniously introduced, was a favourite theme so late as in the time of

James I., and the habit of extemporizing upon such melodies seems to be indicated by Skelton's verse.

Henry VI.'s Reign

The introduction of vocal part-music in the miracle-plays and mysteries (the early attempts at dramatic composition) can be traced to this reign. So much is evidenced by a MS. (in the Towneley collection) in the form of a miracle-play on the subject of the Adoration of the Shepherds. The character of this work amounts almost to farce, in spite of its religious disguise. In the moral play, *Mind, Will, and Understanding* (also dating from Henry VI.'s time), there is the following:—

"*Mynde.* I rejoys of thes; now let us synge.
Undyrstondyng. Ande yff I spare, evell joy me wrynge.
Wyll. Have at you I; lo, I have a sprynge;
Lust makyth me wondyr wylde.
Mynde. A tenour to you both I brynge.
Undyrstondyng. And I a mene for any kynge.
Wyll. And but a trebul I out wrynge,
The devell hym spede that myrthe exyled."

Though the stage direction adds "Et Cantent" (and let them sing), unfortunately the music and words have both disappeared. In another part of this morality, the direction runs—"Here they go out, and in the goying the soule syngyth in the most lamentabull wyse with drawte notes, as yt ys songyn in the passyon wyke."

Although religious parodies were composed in Greek during the fourth century, the true origin of sacred comedy is of later date. During the eighth century, the establishment of public marts, due to Charlemagne, brought together numbers of people, whom the merchants endeavoured to attract and divert by means of shows, in which music and dancing were brought into requisition. The success of these performances led to their interdiction by the priests. Finding opposition useless, the clergy, with a worldly wisdom not always so readily forthcoming, took a leaf out of the secular book, and themselves turned actors. Stories from the Bible were turned into little plays, in which much of the grossness and absurdity of the fairs were still evident. *The Feast of Fools*, the *Prose de l'Âne*, and *La Fête des Innocens* became highly popular. William the Conqueror did for our own country a service similar to Charlemagne's for France. The miracle-play of *St. Catherine*, acted at Dunstaple in 1110, is but one of a number of such pieces popular at the time, especially in London.[1] At Chester in 1327 many such pieces were given at the expense of the trading companies. A few of these plays are thus entitled: *Fall of Lucifer*, *Creation*, *Deluge*, *Abraham*, *Moses*, *Salutation and Nativity*, *The Three Kings*, *Last Supper*, *Resurrection*, *The Ascension*. The plays were in the hands of the clergy, who, however, employed minstrels

[1] Du Cange describes the farces and drolls given at the French Court about the year 1290 in the following terms:—"The company was entertained with the instrumental music of the minstrels, who played on the kettledrum, flageolet, cornet, cittern, flute, trumpet, Moorish cittern, and fiddle. Comedies," says he, "were performed by Farceurs, Jongleurs, and Plaisantins."

for the musical portions of the entertainment. Thus, at Coventry in 1474 there is mention of minstrelsy and organ-playing. As early as 1378, the choristers of St. Paul's Cathedral, London, presented a petition to Richard II. to protect their Christmas plays, upon which much money had been spent, and which were being interfered with "by ignorant and unexperienced persons" acting the same. The St. Paul's children became so expert in these matters that they were not uncommonly in request at Court.[1] At Eton it was customary on the Feast of St. Andrew (November 30th) to select a play for the boys to learn "over against Christmas," when it was publicly presented, in Latin or English, as the case might be. Other schools, about this time, followed the same custom. Such is the briefest possible account of the precursors of the drama, the opera, and the oratorio.

The friars of Coventry, whose history is inseparable from that of our early drama,[2] entertained Queen Margaret (wife of Henry VI.) in 1456 with a presentation of pageants. Later (in 1474), the same famous exhibitors played before the son of Edward IV.; the

[1] In a puritanical pamphlet (1569), entitled *The Children of the Chapel Stript and Whipt*, there is the following:—"Even in her Majesty's chapel do these pretty upstart youths profane the Lord's Day by the writhing of their tender limbs and gorgeous decking of their apparel, in feigning fables gathered from the idolatrous heathen poets."

[2] The old morality of *Everyman*, successfully revived in our time, was originally printed (in black-letter) by John Skot, of *Powle's Chyrche Yarde*, in Henry VIII.'s reign. Pynson reprinted it. (See Hawkins' *Origin of the English Drama*, where it is reproduced).

piece offering such characters as Edward the Confessor, St. George and the Dragon, and so forth. The conduit on which the champion was placed "running wine in four places;" there was also "minstrelsy of organ-playing."

The second half of the fifteenth century was a notable period in the musical history of this country. Already signs were not wanting that a new order of men was springing up which had little or nothing in common with the minstrel class, though practising a higher development—so much must be allowed—of the same art. Dunstable, the most considerable musician which England had so far produced, died in 1453. The confusion into which the Wars of the Roses (1455-71) plunged the country did not entirely suspend the progress of music. In 1456 a commission was formed for impressing youths to supply vacancies among the king's minstrels. Care was to be had that those chosen should be graceful and attractive no less than well-skilled in music, for the better diversion of his Majesty Henry VI. John Hamboys may be mentioned as one of the new school. He is referred to in *Holingshed's Chronicle* as one eminent for learning. Hamboys is said by Hawkins to have been "the first person on whom the degree of Doctor in Music was conferred by either of the universities in this kingdom." The records, it seems, neither disprove nor support the statement. Mention of several graduates occurs about this time. Thus, we read of Henry Habington being admitted a Bachelor of Music at Cambridge in 1463; while in the same year Thomas Saintivex (or Sainwix),

Mus. Doc., was made Provost of King's College (Cambridge), by the founder, Henry VI. A remarkable passage in Erasmus confirms our view that music was now being much cultivated. "As nature has implanted self-love," says this writer, "in the minds of all mortals, so has she dispensed to every country and nation a certain tincture of the same affection. Hence it is that the English challenge the prerogative of having the most handsome women, of being most accomplished in the skill of music, and of keeping the best tables."[1]

Edward IV.

In the ninth year of the reign of Edward IV., on the complaint of some of the king's minstrels that their livery and title was being appropriated and used by certain rude husbandmen and artificers of various trades, a royal charter was granted for the protection of these musicians. Walter Haliday, who had served under the two preceding monarchs, was appointed as Marshal—a title which, it may be noted, had been his since 1464, when he is so described in an instrument granting a pension of ten marks annually for life. The minstrels associated with Haliday were John Cliff, Robert Marshall, Thomas Grene, Thomas Calthorn, William Cliff, William Cristean, and William Eyneysham. It may be observed that three of the minstrels mentioned—namely, Haliday, Marshall, and John Cliff—had been appointed pre-

Royal Charter

[1] "Natura ut singulis mortalibus suam, ita singulis nationibus, ac penè civitatibus communem quandam insevisse Philautium; atque hinc fieri Britanni præter alia, formam, musicam, et lautas mebsas proprie sibi vindicent."—*Moriæ Encomium.*

viously by Henry VI. to provide youths in the room of members of the royal minstrels who were deceased. King Edward's charter granted letters patent to the effect that the Marshal and his seven associates should form "in deed and name one body and cominality, perpetual and capable in the law, and should have perpetual succession; and that as well the minstrels of the said king which then were, as other minstrels of the said king, and his heirs which should be afterwards, might at their pleasure name, choose, ordain, and successively constitute from amongst themselves one marshal, able and fit to remain in that office during his life, and also two wardens every year, to govern the said fraternity and guild."

Edward IV.'s Band

In the king's private establishment provision was made for "Minstrels thirteen, whereof one is virger, who directeth them on all festival days, in their stations of blowing and pipings, to such offices as the officers might be warned to prepare for the king's meats and suppers; to be more readier in all services and due time; and all these sitting in the hall together, whereof some be trumpets, some with the shalmes and small pipes, and some are strange men coming to this court at five feasts of the year, and then take their wages of household after 4d. by day, accordingly as they have been present in court, and to depart after the morrow of the feast, beside their other rewards yearly in the king's exchequer, and clothing with the household, winter and summer for each of them 20s., and they take nightly amongst them all four gallons of ale; and for winter season three wax candles, 6 candles of pitch, 3 taleshieds (bundles of firewood); lodging sufficient by the 'herbengere' for them and their horses, nightly to the court. Also having into court 2 servants to bear their trumpets, pipes, and other instruments, and torch for winter nights, whilst they blow to supper of the Chantrey; and alway two of these persons to continue still in court at wages by the check-roll, whilst they be present 4d. daily to warn the king's riding household when he goeth to horseback as oft as it shall require, and that his household men may follow the more reddier after by the blowing of the trumpets. If any of the two minstrels be let blood in court, he taketh 2 loaves, 2 messes of great meat, one gallon of ale. They part not at no time with the rewards given to the household. Also when it pleaseth the king to have 2 minstrels continuing in court, they will not in nowise that these minstrels be so familiar to ask rewards.

"A Waite[1] that nightly from Michaelmas to Shrove

[1] The Wait was originally a watchman, whose instrument (hautboy) was also known as "wait" or "waight." Stowe states that in 1253, Henry III. established Watches in London, and that at certain seasons (as Midsummer) great processions numbering (on one occasion, at least) 2000 men, with drummers, fifes, and mounted trumpeters going before, perambulated the city, where bonfires and banquettings were prepared in the streets. After Henry VIII.'s time these city watches became less and less; finally, a wait was a town appointment, held by a musician who took part in civic shows. The Waits at Christmas-time are the watchers, or wakes, who greet the anniversary of the Nativity morning.

Thursday pipeth watch within this court four times; in the summer nights three times; and maketh Bon Gayte at every chamber door and office as well for fear of pickers and pillers. He eateth in the hall with minstrels and taketh livery at night a loaf, a gallon of ale, and for summer nights two candles pitch, a bushel of coal; and for winter nights half a loaf of bread, a gallon of ale, four candles pitch, a bushel of coal; daily whilst he is present in court for his wages in check roll allowed 4d. or else 3d. by the discretion of the steward and treasurer, and that after his coming and deserving, also clothing with the hoysehold yeomaen or minstrels, like to the wages that he taketh; an he be sick he taketh two loaves, two messes of great meat, one gallon of ale. Also he parteth with the household of general gifts and have his bedding carried by the controller's assignment, and under this yeoman to be a groom waiter. If he can excuse the yeoman in his absense then he taketh reward clothing meat and all other things like to other grooms of household. Also this yeoman waite at the making of Knights of the Bath, for his attendance upon them by night-time, in watching in the chapel after his fee all the watching clothing that the knight shall wear upon him.

"The Dean hath all corrections of Chapellmen, *in moribus et scientia;* except in some cases to the steward and counting-house; he nor none of the Chapel parteth with the household of no general gifts except vesture.

"Chaplins and Clerks of the Chapel xxiiii. by the Dean's election or denomination, endowed with virtues moral and speculative, as of the music, showing in descant, clear voiced, well relished in pronouncing. Eloquent in readings, sufficient in organs playing, and modest in all other behaviour, sitting in the hall together at the Dean's board, also lodging together within the court in one chamber, or else nigh thereto. And every each of them being in court for his daily wage allowed in the check roll, vii[d]."

The two Epistellers (or Pisteleres) were chosen from the older children of the chapel, in order of seniority. Of the latter there were eight. They were boarded, lodged, and taught singing and the use of the "orgaines" by a master of song appointed for that purpose. Arrived at the age of eighteen years, "and their voyces changed," they were sent at the charge of the king to Oxford or Cambridge, until the king "may otherwise advaunce them." Finally, this curious document mentions the duties of the Master of the "Gramere Schole," who was to be skilled in poetry, grammar, music, etc. If such master was also a priest, he had to sing "our Lady Masse, in the king's chapel, or else read the gospel, and be at the great procession." He was allowed livery for his horses, and permitted to keep "one honest servant."

This charter restores to the king's minstrels a "Fraternity, or perpetual guild—such as, it is understood, the brothers and sisters of the fraternity of minstrels held in times past. The marshal and two wardens were authorized to examine the pretensions of those who exercised the minstrel profession, and to regulate, govern, and punish (where necessary) all such persons, excepting only those of Chester," who, as we have before seen, were specially chartered. A new office appears to have been created during Edward IV.'s reign, for there is mention of a "Serjeant of Minstrels." This was held by one Alexander Carlile. The confidential character of the appointment, it is said, is shown by the fact of the Serjeant having access to the king's chamber at all times. The following anecdote is preserved from a fragment quoted by Hearne[1]:—"And as he was in the north contray in the moneth of Septembre, as he laye in his bedde, one named Alexander Carlisle, that was sarjaunt of the mynstrallis, cam to him in grete haste, and bade him aryse, for he hadde enemys cummyng for to take him, the which were within vi. or vii. mylis, of the which tydinges the king gretely marveylid." This incident is of the same year as the charter just quoted, and it is somewhat singular that the Serjeant is not anywhere referred to.

The importance of this period is sufficiently marked when it is remembered that in 1469 Caxton's *Morte d'Arthur* appeared. Another instance, smaller in its significance but more directly bearing on our subject, is the foundation of the Musicians' Company of the City of London, the charter of which is no other than that already described above, under the mastership of Walter Haliday. It may not be improper to observe that this Company, with its rich endowment, is, at the time of writing, doing much to encourage that art

[1] *Sprotti Chron.*, ed. Hearne. Oxford, 1719.

which in olden times it was the privilege of kings to make or to mar.

The first music-printing is understood to have been the Gregorian tunes issued by Hans Froschauer at Augsburg in 1473. Previously spaces were left, or only a printed stave offered, for the music-character to be afterwards inserted by hand. Higden's *Polychronicon*—from the press of Caxton's pupil, Wynken de Worde—was issued from Westminster in 1495,—important to England as the first native production of the kind. With these brief data, we must pass on to the concluding portion of our sketch. It cannot, however, be too clearly borne in mind that the advent of the printing art was of immense influence in sealing the fate of the wandering minstrel. His productions began to appear ridiculous by the side of the well thought-out and polished performance of the writers of romance and lyric verse. The old minstrel could play and sing, but he could not read or write. The people were now beginning to read,[1] and many of the older pieces were recast and re-polished that they might bear the test of the eye, as well as the ear. This seems to have been the last effort of the better class of minstrel; while his brethren of the poorer sort, who flourished in spite of the royal charters, quickly degenerated into absolute vagrancy.

[1] "Nowadays," writes Aubrey, "books are common, and most of the poor people understand letters; and the many good books and variety of turns of affairs, have put all the old fables out of doors. And the divine art of printing and gunpowder have frightened away Robin Goodfellow and the fairies."

The class of men who now enter into our story were retainers of the nobility and gentry. Every great family had its band of musicians, who still went by the name of Minstrels, though the order was becoming widely separated from its original stock.

Sir John Howard's Minstrels

The household book of Sir John Howard gives numerous details of music and musicians. Thus, we read that the three following were employed as singers:—Nicholas Stapylton, William Lyndsey, and "Little Richard," in addition to six children of the chapel. The chief minstrel was no doubt Thomas "the harperd." Many others of the order were employed, in accordance with the custom of the time, when Sir John visited or took his journeys. Mention is also made of the son of John Colet of Colchester, living with William Wastell, harper, of London, who was to prepare the youth for service as a harper in the said establishment.

"The Battle of Otterburn" and "Chevy Chase"—two of the surviving ballads of the period 1460-1500—may be regarded as genuine minstrel songs, originally written for and sung to the harp. "Chevy Chase" was first printed by Hearne at the end of his edition of William of Newborough. It was preserved by Richard Sheale, a minstrel living in 1548. Much confusion has arisen by a mistake (which seems to have originated with Addison[1]) in supposing Sheale's version to be the popular one. A reference to Percy's *Reliques* will show that the original form preserved by Sheale begins thus—

[1] *Spectator*, 70 and 74.

"Chevy Chase"

"The Perse owt of Northumberlande,
And a vowe to God made he,
That he wolde hunte in the mountayns
Off Chyviat within dayes thre."

And it is of this ballad that Sir Philip Sydney spoke when he exclaimed, "Certainly, I must confess my own barbarousness; I never heard the old song of Percy and Douglas, that I found not my heart moved more than with a trumpet; and yet it is sung but by some blind crowder with no rougher voice than rude style, which being so evil apparelled in the dust and cobweb of that uncivil age, what would it work trimmed in the gorgeous eloquence of Pindar?" To the modern and more widely known version of this ballad we shall presently return.

The air to which the ballad was sung is one of the most famous in all our minstrelsy, and, in accordance with a common custom, was used for numberless other ballads which had no tune of their own. For example, in Philips' *Old Ballads* (1723) this air, known as "Flying Fame," does duty for the following pieces:—"King Alfred and the Shepherd," "King Leir and his 3 Daughters," "King Arthur and the Round Table," "Battle of Agincourt," "The Union of Red and White Rose," "Roman Charity," "Alfonso and Ganselo," "The Wanton Wife of Bath," and the original ballad of Chevy Chase itself.[1]

[1] Other ballads to the same tune are "The Gentleman in Thracia," "When as King Henry rul'd this land," "When Arthur first in court began," and "The Belgick Boar."

"FLYING FAME."

God pros-per long our no-ble King, Our lives and safeties all, A
woe-ful hunt-ing once there did In Che-vy Chase be-fall.

We give a simple harmonization of the air. Many versions of the tune exist. The above appears to be its most dignified form. Perhaps the *worst* is that printed as the first piece in *Pills to Purge Melancholy*, vol. iv. (1719), headed "Three Children sliding on the Thames. Tune: Chivy-Chase," in this way—

Having spoiled the tune, Durfey proceeds to put forth the following doggerel:—

> "Some Christian people all give ear
> Unto the grief of us,
> Caus'd by the death of three children dear,
> The which it happen'd thus."

"John Dory"

The air makes its reappearance on page 289 of the same volume, in association with the modernization of the original ballad, the first verse of which has already been quoted. One cannot help wondering if the minstrels of old gave the complete 270 verses at one audience! Curiously enough, the air crops up for the third and last time at page 326 of the same volume, now degraded into "A Warning to all Custard Eaters." There we take leave of it.

Of about the same period, and of scarcely less popularity, was the old ballad of "John Dory," whose exploits appear to have been entirely mythical. Dryden, in one of his lampoons, refers to it as the most hackneyed thing of the time. (See Ritson's *Ancient Songs;* 1792). The music to this singular ditty is to be found in its best form in Ravenscroft's *Deuteromelia* (1609); another version is in Playford's *Musical Companion* (1687), and the early editions of *Pills to Purge Melancholy.*

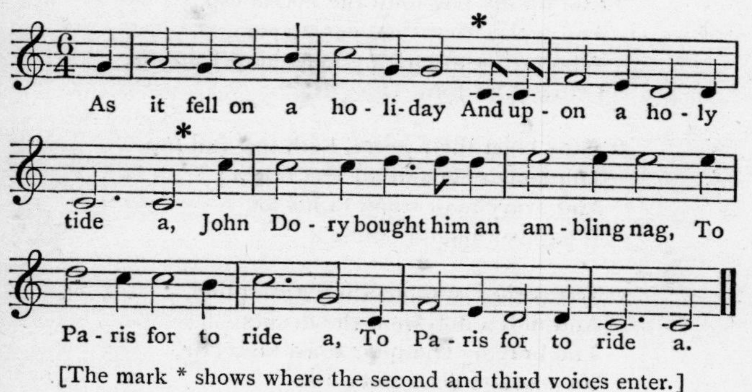

[The mark * shows where the second and third voices enter.]

"And when John Dory to Paris was come,
A little before the gate a,
John Dory was fitted, the porter was witted,
To let him in thereat a.

"The first man that John Dory did meet
Was good King John of France a;
John Dory could well of his courtesie,
But fell downe in a trance a.

"A pardon, a pardon, my Liege and my King,
For my merie men and for me a;
And all the churles in merie England,
Ile bring them all bound to thee a.

"And Nicholl was then a Cornish man,
A little beside Bohide a;
And he made forth a good blacke barke,
With fifty good oares on a side a.

"Run up my boy unto the maine top,
And looke what thou canst spie a.
Who ho! who ho! a goodly ship I do see,
I trow it be John Dory a.

"They hoist their sailes, both top and top,
The meisseine and all was tide a;
And every man stood to his lot,
Whatever should betide a.

"The roring cannons then were plide,
And dub a dub went the drumme a;
The braying trumpets lowd they crie,
To courage both and all a.

"When Fidlers sing at Feasts"

"The grapling hooks were brought at length,
The browne bill and the sword a;
John Dory at length, for all his strength,
Was clapt fast under board a."

Many are the allusions to this old ballad, which, if it could be traced, might date back to the time of Henry VI. Dryden refers to it thus—

"But Sunderland, Godolphin, Lory,
These will appear such chits in story,
'Twill turn all politics to jests,
To be repeated like John Dory,
When fidlers sing at feasts."

Apart from the antiquity of the piece, it must be confessed that there is small merit in either words or music; yet it so held the popular taste as to survive some two centuries, and the last we hear of the ballad is in the time of Charles II.

CHAPTER VII.

Tudor period—Henry VII.'s household expenses—"Westron Wynde"—First dramatic music—Robin Hood—Henry VIII.—"Passetyme"—Maying—Court music—Freemen's songs—Puttenham—Charter renewed—Tusser—Wolsey—Anne Boleyn—"The Hunt is up"—Ghostly psalms—Reformation—Suppression of monasteries—Bow Bells—University influence—Henry VIII.'s obsequies.

Henry VII. (1485-1509)

THE Tudor period, upon which we are now entered, is most important, generally considered, though the reign of Henry VII. in particular is far from being rich in recorded incident. Music's annals can show nothing sensational, such as the discovery of a new continent. The art, however, was not without its inventions, for in 1498 music was first printed with movable types. Josquin des Pres was at the height of his fame; Mouton was as yet a student; and the old master, Ockenheim, was still in the land of the living. With the close of the fifteenth century the race of the Minnesingers ceased. The year 1494 witnessed the birth of the redoubtable Hans Sachs, cobbler of Nuremberg and Mastersinger, whose extant works number over six thousand.

After his decisive victory at Bosworth Field, Henry VII. settled down to a policy which, if characterized by rapacity and extortion, still permitted the peaceful arts to expand and develop under his protection and encouragement. To judge from the long catalogue of musicians and musical instruments, says the editor of his household book, the king's love of music must have been great. In every town he entered, as well as on board the ship which conveyed him to Calais, he was attended by minstrels and waits. Among the first of these entries of household expenses we read—

1492.—Feb. 4th. To the childe that playeth on the records (recorders) - - - - £1 0 0

Another payment in August of the same year reads—

August 1st. At Canterbury. To the children for singing in the gardyn - - - - £0 3 4

Then there are these—

To the maydens of Lambeth for a May - - £0 10 0
For playing of the Mourice Daunce - - - 2 0 0

Morrice and May dances claim numerous payments. On May 21st, 1501, the king expended 13s. 4d. on a lute for the Lady Margaret, his twelve-year-old daughter, afterwards Queen of Scots. In the same year (December 4th) a payment is recorded "To the Princesse stryng mynstrels at Westminster, £2." An early entry records a special fee of 13s. 4d. "to the Queresters at Paule's and St. Steven." Newark (probably William Newark) received £1 "for making a song"; Cornysshe "for a prophecy, in rewarde 13s. 4d."; and Burton, for making a Masse, £1. An interesting note occurs under 1495 (November 27th), when we read that one "Hampton of Wourcestre, for making of Balades, in rewarde" received £1. A few of the entries are mere extravagancies, such as "To a Priest that wrestelled at Ceceter, 6s. 8d.," or the payment of £2 "to the gentlemen of the king's chapel, 'for to drinke with a bucke.'" There are many other sums mentioned as paid to the Waytes of Dover, Canterbury, and Coventry. The minstrels of Sandwich, bagpipyers, harpers, and rymers are further included in this roll, which, however, vouchsafes no further particulars of interest.

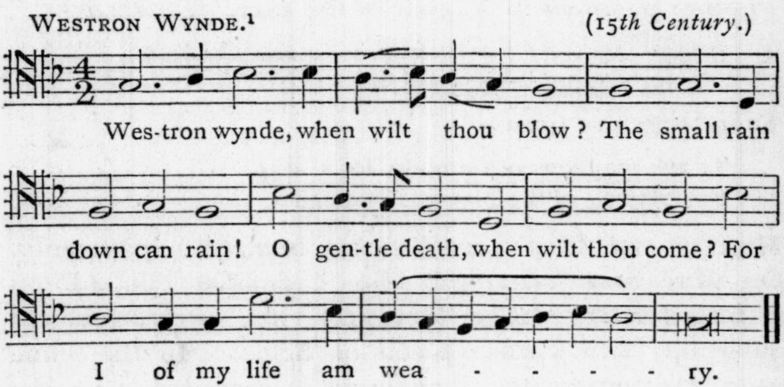
WESTRON WYNDE.[1]
(15th Century.)
Wes-tron wynde, when wilt thou blow? The small rain
down can rain! O gen-tle death, when wilt thou come? For
I of my life am wea - - - - ry.

A manuscript book of songs, written on vellum for the Prince of Wales (Pepysian Library, Magdalene College, Cambridge, No. 87), preserves many of the compositions of Henry VII.'s time by English and foreign musicians. Hawkins and Burney both give extracts from a fifteenth-century quarto (Add. MSS.

[1] John Taverner wrote a Mass on this melody, preserved in a sixteenth-century octavo volume in the British Museum. (See add. MSS. 17802, fol. 25b.)

5465) in the British Museum. Our example is of a popular song which has come down to us from an old MS. in the same Library.[1]

During Henry VII.'s reign moralities and religious pageantry reached the high-water mark. "This sort of spectacle," says Warton, "was now so fashionable that John Rastall, a learned typographer, brother-in-law to Sir John More, extended its province, which had hitherto been confined either to moral allegory or to religion blended with buffoonery, and conceived a design of making it the vehicle of science and philosophy. With this view he published "*A New Interlude* and a mery, of the nature of the iiii Elements, declaringe many proper points of philosophy naturall and divers straunge landys, etc." This work is of great interest to musicians owing to the fact that it contains the earliest known specimen of English dramatic music. So remarkable a piece calls for quotation. Here it is—

1519

Tyme to pas with good - ly sport our

[1] Append. to Royal MSS. 58, fol. 3.

spryte to re - vyve and com - fort,
To pipe, to singe, to daunce, to spryng
with plea - - - - - - - - -
(♭)

"The Four Elements"

"This is copied," says Stafford Smith, "from the *Interlude of the Four Elements, etc.*, by I. Rastel, among Garrick's Plays, British Museum, bound with Rastel's abridgements of the Statutes, first impression, dated October 25th, 11th Henry VIII. It is probably the first printed score or partition in this kingdom." The heading reads, "The Dauncers Syng a Song." Beneath the music is the note—"This may be seyde for nede." The directions after the song run thus—"Then Sensual Apetite syngeth a song and daunceth withall, and evermore maketh countenance accordyng to the mater, and all the other aunswer, 'Daunce we, praunce we, etc.'"

Masques

Masques had not long come in. An account of the first so called is thus given by Edward Hall, who may have been an eye-witness—"On the day of the Epiphany at night, the king with eleven others, was disguised after the manner of Italy, called a Maske, a thing not seen before in England. They were apparalled in garments long and broad, wrought all with gold, with visors and caps of gold.

And after the banquet done, these maskers came in, with six gentlemen disguised in silk, bearing staff-torches, and desired the ladies to dance. Some were content and some refused. And after they had danced and communed together, as the fashion of the maske is, they took their leave and departed; and so did the queen and all the ladies." The chief feature of this class of entertainment was a carefully planned surprise. Much of the early machinery of the pantomime was employed. Dancing, of course, formed a part, and the masque proper was nothing more or less than a spectacular action carried out in dumb show.

"A little Geste of Robin Hood" printed in Fleet Street by Wynken de Worde, like the modern copy of "Chevy Chase," affords an instance of old minstrelsy subjected to the refining influences of writing and printing. No air is known in connection with this fine old ballad; but it would be possible to sing it to "Flying Fame," just as was the older ballad. A whole collection of Robin Hood ballads was issued by Chepman and Myllar in Edinburgh about the year 1506. The importance of these early pieces cannot be over-estimated when it is remembered that few we possess can be placed further back than the time of Elizabeth.

It remains to add that during Henry VII.'s reign monastic education was fast falling into neglect. No less than twenty grammar schools in addition to several university colleges were founded, and there is no doubt that in all of these music was cultivated to some extent. Doubtless, one of the most enduring monuments of the period is that mentioned by Stow in the following words :—

"King Henry the Seventh, in the yeere 1502, bestowed 14000 pounds on the East side [of Westminster Abbey], where he built a Chappell of admirable beauty (which Leland calles *The Miracle* of the World; for any man that sees it, may well say, that all elegancy of workemanship and matter is couched in it) to be a place of Sepulture for himselfe, and all his posterity; wherein (at this day) is to bee seene his owne Tombe, most gorgeous and great, made all of solid Brasse."

Henry VII.'s Chapel

"Men might say,
Till this time pomp was single, but now married
To one above itself."

—*Henry VIII.*, Act I. Sc. I.

With the ascension of Henry VIII. to the throne, a new and important epoch is begun. He was in his eighteenth year, and was well-skilled in music. Being the younger of two brothers, his chance of the throne was thought remote, and it is understood that he was originally qualifying for the post of Archbishop of Canterbury. However this may be, there is no doubt that Henry could both sing and play, as well as write music. Lord Herbert of Cherbury (Henry's biographer) speaks of two complete services by his royal master. There is a three-part serenade beginning "Quam pulchra es" in Hawkins' *History*. Mention may also be made of

Henry VIII. (1509)

the anthem or motet "O Lord, the maker of each thing," which, on the authority of Dr. Aldrich, is by Henry VIII. Among the MSS. in the British Museum there are the originals of the famous "Passetyme with Goode Company" (or "The Kynge's Balade") and eighteen songs and fifteen instrumental pieces also from the royal and august pen. Henry's diversions (to quote Hollinshed) included daily exercise "in shooting, singing, dancing, wrestling, casting of the bar, playing at the recorders, flute, virginals, in setting of songs and making of ballads." We shall proceed to give an example of this gifted monarch's powers:—

PASSETYME WITH GOODE COMPANY. *Henry VIII.*

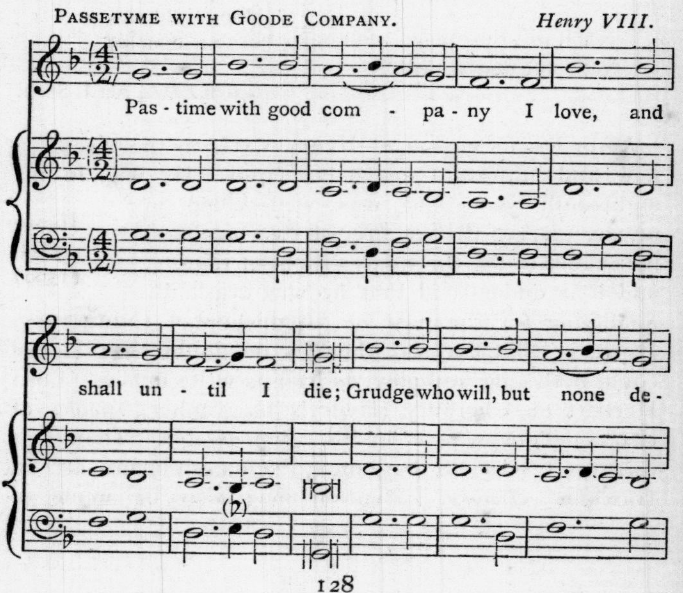
Pas - time with good com - pa - ny I love, and
shall un - til I die; Grudge who will, but none de -

"Passetyme"

- ny, So God be pleas - èd this life will
(♮)
I For my pas - tance, Hunt, sing and dance, My
(♮)
(♮)
heart....... is set, All good - ly sport, To

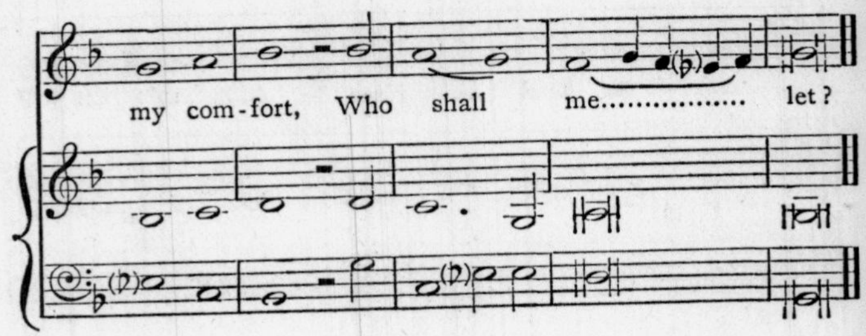
my com-fort, Who shall me.................. let?

II.

Youth will needs have dalliance,
Or good or ill some pastance ;
Company me thinketh best
All thoughts and fantasies to digest.
For idleness
Is chief mistress
Of vices all ;
Then who can say
But pass the day
Is best of all?

III.

Company with honesty
Is virtue and vice to flee.
Company is good or ill,
But every man has his free will.
The best I sue,
The worst eschew ;
My mind shall be
Virtue to use,
Vice to refuse,
I shall use me.

May-day

The popularity of this royal hymn is well shown by the number of MSS. which contain one or another form of it. As these differ, the text is founded on what appeared the most musical version—namely, the Additional MS. 5665, fol. 133 (British Museum). The notes are copied exactly, but the bar lines were not in the original, and the voice parts were written, not in score, but one after the other, in the manner usual in the sixteenth century.

"In the Moneth of May—namely, on May-day in the morning, every man, except impediment, would walke into the sweete meddowes and green woods, there to rejoice their spirits with the beauty and savour of sweet flowers, and with the harmony of birds, praysing God in their kind. And for example hereof, Edward Hall hath noted, that King Henry the 8 as in the 3 of his reigne, and divers other yeeres, so namely in the seventh of his reigne, on May-day in the morning, with Queen Katherine his wife, accompanied with many Lords and Ladies, rode a Maying from Greenwitch to the high ground of Shooters-hill, whereas they passed by the way, they espied a company of tall yeomen cloathed all in greene, with green whoods, and with bowes and arrows, to the number of 200. One being their chieftaine, was called Robin Hood,[1] who required the king and all his company to stay and see his men shoote; whereunto the king granting, Robin Hood whistled and all the two hundred archers shot off,

[1] Not, of course, the original Robin Hood, who was famous in Edward III.'s day.

loosing all at once, and when hee whistled againe, they likewise shot againe, their arrowes whistled by craft of the head, so that the noyse was strange and loud, which greatly delighted the King, Queen, and their company.

"Moreover, this Robin Hood desired the King and Queene, with their retinue, to enter the greene Wood, where, in Arbours made with boughes, and decked with flowers, they were set and served plentifully with venison and wine, by Robin Hood and his meyny, to their great contentment, and had other Pageants and Pastimes, as ye may reade in my said Author.

"I find also, that in the Moneth of May, the Citizens of London (of all estates) lightly in every parish, or sometimes two or three Parishes joining together, had their several Mayings, and did fetch in Maypoles, with divers warlike shewes, with good Archers, Morice-dauncers, and other devices for pastime all the day long; and towards the evening, they had Stage-playes, and Bonfiers in the streets."[1]

After the May-day celebrations at Greenwich in 1515, dinner being over, a large company adjourned to certain rooms in the palace where were a number of organs, virginals, flutes, etc. Here the Secretary to the Venetian Embassy, Signor Sagudino, played with notable skill upon both virginals and organ. The prelates present informed him that the king would certainly expect him to play in his Majesty's own apartment, and that their royal master practised music both day and night. A contemporary writer adds that

[1] Stow's *Survey*, pp. 150-51, ed. 1618, Blackletter.

his Majesty "plays well on the lute and virginals, and sings from book at sight." A monarch so predisposed towards the art could not but have a powerful influence in spreading and developing its resources. The court music was now in a flourishing state, as we may see from the opinion of Pasqualigo of Venice,—an ambassador who had held appointments in the principal capitals of Europe. "We attended Mass," writes he, "which was chanted by the Bishop of Durham, with a superb and noble descant choir." To this, the secretary above-mentioned adds—"High Mass was chaunted, and it was sung by his Majesty's choristers, whose voices are really rather divine than human; they did not chaunt, but sung like angels; and as for the deep bass voices, I do not think they have their equals in the world." An incident related concerning Thomas Cromwell (afterwards Earl of Essex) introduces us to mention of the Three-man's (or Freeman's) Song, a favourite English composition of the period. Cromwell journeyed from Antwerp to Rome to obtain from Pope Julius II. a renewal of the "greater and lesser pardon" for the town of Boston. He was loth to spend much time, and still more loth to waste his money, among "the greedy cormorants of the Pope's court."[1] The ordinary diplomatic channels being thus closed, Cromwell's arts were directed towards captivating the papal ear and palate. Having, therefore, prepared certain rare dishes, Cromwell's men bearing these advanced, singing a "three-man's song" the

Court Music

[1] See *Foxe's Acts and Monuments.*

while, and proffered them to the Pope, who had just returned from hunting. The success of the ruse flattered its author's knowledge of men; for as soon as his Holiness perceived the musicians coming not empty-handed, he inquired as to the gift and its meaning. His cardinal first tasted and approved; after him the Pope, who was so pleased that, "without any more ado, he stamped both their pardons, as well the greater as the lesser."

Our knowledge of the "three-man's song" is chiefly derived from Ravenscroft's fine collection, entitled—*Deuteromelia; or, the second part of Musicke's Melodie, or melodious musicke of pleasant roundelayes. K(ing) H(enry's) Mirth or Freemen's Songs*" (1611). Doubtless "Three-men's Songs" was the original description, softened in practice to "Freemen's"; just as *thills* (wagon-shafts) became *fills*, and *Thrift* St. changed to *Frith* St. Such songs were in use in the time of Henry VI., being for any number of voices—though three and six were most usual.[1] Thus, in the "Turnament of Tottenham" (*circa* 1456), there is the following:—

"Mekyl myrth was them amang;
In every corner of the house
Was melody delycyous,
For to her precyus
Of six menys sang."

---

[1] In Vowell's *Life of Sir Peter Carew* we read—"For the king himself being much delighted to sing, and Sir Peter Carew having a pleasant voice, the king would often use him to sing with him certain songs they call *Freemen Songs*, as namely, 'By the banke as I lay,' and 'As I walked the wode so wylde.'"

"Cantabanqui"

Quite apart from the minstrels in regular employment, such as might be expected to take part in ordinary entertainments, a large number of men abounded in the time of Henry VIII. who sought their living by stories, rhymes, and moral speeches, either for singing or recitation, delivered in the taverns and places of popular resort. Nor were these people content with such a sphere for their performances; they pushed into the houses of the great—"Irrumpunt in convivia Magnatum," says Erasmus—and expected the treatment accorded the fully recognized minstrel order. Puttenham no doubt had this class of person in mind when writing of "small and popular musickes, song by these *Cantabanqui* upon benches and barrels-heads, where they have none other audience than boys or countrey fellowes that passe by them in the streete, or else by blind harpers or such like tavern minstrels, that give a fit of mirth for a groat, and their matters being for the most part stories of old time, as the tale of Sir Topas, the reports of Bevis of Southampton, Guy of Warwicke, Adam Bell, and Clymme of the Clough, and other such old romances or historical rhymes, made purposely for recreation of the common people at Christmasse dinners and brideales, and in taverns and alehouses, and such other places of base resort; also they be used in carols and rounds, and such light poems, which are commonly more commodiously uttered by these buffoons in plays than by any other person. Such were the rhymes of Skelton (usurping the name of a poet laureate); being indeed but a rude railing rhymer and all his doings ridiculous, he used both short distaunces (periods) and short measures, pleasing only the popular ear; in our courtly maker we banish them utterly."[1] In accepting Puttenham's picture of the common minstrel, we need in no sense endorse his view of Skelton, whose "Colin Clout" is a true representation of popular feeling against the corruption of the Church. Contrast Erasmus's statement that Skelton was the glory and light of English letters, or Caxton's that he uplifted our language.

The most considerable court musician of this time was William Cornyshe, who appears to have been in durance at the Fleet prison about the time of Henry VIII.'s coronation. In 1493 there is mention of a sum of 13s. 4d. being paid "to one Cornyshe for a prophecy in rewarde." A similar sum was paid to Cornyshe by Henry VII.'s queen, "for setting of a carralle upon Christmas Day." However, it chanced that this musician was placed in the Fleet, from thence we find him petitioning for his release, in a *Treatise between Trouth and Informacion.*[2] He was successful, and in 1509 supplanted William Newark as master of the children of the Chapel Royal. He speedily became a favourite with Henry VIII. In the masques and early pieces of the same type which admitted of music's aid, Cornyshe certainly took a prominent part. The large sums he received help to illustrate our remark. Thus,

[1] *Arte of English Poesie.*

[2] Hawkins quotes 112 verses from this curious document. (*Hist.*, bk. lxxv.)

in the eighth year of Henry VIII., in November there was paid "to Master Cornyshe, gentylman of the King's Chapell, upon a warraunt, in rewarde, £200." One other item, and we may dismiss the matter. In 1508 there is an entry (among the court payments) as follows:—"To Mr. Kite, Cornyshe, and other of the Chapell that played affore the King [Henry VII.] at Richmonte, £6 13s. 4d." No doubt some of these payments would relate to miracle-plays, mysteries, pageants,[1] and the like. There seems no reason, however, to disbelieve the statement that "prior to the introduction of what may be termed operatic masques in this country, the plays or masques exhibited before the court and nobility were acted by the children of St. Paul's, Windsor, and the royal chapel." The writer adds that "the situation of master of the children was always held by a competent musician, and it is but fair to conjecture that the holders of that office were the chief contributors to the musical portion of the entertainments."

With the earliest history of these plays we are scarcely concerned, though it is impossible to believe that music did not play some notable part in them.[2]

Passing to the more critical years of Henry VIII.'s

[1] He attended the king at the Field of the Cloth of Gold, where he devised the pageants at the banquet.

[2] Stow observes, under so early a date as 1409, that "a great play at Skinner's Well" was performed. This, he says, "lasted eight daies, and was of matter from the creation of the world: the most part of all the great Estates of England were there to behold it."

reign, we read that in 1520 (the year of Tallis's birth) the king renewed the charter (of Edward IV.) to John Gilman, his Marshal, and to seven others of his minstrels. Nine years later, this Gilman was succeeded by Hugh Wodehouse. The charter (as we before saw) allowed of boys being impressed for the services of the Church. Thomas Tusser, author of *Five Hundred Points of Good Husbandry*, relates, in verse, how he came of good lineage, and was sent by his father to a music-school at Wallingford College, where he was "impressed" and taken to St. Paul's School. His lot might have been worse, for Dean Collet's foundation had recently been made (namely, in 1512), providing for 353 poor men's sons;[1] though, it must be allowed, that the cathedral-school may even then have been a separate establishment. Tusser thus refers to this event:—

"Thence for my voice I must (no choice)
Away of force, like posting horse,
For sundrie men had placards then
Such child to take."

The child then, to his great content, became a pupil of John Redford, organist of St. Paul's Cathedral.

In the year 1526 the king's band of musicians was constituted as follows:—15 trumpets, 3 lutes, 3 rebecks, 3 taborets, 1 harp, 2 viols, 10 sackbuts, a fife, and 4 drumslades. We have a further record of this band, four years later, when we find the number increased by

[1] Stow's *Survey*, p. 170.

the addition of a trumpet, a lute, 3 minstrels, and a player of the virginals; while, on the other hand, the withdrawals included a sackbut, the fife, and two drum-slades. Many of the great prelates and lay lords had large musical establishments. For example, Cardinal Wolsey, in addition to four regular minstrels, maintained the following for daily service in his chapel:—"a Deane—a great divine, and a man of excellent learning; a Sub-deane, a Repeater of the Quire, a Gospeller, a Pisteller; of Singing Priests tenne, a Master of the Children; twelve seculars, being singing men of the chappel; ten singing children, with a servant to attend upon the children. In the Revestry, a yeoman and two grooms; over and beside divers retainers, that came thither at principall feasts."[1] This note is supplemented in the same writer's *Annals* (p. 535), where we read that upon one occasion "there was not only plenty of fine meats, but also much mirth and solace, as well in merry communication as with the noise of my Lord's minstrels, who played there all that night so cunningly, that the King took therein great pleasure; insomuch that he desired my Lord to lend them unto him for the next night, and after supper their banquet finished, the ladies and gentlemen fell to dancing, among whom, one Madame Fontaine, a maid, had the prize. And thus passed they the most part of the night ere they departed. The next day the King took my Lord's minstrels, and rode to a nobleman's house where there was some image to whom he vowed

[1] Stow's *Survey*, p. 137.

a pilgrimage, to perform his devotions. When he came there, which was in the night, he danced and caused others to do the same, after the sound of my Lord's minstrels, who played there all night, and never rested, so that whether it were with extreme labour of blowing, or with poison (as some judged) because they were commended by the King more than his own, I cannot tell, but the player on the shalme (who was very excellent on that instrument) died within a day or two after."

We have ventured this somewhat lengthy extract because it shows, as nothing else can, the court minstrel (or musician,[1] as he may now be called) in the exercise of his duties. The real distinction which always existed between those employed in the service of the Church and the secular performer, was rapidly vanishing in Henry's time. The employment of choristers in the masques of the day assists our argument.

Before quitting this part of my subject, I add a few extracts from Hawkins, who devotes much space to the household establishment of "Henry Algernon Percy, the fifth Earl of Northumberland, at his castles of Wresill and Lekingfield, Yorkshire." This document shows that twenty-three gentlemen and children of the chapel took part in the daily Mass. One of the entries reads—"Oone for the orgayns," which means that one of these "gentlemen" was organist. The

[1] Both Percy (in the *Reliques*) and Hawkins (*History of Music*) point out that "minstrel" at this time referred to performer or musician.

office, however, was rotated, as is seen from this direction—

"The ordering for keeping weekly of the organs one after another as the names of them hereafter followeth weekly :—
The master of the children, if he be a player, the first week.
A countertenor that is a player the 2nd week.
A tenor that is a player the 3rd week.
A Bass that is a player the 4th week.
And every man that is a player to keep this course weekly.'

The date of this record is 1512. On the death of the then Earl, Cardinal Wolsey, jealous (it is said) of this great establishment, found a way of reducing it by the simple expedient of borrowing indefinitely all the books used in the service of the chapel.

It is recorded that at the coronation of Anne Boleyn, choirs of men and boys were placed on the leads of St. Martin's Church, to sing new ballads in praise of her Majesty. Anne Boleyn is known to have excelled in music and dancing. It is left on record that "she doated on the compositions of Jusquin and Mouton," and had collections of them made for the private practice of herself and her companions. There is some ground for believing her also possessed of uncommon poetical powers. Her song "O death, rocke me on slepe" has been recently reprinted, together with the music.[1] Certainly its character is in keeping with the tragic fortunes of this unhappy lady. "For," saith an old

[1] It is reprinted in a curious collection entitled *Kings' Music* (Augener), edited by the present writer.

chronicle, "within one and the same month was Queen Anne flourishing, accused, condemned, executed, and another assumed into her place. The first of May (1533) she was informed against; the 2nd, imprisoned; the 15th, condemned; and the 17th, deprived of her brother and friends, who suffered in her cause, and the 19th, executed. On the 20th, the King married Jane Seymour, who on the 29th was publicly shown as Queen." Among those implicated was a minstrel of the name of Mark Smeaton, who was treated with greater savagery than his noble companions. The fate allotted this unfortunate person brought him to the Tower, where he was loaded with chains, and after a hasty trial, hanged, drawn, and quartered. His crime, if Anne Boleyn spoke truly, was no more than that he had once, and once only, entered her chamber to play to her. She asked him why he looked so sad, and the minstrel replied that a look from her sufficed him. Among the gentlemen of the court who shared the same penalty, was Henry Norris, a favourite of the king, who was offered a free pardon if he would confess. "I would rather die a thousand deaths than betray the innocent!" The recording angel must have blushed as he traced the king's reply—"Hang him up, then; hang him up!"

Smeaton

In this same year (1533) a proclamation was issued suppressing "fond books, ballads, rhimes, and other lewd treatises in the English tongue." We reserve our remarks on the ballad for another chapter, and now merely note that this proclamation was put in force against one John Hogon, who, it appears, had the temerity to sing a political ballad "with a crowd or a fyddyll" to the tune of "The hunt is up." Hogon's ballad in the fragment that is preserved ran thus—

"The hunt is up! the hunt is up! and now 'tis almost day;
The masters of arte and doctours of dyvynyte
Have brought this realme out of good unyte.
Thre nobyll men have take this to stay,
My Lorde of Norffolk, Lorde of Surrey,
And my Lorde of Shrewsbyrry;
The Duke of Suffolk myght have made Inglond mery."

—Payne Collier's *Roxburghe Ballads* (1847).

More than one air is credited with being the actual melody sung by Hogon. Here is the best of these, but it is plain that it fits the words extremely ill:—

The hunt is up, the hunt is up, and now 'tis almost day, &c.

Puttenham alludes to a song of this title, in *The Art of English Poesie*, in these words—"And one Gray what good estimation did he grow unto with the same King Henry, and afterwards with the Duke of Sommerset, Protectour, for making certaine merry Ballades, whereof one chiefly was, 'The Hunte is up, the hunte is up.' And Queene Mary his daughter for one Epithalamie or nuptiall song made by Vargas a Spanish Poet at her marriage with King Phillip in Winchester gave him during his life two hundred Crownes pension; nor this reputation was given them in auncient times altogether in respect that Poesie was a delicate arte, and the poets themselves cunning Prince-pleasers, but for that also they were thought for their universall knowledge to be very sufficient men for the greatest charges in their common wealthes, were it for counsell or for conduct, whereby no man neede to doubt but that both skilles may very well concurre and be most excellent in one person." The reference here is probably to the Scalds, whose art (briefly mentioned in our earlier pages) was looked upon as something divine. Sir Philip Sydney, writing a few years before Puttenham, had observed that "I think (and think I think rightly) the laurel crown appointed for triumphant captains doth worthily, of all other learnings, honour the poet's triumph." The pages of this book sufficiently show that the minstrels (speaking generally) did not go without rewards; but whether these were given to the "Prince-pleasers" and the less substantial laurel awarded the poet it is vain to inquire.

It would seem that the attempt to put down popular ballads and songs had its sympathizers—at least, amongst the readers of Miles Coverdale's "Address to the Christian." This address written in 1538, six years after its author had concluded his share of the translation of the Bible, will be found prefixed to *Goastly*

Psalmes and Spirituall Songes, and gives utterance in the following terms:—"Wolde God that our Mynstrels had none other thynge to play upon, neither our carters and plowmen other thynge to whistle upon, save psalmes, hymns, and such like godly songes." The austere old friar would go further, for he lays it down in a no less confident manner that "if women at the rockes [distaffs] and spinnynge at the wheles, had none other songes to pass their tyme withal than such as Moses' sister songe before them, they should be better occupied than with 'Hey, nonny, nonny: Hey, trolly, lolly,' and such like fantasies." How little did Coverdale imagine that as the centuries passed his lines would be eagerly scanned, if perchance they preserved the very names of those "fantasies" which he detested!

The immediate effect of the Reformation must be considered disastrous to secular music, which does not seem to thrive in times of political ferment 1539
and change. It is only too likely that the music of the Church, despite the Masses of Josquin and Mouton (merely to mention Anne Boleyn's favourites) was doing its best to bring discredit upon itself. Secular melodies were introduced into sacred compositions, and though England does not appear to have been so extravagant in her services as her continental neighbours, some ground there was for Erasmus, once a chorister himself, making the following indictment:—"We have brought a tedious and capricious kind of music into the house of God, a tumultuous noise of different voices, such as I think was never heard in the theatres either of

the Greeks or Romans, for the keeping up whereof whole flocks of boys are maintained at great expense, whose time is spent in learning such gibble-gabble, while they are taught nothing that is either good or useful. Whole troops of lazy lubbers are also maintained solely for the same purpose; at such an expense is the Church for a thing that is pestiferous." The learned prelate concludes his charges by estimating how many poor men could be kept out of the salaries of such singers, and gives a final rap at England for admiring and encouraging such services.

The statement in the "Seventy-eight Faults and Abuses of Religion," presented to Henry in 1536, goes if anything still further. Here is a choice specimen:—"Synging and saying of Mass, Matins or Evensong, is but roryng, howling, whistelyng, mummying, conjuryng, and jogelyng, and the playing at the organys a foolish vanitie." It is known that, after the king's breach with Rome, only slight alterations were made in the Liturgy, which was still in Latin, and sung in the usual manner. The King's Primer, published in English in 1535, was followed by Tyndal's translation of the whole Bible—a folio volume issued in 1538. In *A Book of Ceremonies*, published the following year, there is this passage, which views church music in a better light:—"The sober, discreet, and devout singing, music, and playing with organs, used in the church in the service of God, are ordained to move and stir the people to the sweetness of God's word, the which is there sung; and by that sweet harmony both to excite them to prayer and devotion, and also to put them in remembrance of the heavenly, triumphant Church, where is everlasting joy, continual laud, and praise to God."

The suppression of the monasteries, which took place in 1540, is of some importance to our story. We quote the simple entry in Stow's *Survey* in reference to the sale of the minstrel's priory:—"This priory, at the late surrender, the 30 of Henry the 8, was valued at 653*l.* 15*s.* by yeere." A portion of the building was pulled down, while the choir was annexed to the old parish church adjoining. A set of six bells was sold to the St. Sepulchre's parish, while the major portion of the priory went to Sir Richard Rich, who was concerned in the executions of Bishop Fisher and Sir Thomas More. In these transactions of Henry VIII., the libraries were included as part of the purchase. Priceless books and MSS. were treated as mere waste-paper. Some were shipped abroad to the foreign bookbinders. The red letters and the embellished figures on the illuminated missals and manuscripts were sure passports to destruction.[1] The few works that escaped the popular fanaticism were those that had been buried underground, or hidden in the walls of old buildings; and in such cases damp commonly obliterated what time had spared. It is, of course, quite impossible even to guess at the extent of the loss to music which such ruthless destruction may have caused; that

Priory of St. Bartholomew

[1] "We still find such volumes mutilated of the gilt letters and elegant flourishes, but the greater number were annihilated."—ISAAC D'ISRAELI.

it was serious is certain when we remember that the monasteries, from times long before the good St. Dunstan, were the only repositories of books and manuscripts of poetry and music.

A singular and unanticipated effect of the publication of Marot's Psalter (in 1540) may be briefly noticed in passing. The psalms simply leaped into popularity. From the court downwards, every one sang them; but, strangely enough, to *merry tunes.* Shakespeare's "Psalms to hornpipes" was no more than a literal fact. The queen sang "O Lord, rebuke me not" to a fashionable jig. The King of Navarre's favourite was "Stand up, O Lord" to a Poitou dance-tune. Every one followed suite.

About this time—namely, 1544—it is recorded that the Princess (afterwards Queen) Elizabeth resided at Hatfield House, in Hertfordshire, in the custody of Sir Thomas Pope. Here she was visited by Queen Mary. One of the diversions after Mass in the morning was a grand bear-baiting, with which their highnesses "were right well content." Towards evening, the chamber was adorned with a sumptuous tapestry, representing the "Hanging of Antioch." After supper, a play was presented (perhaps *Holophernes*) by the children of St. Paul's. The Princess was so delighted with the choristers from St. Paul's Cathedral, that on the next day she sent for one Maximilian Poines, who had taken a part, and made him sing to her, while "she played at the virginals." From this quiet entertainment we pass to a popular and noisier diversion.

"Bow Bells"

An old writer observed that the English were fond of great noises that fill the ear, such as the ringing of

bells, the firing of cannon, or the beating of drums. "It is common," he affirms, "for a number of them that have got a glass in their heads to get up into some belfry, and ring the bells for hours together for the sake of exercise." Every one has heard of Bow Bells. The church which they rang into world-wide fame was originally of the reign of William the Conqueror; and being the first in the city built upon stone arches, was called New Mary Church of St. Mary de Arcubus, or "Le Bow in West Cheaping." In 1196 William Fitz Osbert took possession of Bow Steeple, fortifying and provisioning the same for a siege. This hero, it appears, was dislodged by fire and smoke; and, in due course, he and nine of his followers were drawn by the heels to the Elms in Smithfield and there hanged. In 1271 one Laurence Ducket, a goldsmith, took refuge in this steeple. His enemies, however, came upon him in the night, and hanged him from the window, in such a manner as to lead to a verdict of suicide. But a boy witnessed the scene, and in due time his evidence led to the hanging of sixteen men, and the burning of "a certain woman named Alice, who was the chief causer of the said mischief." The church was then, for a time, interdicted, and the windows and doors stopped up with thorns. Passing to 1469, we find that it was ordained in Common Council that Bow Bell should be rung nightly at the hour of nine. But the Clerk being somewhat unpunctual, had this rhyme made upon him by the young apprentices of Cheap—

"Turn again, Whittington"

"Clarke of the Bow-bell with the yellow locks,
For thy late ringing, thy head shall have knocks."
[Whereto the Clerk replied—]
"Children of Cheape, hold you all still,
For you shall have the Bow-bell rung at your will."[1]

Stow mentions that "it appeareth that the lanthornes on the toppe of this steeple were meant to have been glazed, and lightes in them placed nightly in the winter, wherby travellers to the city might have the better sight thereof, and not to misse of their wayes."

A scrap of information comes to us under date 1542, when William Crane, who had succeeded William Cornyshe as master of the children at the Chapel Royal sixteen years previously, obtained a somewhat remarkable privilege. This was no less than the sole right to buy and export for his advantage 400 tons of double

[1] After a long period, during which Bow Bells merely rung the conventional quarters, the chimes have been recently restored. They are arranged by Sir C. Stanford, and founded on the old air, "Turn again, Whittington." First quarter: the four notes (numbered); second quarter: the six notes (numbered); the hour: all the notes; third quarter, as below:—

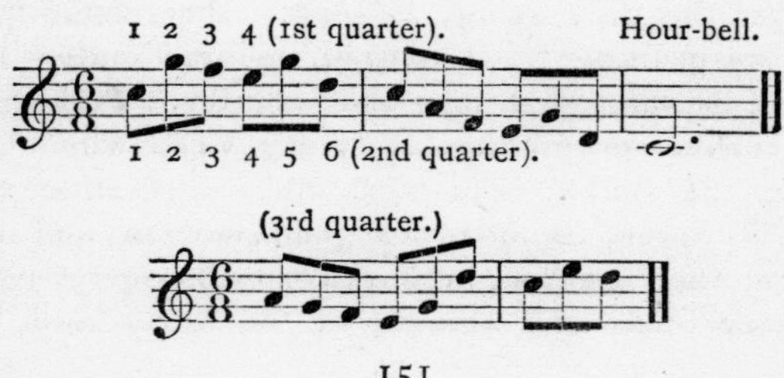

beer. Such grants, however, were not uncommon at the time, as is seen from the privy seals, in the Rolls Chapel.

Not content with the proclamation of 1533, an Act was passed in 1543 going further, and treating the printers with greater severity. This is entitled "An Act for the advancement of true religion, and for the abolishment of the contrary." It recites that "froward and malicious minds, intending to subvert the true exposition of Scripture, have taken upon them, by printed ballads, rhymes, etc., subtilly and craftily to instruct his highness' people, and specially the youth of this his realm of all such books, ballads, rhymes, and songs as be pestiferous and noisome. Therefore, if any printer shall print, give, or deliver any such, he shall suffer for the first time imprisonment for three months, and forfeit for every copy £10; and for the second time, forfeit all his goods and his body be committed to perpetual prison." In the list of exceptions which follows, *The Canterbury Tales*, Chaucer's books, Gower's, etc., are named; so also are all books printed before 1540, entitled Statutes, Chronicles, and Biographies. This sweeping Act accomplished its purpose, for the time being, at least. One result was to drive the printing trade abroad, printed matter being afterwards smuggled into the country. Perhaps the most curious prohibition of Henry VIII. was that of reading the Bible. The high officers of state might scan its pages, as also the gentlewoman and noble lady "in their garden, orchard, or other secret place"; but those (men and women) of the lower rank were neither to read nor to have it read to them. The Pope himself could have gone no further.

Among the chief musicians of the reign we have already mentioned William Cornyshe, senior, and some others. To these may be added the names given in Morley's *Plaine and Easie Introduction to Practicall Musicke* (1597). The author states in his preface that some of the names "had been buried in perpetual oblivion" had it not been for his notice of them. Taverner, Fairfax and Cooper are cited in Morley's Preface, in the sense of theorists. Compositions are extant of all three, if the Robert Cooper is the Dr. Copere[1] of the Royal MSS. 58 (App.), British Museum. We give a facsimile of the first folio contained in this early sixteenth century quarto.[2] At the end of his book Morley sets the following names, the greater number being those of musicians flourishing before the Reformation:—M. Pashe, Robert Jones, Jo. Dunstable, Leonel Power, Robert Orwel, M. Wilkinson, Jo. Gwinneth, Robert Davis, M. Risby, D. Farfax, D. Kirby, Morgan Grig, Tho. Ashwell, M. Sturton, Jacket, Corbrand, Testwood, Ungle, Beech, Bramston, S. Jo. Mason, Ludford Farding, Cornish, Pyggot, Taverner, Redford, Hodges, Selby, Thorne, Oclande Averie, D. Tye, D. Cooper, D. Newton, M. Tallis, M. White, M. Persons, M. Byrde. We have no space to examine Morley's list of musicians in detail; nor, indeed, is there

[1] Dr. Cooper (or Coperario), Morley's contemporary, must not be confused with his namesake, who lived a century earlier.

[2] See page 154.

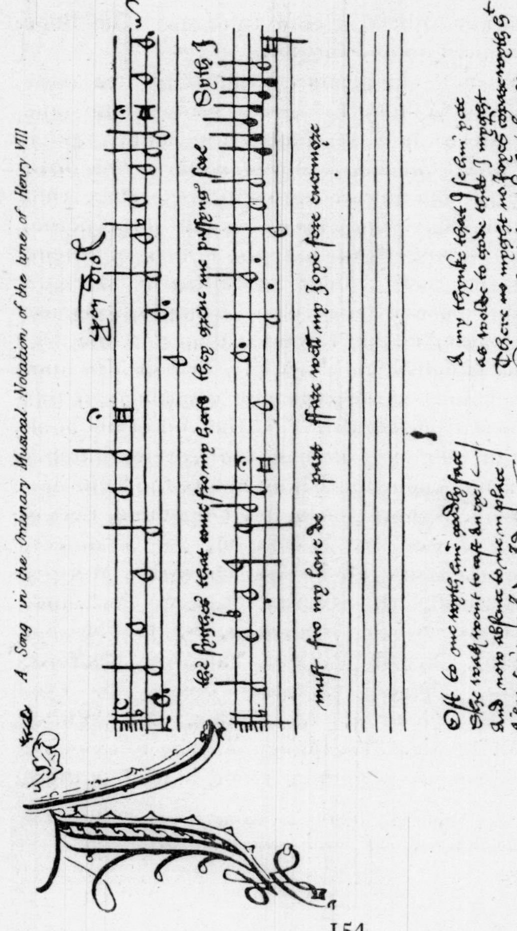

A Song in the Ordinary Musical Notation of the time of Henry VIII

FIG. 7.—"A THE SYGHES."

sufficient material now remaining to enable us to do so with any completeness. It may be observed, however, that the names cover a wide period; for example, Dunstable died in 1453, while Byrde was not born until 1538. Some of these musicians[1] were also priests; several held good positions—such as S. J. Mason, who was master of the choristers, Magdalen College, Oxford, in 1508; or White, who succeeded Tye (in 1562) as organist of Ely Cathedral. Many scattered compositions remain among the MSS. of the Museum and College libraries, and a few are printed by Hawkins and Burney. Tallis appears to have been a chorister of the Chapel Royal during Henry VIII.'s time, but both he and Byrde more properly belong to the Elizabethan period.

The cultivation of music at the university centres was making its influence a real factor in the history of the art. Between 1504-1516, there were sixteen degrees granted in the faculty of music at Oxford. There is evidence that practical composition was required by the examiners; as, for example, from Christopher Wodde,

[1] It would be passing strange if in so remarkable a reign—when the fortunes of his subjects lay at the mercy of the king's moods—music had not contributed her share of martyrs. Taverner, Fryer, and Frith, while at Oxford, became Lutherans. Fryer was arrested, and while in the Savoy prison "did much solace himself with playing on the lute." Frith fared worse, being burned (together with one Andrew Hewet), at Smithfield in 1533. Testwood (a singing man of Windsor) came to a similar end in 1544; while Marbeck narrowly escaped the same terrible fate, having tempted fortune and the wrath of the Church by compiling so harmless a thing as an English Bible Concordance.

who had to compose a complete Mass with antiphon. Singing—at Cambridge, at least—was expected of candidates for fellowships, though it was not compulsory.

Some of the publications of Henry VIII.'s time call for passing notice. Thus, in 1530 Wynken de Worde issued the first song-book printed in England, which contained nine pieces by Cornyshe, Pyggot, Gwinneth, Robert Jones, Dr. Cooper, and Fayrfax. The British Museum has this copy, which contains the *Bass part* only of the songs. No other copies are known. Another publication worthy of mention is Day's issue of the Church Service in 1560. Still more important was Day's second venture—namely, "The whole Booke of Psalmes collected into English metre by T. Sternhold, J. Hopkins, and others, conferred with the Ebrue, with apt Notes to sing them withall." A perfect copy of this work is preserved in the Ryland's Library, Manchester, while the British Museum has recently acquired a valuable though not perfect specimen. The "apt notes" referred to in the title signify merely the melody. An edition with four-part harmony followed in 1563, the joint work of Tallis, Parsons, Edwards and others. Puttenham's amusing reference to the literary part of the work mentions that "King Henry VIII., for a few Psalms of David turned into English metre by Sternhold, made him groome of his privy chamber, and gave him many other good gifts."[1] No doubt the reference is to the first instalment of

[1] *Arte of Poesie*, p. 12; reprint p. 32.

nineteen Psalms which had appeared without any music in 1549, the year of Sternhold's death.[1]

Henry VIII.'s funeral ceremony was carried out with the full ritual of the Catholic Church and the Latin service. When the Lord Chamberlain and the bishops brake their staves, with "sighs and tears, and exceeding sorrow," then "the trumpets sounded with great melody and courage, to the comfort of all them that were present." Roger North describes the music of Henry's church as "at its perfection." He continues, "There was small show of skill in music in England, except what belonged to the cathedral churches and monasteries (when such were), and for that reason the consortiers wherever they went (from 'ministers,' as the word was) were called Minstrels, and then the whole faculty of music—'The Minstrelsie.'"

[1] Robert Crowley's Psalter of 1549 is described in Professor Wooldridge's excellent article in *Grove's Dictionary*, p. 752, Appendix, and iii. 832, new ed.

CHAPTER VIII.

Cranmer's Liturgy — Dr. Tye — Richard Sheale — Edward VI.'s Musicians and Players—John Heywood—"Little John Nobody" —Gentlemen of the Chapel—Tallis and Byrde—Mary Tudor—Clerks of London—Sir William Forrest.

WITH the service of the Church we are not directly concerned; but, as it has been seen that Henry VIII.'s funeral ceremony was performed with full Catholic rites, in order not to give a mistaken impression of the results of the Reformation, the following quotation from Heylin is to our purpose:—"On the 18th day of the moneth of September 1547"—that is, seven months after the young king had come to the throne—"the letany was sung in the English tongue in St. Paul's Church between the quire and the high altar, the singers kneeling, half on the one side and half on the other. And the same day the epistle and gospel was also red at the high mass in the English tongue." Cranmer's English Liturgy, composed in 1548, was printed and used the following year. A statute imposed penalties on those who neglected or depraved its use. This was followed in 1552 by a revised version, again confirmed by statute. Marbeck's *Book of Common*

Prayer Noted had appeared in 1550. In the same year he issued his *Concordance of the Bible*. It was during the preparation of this work that the musician so narrowly escaped being burned at the stake. Thomas Tallis (1520-85) was at this time a Gentleman of the Chapel Royal, and served, says Hawkins, for sevenpence-halfpenny per diem. Among Tallis's fellow-singers was Christopher Tye, who at one time had acted as music-master to Edward VI., and probably to the Princesses Mary and Elizabeth. Tye had become Doctor in Music (Cantab.) in 1545. His *Acts of the Apostles*, of which Hawkins quotes a specimen, appeared in 1553, and were for a brief time sung in the Chapel Royal. Another musician, Richard Edwardes, also of this reign, is briefly referred to later in our pages.

Of more importance to our story is the surviving information concerning Richard Sheale, a minstrel who was in the service of Edward, Earl of Derby (died 1574). From the MS. printed by Hearne the old copy of "Chevy Chase" is seen to be subscribed, after the manner of old poetry, "expliceth quoth Rychard Sheale." We may, therefore, assume that Sheale copied or set down the old ballad which we have previously referred to. (See p. 114.) A *chant* by this unfortunate minstrel sets forth how he was robbed on Dunsmore Heath. This is quoted at length in the *British Bibliographer* (vol. iv. p. 100). The portion dealing with the effect the robbery had on the minstrel's spirits is thus given:—

"After my robbery my memory was so decayed
That I could neither sing nor talk, my wits were so dismayed,
My audacity was gone and all my merry talk.
There are some here have seen me merry as an hawk,
But now I am so troubled with fancies in my mind
I cannot play the merry knave according to my kind;
Yet to take thought I perceive is no the next way
To bring me out of debt my creditors to pay.
I may well say that I had but evil hap
For to lose about three-score pounds at a clap.
The loss of my money did not grieve me so sore,
But the talk of the people did grieve me much more.
Some said I was not robbed, I was but a lying knave,
It was not possible for a minstrel so much money to have.
Indeed, to say the truth, it is right well known
That I never had so much money of my own;
But I had friends in London, whose names I can declare,
That at all times would lend me two hundred pounds of ware;
And with some again such friendship I found
That they would lend me in money nine or ten pound.
The occasion why I came in debt I shall make relation:
My wife indeed is a silk-woman by her occupation;
In linen cloths most chiefly was her greatest trade,
And at fairs and markets she sold sale-ware which she made
As shirts, smocks, and partlets, head-clothes and other things
As silk thread and edgings, skirt bands and strings.
At Lichfield market and Atherston good customers she found;
Also at Tamworth, where I dwell, she took many a pound.
When I had got my money together my debts to have paid,
This sad mischance on me did fall, that cannot be denied.
I thought to have paid all my debts and to have set me clear,
And then what evil did ensue ye shall hereafter hear.
Because my carriage should be light I put my money into gold,
And without company I rode alone, thus was I foolish bold;

I thought by reason of my harp no man would me suspect,
For minstrels oft with money they be not much infect."

We have already related how Tusser was seized under a warrant and taken to St. Paul's to serve as a chorister. This arbitrary practice was continued in Edward VI.'s reign. Strype records that in 1550 a commission was granted to "Philip van Welder [or Wilder], Gentleman of the Privy Chamber, in any churches or chappells within England to take to the king's use such and as many singing children and choristers as he or his deputy shall think good." This warrant was renewed in the very next year, when we read that the Master of the King's Chapel is licensed "to take up from time to time as many children to serve in the king's chapel as he shall think fit." The record of Edward VI.'s "musitions and players" is thus given in *Liber Niger Domus Regis*, p. 271:—

		Fee.		
Serjeante - - -	Benedicte Browne - - -	£24	6	8
Trumpeters (sixteen each by the year, £24 6s. 8d.) - -		389	6	8
Luters - - -	Philip van Welder Peter van Welder } - - -	40	0	0
Harpers - - -	William Moore - - -	18	5	0
	Bernard de Ponte - - -	20	0	0
Singers - - -	Thomas Kent - - -	9	2	6
	Thomas Bowde - - -	9	2	6
Rebeck - - -	John Severnecke - - -	24	6	8
Sagbutts (six): five @ £24 6s. 8d., one @ £36 10s. -		158	3	4
Vyalls (eight): six @ £30 8s. 4d., one @ £20, another @ £18 5s. - - - - - - - - -		220	15	0

		Fee.		
Bagpiper - - -	Richard Woodward - -	£12	3	4
Minstrelles (nine): seven @ £18 5s., one @ £24 6s. 8d., one @ £3 6s. 8d. - - - - - - - -		155	8	4
Dromslades (three) -	Robert Bruer (master) - -	18	5	0
	Alexander Pencax - - -	18	5	0
	John Hodgkin - - - - -	18	5	0
Players on Flutes -	Oliver Rampons - - -	18	5	0
	Pier Guye - - - - - -	34	8	4
Players on Virginals -	John Heywoode - - -	50	0	0
	Anthony de Chounte - - -	30	8	4
	Robert Bewman - - - -	12	3	4
Musicians Straungers, The four brethren Venetians—viz., John, Anthonye, Jasper, and Baptiste - - -		16	6	8
	Augustine Bassane - - -	36	10	0
	William Trosses - - -	38	0	0
	William Denivat - - -	38	0	0
Players of Interludes in number eight: Each of them @ £3 6s. 8d., by yeere £26 13s. 4d. In camera, seven: £23 6s. 8d.; in Sccio, one, £3 6s. 8d.		26	13	4
Makers of Instruments:	William Beton, Organ-maker -	20	0	0
	William Tresorer, Regal-maker -	10	0	0
	[1] Summa totalis ...	£1732	5	0

Total number of persons, 73.

A comparison of King Edward's "Musicians and Players" with the number employed by Henry VIII., shows that the former had increased the royal band by a harper, 2 singers, 6 viols, 6 minstrels, a drumslade,

[1] The figures are quoted from Hawkins, but there is an error of £265 15s., which may possibly occur in the item for Players of Interludes, who would each need to receive £36 11s. 0½d. to render a correct total.

2 flutes, 2 virginals, in addition to the 7 "musicians straungers," 8 players of interludes, and the two makers of instruments. Among the reductions are the following:—2 luters less; 2 rebecks less; 3 sagbutts less; and the 3 taborets done away with altogether.

Several noteworthy names occur in the above list. John Heywood (or Heiwood) made more reputation as an epigrammatist than in music. Henry VIII. was especially fond of his wit, and rewarded him liberally. "To his talents of jocularity in conversation he joined a skill in music," says Warton, "both vocal and instrumental." Heywood's chief work was "The Spider and the Flie"—a long poem, of which Warton gives some extracts of little interest. Other pieces by this literary musician comprised comedies, interludes (a popular form at this time), and the aforesaid epigrams, which last numbered no less than six hundred. One song by Heywood is preserved in a sixteenth century folio in the British Museum (Add. MSS. 4900, fol. 55), beginning "What harte can thinke." Puttenham mentions that Heywood came to be well benefited by the king (Henry VIII.), "for mirth and quickness of his conceits more than for any good learning" that was in him. Heywood died in 1565, at Mechlin (Brabant), having quitted his native country on the death of Queen Mary, to whose religion he had been a faithful adherent.

Of the remaining musicians, it may be observed that Philip van Welder, chief lutenist, had been empowered to impress youths for his Majesty's choral services.[1] The maintenance of an organ-maker on the music-staff seems unusual; and as for the regal-maker, there is no mention of players for this particular instrument. A glance at the fees received by the various musicians, indicating as it does the degrees of estimation in which they were held, shows that the singers, minstrels, and harpers, and the four "brethren Venetians" received the leanest salaries; while the £50 per annum paid to Heywood (player of the virginal) was an unusually large sum at this period.

FIG. 8.—A REGAL PLAYER.

It appears that the young king, who had received an extremely good education, was able to handle the lute; for it is mentioned in the royal diary that on the occasion of a visit from the French Ambassador (July 19th, 1551), Edward performed on the lute, to the great satisfaction of his audience.

"The alterations made in the established religion by Henry VIII., the sudden changes it underwent in the three succeeding reigns within so short a space as eleven or twelve years, and the violent struggles between expiring Popery and growing Protestantism, could not but interest all mankind. Accordingly, every pen was engaged in the dispute. The followers of the old and

[1] In 1551 a yearly allowance was made "to find six singing children for the king's privy chamber." The sum named is £80.

new profession (as they were called) had their respective ballad-makers; and every day produced some popular sonnet for or against the Reformation." Dr. Percy, in support of the above remarks, proceeds to quote "A Ballad of Luther, the Pope, a Cardinal, and a Husbandman," together with one entitled "Little John Nobody," both written in Edward VI.'s time. One stanza of the latter ballad gives a hint of its general style. Its versification is that of "Pierce Plowman's Visions." Rhyming at this period was coming into general use:—

"For our reverend father hath set forth an order,
Our service to be said in our seignours tongue;
As Solomon the sage set forth the scripture;
Our suffrages, and services, with many a sweet song,
With homilies, and godly books us among,
That no stiff, stubborn stomacks we should freyke[1];
But wretches nere worse to do poor men wrong;
But that I little John Nobody dare not speake."

From quite early in the sixteenth century, it appears that the chaplains in the employ of the royal and noble households were expected to compose plays for domestic use. This is shown by the Earl of Northumberland's household book (1512-25). One entry reads—"My Lorde's Chapleyns in Household VI., namely, the Almonar, and if hy be a maker of Interludys, then he to have a servaunt to the intent for writynge of the Parts; and ells to have none." Further entries confirm that

[1] *Freyke*, indulge, humour.

quoted. Christmas Day had its Play of the Nativity, which, if my lord were home, the servants of the chapel presented in the morning, and received in reward the sum of 20s. Only half that amount was expended on the "Shrof Tewsday" play, which was given yearly, at night. "Estur Day" had its Play of the Resurrection, and the reward was the full sum of 20s. A further entry in this household book shows that strangers taking part in the Christmas plays received only 20 pence. During the year some twenty plays seem to have been given. The value of money early in the sixteenth century may be estimated from the fact that a fat ox cost 13s. 4d., a lean one 8s. Twenty times the money would scarcely tempt our modern cattle-dealers. Having shown the intimate connection between diversions of leisure and the more solemn employments of chaplains and singing men, we shall close our account of Edward VI.'s reign by quoting a list of the Officers of the Chapel, adding a few remarks on the most conspicuous of the members.

Officers of the Chappell.

Master of the Children, Richard Bowyer. -	Fee, £40 0s. 0d. Largesse to the children at high feasts, £9 13s. 4d. Allowance for breakfast for the children - £16	£65 13s. 4d.

Gentlemen of the Chappell, 32; each of them 7d. ob. a day.	Emery Tuckfield.	John Kye.	£365
	Nich. Archibald.	John Angel.	
	William Walker.	William Huchins.	
	R. Chamberleyn.	Robert Phelipps.	
	W. Gravesend.	Thomas Birde.	
	Richard Bowyer.	Robert Perry.	
	William Barber.	Thomas Wayte.	
	R. Richmounte.	Thomas Talles.	
	Nicholas Mellowe.	Thomas Wright.	
	John Bendebow.	Robert Stone.	
	William Mawpley.	J. Shepharde.	
	George Edwards.	Wil. Hynnes, or Hunnis.	
	Robert Morecock.	Thomas Manne.	
	R. Alyeworth.	Roger Kenton.	
	T. Palfreman.	Lucas Caustell.	
	Richard Farrant.	Edward Addams.	

2 at 4d. ob. a daye either of them	£13	13s.	9d.	£46 2s. 1d.
5 at 4d. the daye each of them	30	8s.	4d.	
Hugh Williams at 40s. a yeere -	2	0s.	0d.	
			Summa Totalis -	£476 15s. 5d.

Number of persons—	73	Musicians - - -	£1732	5	0
Do.	41	Officers of the Chappell	476	15	5
Total of both	114	- - - - - -	£2209	0	5

Several of the above musicians claim some notice. William Hunnis in 1549 published some settings of Sir Thomas Wyatt's Penitential Psalms. After being Gentleman of the Chapel Royal in Edward VI.'s reign, he was dismissed by Queen Mary for taking part in plots against the Catholics. Elizabeth restored him, however, and he became custodian of the gardens and orchards at Greenwich (1562). He succeeded Edwardes as master of the children in 1566. Some of the titles of his works are extremely curious; as, for example, "A Hive full of Hunnye, containing the first book of Moses," etc. There is another one entitled "Seven Sobs of a Sorrowful Soule for Sinne, . . . whereunto are annexed his handful of honisuckles" (1583). The punning of the name Hunnis cannot escape attention. He died in 1597. Richard Farrant (1530, *circa* -1580) is still remembered by his anthem, "Lord, for thy tender mercies' sake," and services and anthems. He became organist and lay-vicar of St. George's Chapel, Windsor. Byrde and Tallis (or Talles) were the most conspicuous musicians of their day. Tallis, probably a chorister of the Chapel Royal, became successively organist of Waltham Abbey (until 1540), Gentleman of the Chapel during a part of Henry VIII.'s reign, and through that of Edward VI., Mary, and Elizabeth. He died in 1585. Byrde studied under this famous church-composer. Senior chorister of St. Paul's in 1554, Byrde afterwards became organist of Lincoln Cathedral (1563-72). In 1575 he was appointed joint-organist with his old master, Tallis, at the Chapel Royal. Nor did the association end there; for we find the two men appointed joint patentees in the exclusive right to print music from January 22nd, 1575, until Tallis's death in 1585. The patent, granted by Queen Elizabeth, included printing and selling music and music-paper, English and foreign. It lasted 21 years. In the first year of this monopoly, Byrde's

Cantiones were issued, the printer being Thomas Vautrollier. The value is understood to have been only small; though the fact of this monopoly being continued by Byrde, after Tallis's death, and again renewed in conjunction with Thomas Morley, proves that the composer was not willing to part with it. Tallis is everywhere known through his "Responses"; though some of his great works, such as the famous motet "Spem in alium non habui" (reprinted by Dr. Armes, of Durham), are prized by students of the important ecclesiastical period to which it belongs. Byrde's place in music is perhaps still more exalted than that of Tallis. The younger musician possessed some of the majestic power of Palestrina; he was also a melodist of supreme merit. His Virginal music in the Fitzwilliam Collection is a splendid monument to his mastery of the instrumental forms of his day.

Mary Tudor (1553-58)

We hear little of the minstrels during the brief reign of Mary Tudor. Their quiet calling would doubtless be pursued in the establishments of the great houses, in the city taverns, and in the holiday sports of many a village green. The queen, like the other members of Henry VIII.'s family, had some talent for music, and a good hand for the lute or virginals. In reversing the religious policy of her predecessors, the Mass in all its glory was restored to the Church. At the funeral obsequies of Edward VI., it is interesting to note, the Latin Requiem performed at the Tower was followed by a Protestant service in English at the

Abbey. The coronation was celebrated in a "godly psalm," composed by one Richard Bearde, parson of St. Mary-hill, the tenor of which is seen in the opening couplet—

> "A godly psalm of Mary queen, which brought us comfort all,
> Thro' God whom we of duty praise that gave her foes a fall."

The duodecimo containing the psalm, includes tunes in four parts.[1]

In 1554 the procession and Mass of the Clerks of London were celebrated with much circumstance. "May the sixth," relates Strype, "was a goodly evensong at Guildhall college, by the Masters of the Clarks and their fellowship, with singing and playing; and the morrow after was a great Mass, at the same place, and by the same fraternity, when every clark offered an halfpenny. The Mass was sung by diverse of the queen's chapel and children. And after Mass was done, every clark went their procession, two and two together, each having on a surplice and a rich cope, and a garland. And then fourscore standards, streamers, and banners, and each one that bare them had an albe or a surplice. Then came in order the waits playing, and then thirty clarks singing *festa dies*. There were four of these choirs. Then came a canopy, borne over the sacrament by four of the masters of the clarkes, with staffe torches burning." Incorporated by Henry III. about 1240, under the patronage of St.

[1] Warton.

Nicholas, the Clerks of London gradually attracted to their ranks many distinguished ladies and gentlemen, ecclesiastics and lovers of music. The society became richly endowed, and its services as a band of musicians or choir were in constant requisition at great ceremonies. In 1390 and 1409 eight-days' plays were enacted before the nobility and gentry of the kingdom. A memorial of these events survives in the name Clerkenwell. "In the ignorant ages," says Warton, "the parish clerks of London might justly be considered as a literary society."

Not content with the ordinary religious celebrations, the queen revived all the pageantries and mummeries of ancient superstition. One of these may be briefly referred to. The curious ceremony of the boy-bishop had been forbidden in 1542 by a statute of Henry VIII. It appears that on the festival of Saint Nicholas (December 6th), and for the twenty-two days succeeding, a chorister was annually invested with the name and state, crosier-staff and mitre of a bishop. This *episcopus puerorum,* with his child-prebendaries, directed the cathedral services, preached the sermon, and (in the fourteenth century, at least) celebrated high Mass. The boy-bishop, further, received certain rents, capons, and emoluments. In France, where the custom was equally popular, a boy-bishop actually disposed of a prebend which fell vacant during his tenure of office. A monument exists at Salisbury showing that in case of death the boy-bishop received full pontifical rites. The origin of this singular ceremonial has been traced to the Constantinople Synod of 867 or 870. It obtained in England during the fourteenth, fifteenth, and sixteenth centuries, at many of the cathedral and collegiate churches, notably at Salisbury, Winchester, York, St. Paul's Cathedral, London, Eton College (whose *ad montem* is probably a survival of these solemn theatricals), Beverley, and last and least, Rotherham, Yorkshire (1481). Though forbidden by Henry VIII.'s statute, only thirty years previously Dean Collet, as founder, provides in the statute of St. Paul's School that the scholars "shall every Childermas day come to Paulis churche and hear the chylde-byshop sermon, and after to be at the hygh-masse, and each of them offer a 1d to the chyld-byshop, and with them the maisters and surveiours of the scole."

A poem founded on this ridiculous custom, written by Hugh Rhodes (described as a musician or Gentleman of the Chapel Royal), was sung before the queen in her privy chamber, St. James', on St. Nicholas' Day and Innocents' Day, 1555. "Mysteries and miracles were also revived," says Warton, "as an appendage of the papistic worship." In the year 1557, Strype mentions that "on the 30th of May was a goodly May-game in Fenchurch Street, with drums and guns, and pikes, with the Nine Worthies, who rode. And each made his speech. There was also the Morice-dance, and an elephant and castle, and the lord and lady of the May appeared to make up this show." During Mary's reign, John Heywood, as we have previously stated, enjoyed a full share of royal favour and some popularity.

Although Mary put down the ballad-makers by an edict of her first year, it would seem that she tolerated those in her praise. Sir William Forrest,[1] priest, queen's chaplain, amongst his other literary labours, issued "A New Ballade of the Marigolde." The metre is that of "The Leather Bottel," and there is some ground for believing that it was sung to that melody. From the copy preserved in the library of the Society of Antiquaries, two stanzas may be quoted:—

"The God above for man's delight
Hath here ordayned every thing,
Sonne, Moone, and Sterres shinying so bright,
With all kind fruits, that here doth spring,
And flowres that are so flourishing;
Amonges all which that I beholde
(As to my minde best contentyng),
I doo commende the Marigolde.

"To Marie our Queene, that flowre so sweete,
This Marigolde I doo apply,
For that the name doth serve so meete
And properlee in each partie,

[1] Forrest, who had an annuity of £6 from Christ Church, Oxford, was a good musician, and collected many contemporary compositions, such as those of Taverner, Marbeck, Fayrfax, Tye, Sheppard, and Norman. The MSS. are preserved in the Library of the Music School, Oxford.

For her enduryng paciently
  The stormes of such as list to scolde
At her dooynges, without cause why,
  Loth to see spring this Marigolde."

Another ballad, by John Heywood, celebrated the marriage of Queen Mary and Philip. A third, entitled "The Lamentable Complaint of Queen Mary for the unkind Departure of King Philip, in whose absence she fell sick and died," to the tune of "Crimson Velvet," became popular soon after Mary's demise. It is quoted by Ambrose Philips: *Old Ballads*, iii. p. 83 (1723).

CHAPTER IX.

Elizabethan period—Church ceremonies—Byrde's "Reasons"—Morley —Masques—"Preces Deo Fundamus"—Elizabeth's Progresses—Burney's absurdities—A carol—Gresham College—Dowland—Este—Beggars and rogues.

Elizabethan Period

WHEN tidings reached Elizabeth, on November 17th, 1558, of her accession to the throne, she fell on her knees and repeated the words of the Psalmist, "A Domino factum est istud; et est mirabile in oculis nostris."[1] It is said that more poetry was written during her long reign than in the two preceding centuries. We shall not go so far as to pretend that the same holds good in regard to music. That the art awoke to a fresh impulse there is overwhelming proof; yet, in the rise of the cultivated musician, the minstrel order rapidly degenerated. The actual number retained at court remained much the same as in the two previous reigns; for we read that Elizabeth maintained a band of musicians, consisting of 16 trumpets, lutes, harps, a bagpipe, 9 minstrels, 2 rebecks, 6 sackbuts, 8 viols, and 3 players of the virginals. "Upon the accession of Queen Elizabeth,"

[1] "This is the Lord's doing; it is marvellous in our eyes."—Ps. cxviii. 23. The Latin words were afterwards stamped on the gold coin of the realm.

says Hawkins, "and the resolutions taken by her to reform the choral service, Richard Bowyer, who had been Master of the Children under King Henry VIII., Edward VI., and Queen Mary, was continued in that station;[1] Dr. Tye—who seems to have been out of employ during the reign of Queen Mary—and William Blitheman were made organists, and Tallis continued a Gentleman of the Chapel Royal. As to Byrde, there seems to have been no provision made for him at court; on the contrary, he went to Lincoln, of which cathedral he had been chosen organist in 1563; nor does it appear that he had any kind of employment in the Chapel till the year 1569, when he was appointed a Gentleman thereof in the room of Robert Parsons, who about a month before, by accident, was drowned at Newark-upon-Trent. Upon his being elected into the Chapel, Byrde was permitted by the Dean and Chapter to execute his office of organist of Lincoln Cathedral by a substitute named Butler, of whom there are no memorials remaining."[2] Thomas Butler became organist and master of the choristers in 1572, on the recommendation of Byrde; it therefore seems probable that the latter returned to London at that date.

Church services were scarcely less ceremonial after Elizabeth restored (by statute) the second liturgy of

[1] Thomas Gyles (Master of St. Paul's Children) was empowered in 1585 "to take up such apt and meet children as are most fit to be instructed and framed in the art and science of music" throughout England and Wales. (Sloane MSS. 2035, fol. 116.)

[2] *History of Music*, bk. x. chap. xcvi.

Edward VI. We read that "the altar was furnished with rich plate, with two gilt candlesticks, with lighted candles, and a massy crucifix in the midst; and that the service was sung not only with organs, but with the artificial music of cornets, sacbuts, etc., on solemn festivals. That the ceremonies observed by the Knights of the Garter in their adoration towards the altar, which had been abolished by Edward VI., and revived by Queen Mary, were retained. That, in short, the service performed in the Queen's Chapel, and in sundry cathedrals, was so splendid and showy, that foreigners could not distinguish it from the Roman, except that it was performed in the English tongue." Attracted by such observances, it is said, most of the popish laity came regularly to church for upwards of nine or ten years—indeed, until the Pope, being out of all hopes of an accommodation, excommunicated the queen and laid the whole of England under an interdict. Archbishop Parker, a skilful musician, assisted with the revision of the liturgy, which in 1559 was published and enforced by the Act of Uniformity. One of the curious requirements of the Act was the imposition of a fine of one shilling on all who absented themselves from church on Sundays or holy days.

We learn from Strype that in September 1559, "on a day of this month, began the true morning prayer at St. Antholin's, London, the bell beginning to ring at five, when a psalm was sung after the Geneva fashion, all the congregation, men and women and boys, singing together." In the following year, Bishop Juel states that the singing of psalms was begun in the town and quickly spread to the city and neighbouring places. At St. Paul's Cross[1] sometimes as many as 6000 people sang together. Choral singing was made possible for congregations by the publication of *Day's Psalter* (for four and three voices), during this same year (1560). Before quitting these remarks on ecclesiastical music, it may be added that a few years later (1564), the Council of Trent were on the point of forbidding polyphonic music in the churches; and that the genius of Palestrina saved the situation, by bringing forth the three famous Masses, models of what the Church might reasonably allow.

Popular singing during Elizabeth's reign flourished with extraordinary vigour. Byrde's "Reasons briefely set downe by th' auctor, to perswade every one to learne to sing" are as follows:—

"First, it is a knowledge easily taught, and quickly learned, where there is a good master, and an apt scholar.

2. The exercise of singing is delightful to Nature, and good to preserve the health of man.

3. It doth strengthen all parts of the breast, and doth open the pipes.

4. It is a singular good remedy for a stuttering and stammering in the speech.

5. It is the best means to procure a perfect pronunciation, and to make a good orator.

6. It is the only way to know where Nature hath bestowed the benefit of a good voice, which gift is so rare, as there is not

[1] The Dean of St. Paul's announced the defeat of the Spanish Armada in 1588, at the Cross, where, in ancient times, public announcements were usually made.

one among a thousand that hath it; and in many, that excellent gift is lost, because they want art to express Nature.

7. There is not any music of instruments whatsoever, comparable to that which is made of the voices of men, where the voices are good, and the same well sorted and ordered.

8. The better the voice is, the meeter it is to honour and serve God therewith; and the voice of man is chiefly to be employed to that end.

> Since singing is so good a thing,
> I wish all men would learn to sing."

It seems almost as if all men were attempting music, in one form or another, at the time of which we write. Morley's *Plain and Easy Introduction to Practical Music* (1597), relates that when supper was ended, and the customary music-books were brought forth, "the mistress of the house presented me with a part, earnestly requesting me to sing." But when this visitor protested his utter inability to join in, "every one began to wonder; yea, some whispered to others, demanding how I was brought up." The person thus "upon shame of his ignorance," wisely sought out a teacher, and proceeded to remedy the defect in his education. Ladies and gentlemen no longer neglected their musical studies. At such schools as the Bridewell and Christ's Hospital, boys of humble parentage were taught music, as a class of accomplishment that would secure them good positions as servants, apprentices, or husbandmen. In the drawing-rooms of the better classes, a bass-viol was commonly provided for the use of visitors awaiting their turn to be admitted to the owner's presence.

Similarly, in places of common resort—such as the barbers' shops—lutes, citterns, and virginals were provided for the diversion of customers.

When George Gascoigne's tragedy of *Jocasta* was acted at Gray's Inn in 1566, the orchestra—such as it was—included viols, cythren, bandores, flutes, cornets, trumpets, drums, fifes, and stillpipes." Mention of organs and recorders is met with soon afterwards. A list of masques and plays produced before the closing of the theatres in 1642 gives pride of place to *Jane Shore*,[1] a Latin play written by Henry Lacy of Trinity College, Cambridge, in 1586. The following description appears in the MS.[2]:—

PROCESSIO SOLEMNIS.

The Show of the Procession.

1. Tipstaffe.
2. Shore's Wife in her pettycote, having a taper burning in her hande.
3. The Verger.
4. Queristers.
5. Singing men.
6. Prebendaryes.
7. The Bishoppe of London.
8. Citizens.

This procession alludes to the well-known historical incident of Shore's wife being publicly conducted to

[1] The earliest so-called musical drama is said to be Richard Edward's *Damon and Pytheas*, acted in 1565.

[2] See Harl. MSS. 6926 and 1412. There is also a reprint in *Musica Antiqua*.

church to do penance. As Byrde's setting of the processional is no doubt unique, we quote his music:—

𝄋 Triplex.
Pre - ces De - o fun - da - mus, fun - da - mus o - re
sup - pli - ces ne sit no - ta pol - lu - ta meus
a - dul - te - râ, ne sit no - ta pol - lu -
- ta meus a - dul - ter - a, meus a - dul - ter - a.
Verse.
Fi - dem tu - e - re con - ju - gum lec - tum - que pro -
Quem - cum - que fac - ti pœ - ni - tet pur - ga sol - u -
- bo li - ber - a de - fen - de, de - fen - de pri - va -
- tum cri - men - e ex - em - pla, ex - em - pla fa - vent
- tos tho - ros fur - ti - va ne le - dat Ve - nus.
pos - te - ros fur - ti - va ne fœ - dat Ve - nus.
Medius.
Pre - ces De - o, Pre - ces De - o.
Mr. Bird.

The remaining piece quoted in this list as staged during Elibabeth's reign is *Cynthia's Revels*, by Ben Jonson, with music by Henry Youle, or Youll (1600). Robert Johnson, a famous lutenist and composer of the period, was at this time in the service of Thomas Kytson, of Hengrave Hall, Suffolk. He is mentioned several times in the household book. In 1575, for example, there is this entry:—"In reward to Johnson the musician, for his charges in awaiting on my Lord of Leicester at Kenilworth, ten shillings." This refers to the Earl of Leicester's entertainment of Queen Elizabeth, at Kenilworth Castle—a splendid occasion, recorded in Laneham's Letter, and mentioned in Scott's famous novel. A royal progress such as the queen then undertook must have found employment for all the available minstrels *en route*, for music was in demand at every turn. Trumpets sounded a welcome, groups of musicians, concealed or otherwise, provided harmony suited to each special occasion. Dancing brought in its train numerous stately movements, such as the Corantos, Galliards, the Haye, the Morris, or old country jigs of the Trenchmore and Cushion pattern. In such dances as the last named, "all the company took part—lord and groom, lady and kitchenmaid, no distinction," says Seldon. Perhaps the most laughable music, mentioned of Laneham, is that referred to in the following description:—"Proteus appeared upon a huge dolphin that was conveyed through the water upon a boat, the oars of the concealed rowers of which were made to resemble the animal's fins; a band of musicians being concealed within the dolphin, who burst into a glorious concert of melody, while the sea deity sang the thanks of the delivered enchantress, and of all the nymphs and gods of the sea, to the mighty, the chaste, and the beautiful Queen of England." Laneham—originally a groom in the royal stables—was promoted by the Earl of Leicester to the position of guarding the council-chamber door from spies and eavesdroppers. He describes his own accomplishments in the manner following:—"Sometimes I foot it with dancing; now with my gittern, and else my cittern, then at the virginals (ye know nothing comes amiss to me); then carol I up a song withal; that by-and-by they come flocking about me like bees to honey; and ever they cry, 'Another, good Laneham, another.'" The queen was a good sportswoman, and many a fine hunting-song must have called her to the field. The number of "Hunt's-ups" and songs of the chase was never more varied than then. Some of these have survived; such are "Blow thy horn, hunter"; "Willy, prithee go to bed"; "The hunt is up"; and "Henry, our royal king, would ride a-hunting." That the queen herself rode a-hunting, and to some purpose, is sufficiently shown in her progress to Berkeley Castle, on which occasion, during the owner's absence, twenty-seven prime stags were accounted for in the course of a single day.

Dr. Burney wrote of Queen Elizabeth that "this heroic daughter [of Henry VIII.] used to be regaled during dinner with twelve trumpets and two kettledrums; which together with fifes, cornets, and side-drums, made the hall ring for half an hour together." This absurd account is founded on a passage in Hentzner, who described what he witnessed at the palace of Greenwich. The half-hour's fanfare was no more than a summons to dinner. The original words run thus:—"During the time that this guard, which consists of the tallest and stoutest men that can be found in all England—being carefully selected for this service—were bringing dinner, twelve trumpets and two kettledrums made the hall ring for half an hour together. At the end of this ceremonial, a number of unmarried ladies appeared, who, with particular solemnity, lifted the meat off the table, and conveyed it into the queen's inner and more private chamber, where, after she had chosen for herself, the rest goes for the ladies of the court." "The queen," adds this writer, "dines and sups alone, with very few attendants; and it is very seldom that anybody, foreigner or native, is admitted at that time, and then only at the intercession of somebody in power." It was a popular practice both at dinner and supper to introduce vocal music. At Christmas-time it was not unusual to sing a "jolly carol" between each course, or dish. Such a song as that of the "Boar's Head," printed by Wynkyn de Worde in 1521, and preserved in the fragment of that book found by Hearne, or the carol of "Remember, O thou man," which found a place in Ravenscroft's *Melismata* (1603), must have helped to cheer the long winter hours at many an English hearth in "good Queen Bess's" days.

" My Dancing Day "

The following example is copied from William Sandys' Collection of Carols (1838). Without vainly speculating as to its age, it may safely be pronounced an ancient piece; it is also remarkable for its fantastic legendry. Dancing as an expression of religious ecstasy belongs to a remote age. The prophet pictured David as dancing " before the Lord, with all his might."

TO-MORROW SHALL BE MY DANCING DAY.

Chorus.
Sing oh! my love, Oh! my love, my
love, my love; This have I done for my true love.

To-morrow shall be my dancing day,
I would my true love did so chance
To see the legend of my play,
To call my true love to my dance.
Sing, oh! my love, oh! my love, my love, my love,
This have I done for my true love.

Then was I born of a Virgin pure,
Of her I took fleshly substance;
Thus was I knit to man's nature,
To call my true love to my dance.
Sing, oh! etc.

In a manger laid and wrapped I was,
So very poor, this was my chance,
Betwixt an ox and a silly poor ass,
To call my true love to my dance.
Sing, oh! etc.

My True Love's Dance

Then afterwards baptized I was,
  The Holy Ghost on me did glance,
My Father's voice heard from above,
  To call my true love to my dance.
      Sing, oh ! etc.

Into the desert I was led,
  Where I fasted without substance ;
The Devil bade me make stones my bread,
  To have me break my true love's dance.
      Sing, oh ! etc.

The Jews on me they make great suit,
  And with me made great variance,
Because they lov'd darkness rather than light,
  To call my true love to my dance.
      Sing, oh ! etc.

For thirty pence Judas me sold,
  His covetousness for to advance ;
Mark whom I kiss, the same do hold,
  The same is he shall lead the dance.
      Sing, oh ! etc.

Before Pilate the Jews me brought,
  Where Barabbas had deliverance ;
They scourg'd me and set me at nought,
  Judged me to die to lead the dance.
      Sing, oh ! etc.

Then on the cross hanged I was,
  Where a spear to my heart did glance ;
There issued forth both water and blood,
  To call my true love to my dance.
      Sing, oh ! etc.

Then down to hell I took my way
  For my true love's deliverance,
And rose again on the third day
  Up to my true love and the dance.
          Sing, oh! etc.

Then up to heaven I did ascend,
  Where now I dwell in sure substance,
On the right hand of God, that man
  May come into the general dance.
          Sing, oh! etc.

In 1579 Sir Thomas Gresham (who had built the Royal Exchange) left by will provision for several professorships, one of which was to be in music. Effect was given to this bequest in 1596, when the Gresham Professorship of Music was placed in the hands of Dr. John Bull, on the recommendation of the queen. Being unable to lecture in Latin, Bull was specially permitted to use his native tongue. His salary amounted to £50 per annum, and he held the post for about ten years. Among Bull's successors were parsons and physicians and an organ-builder, who, among them, usurped the intended educational foundation for upwards of 150 years, when a better order of things was instituted. The success of the present professor (1907) has raised the chair from a position of obscurity to one of high standing.

In an age when every trivial affair of daily life had its ballad, it would have been astonishing if so great an event as the defeat of the Spanish Armada had been passed over in silence. Two ballads survive recording the event, though neither possesses any degree of musical interest; both were sung to the tune of "Hanskin," better known in connection with "Jog on, jog on the footpath way."[1]

In this same year, John Dowland (1562-1626) took his degree (Mus. Bac.) at Oxford. This celebrated lutenist was a great traveller in his day, and visited France, Germany, and Italy, spending at least four years abroad. His most noted air, still popular, is the "Frog Galliard," or "Now, oh now, I needs must part." It first appeared in *Songs or Ayres of Four Parts* (1597), and achieved widespread success as a ballad tune. Dowland was the friend of Shakespeare, who was long credited with the following verses:—

"If music and sweet poetry agree,
As they must needs (the sister and the brother),
Then must the love be great 'twixt thee and me,
Because thou lov'st the one, and I the other.
Dowland to thee is dear, whose heavenly touch
Upon the lute doth ravish human sense;
Spenser to me, whose deep conceit is such,
As passing all conceit needs no defence;
Thou lov'st to hear the sweet, melodious sound

---

[1] The older ballad, beginning "In eyghtye-eyght, ere I was born," s contained in Harleian MSS. 791, fol. 59, and reprinted in Ebsworth's *Westminster Drollery* (Appendix, p. xxxviii.). The second ballad (in same volume) begins "Some years of late, in eighty-eight" (p. 93 text). The latter, with tune, is in *Pills to Purge Melancholy* (iv. p. 37). Both versions are given in Chappell's *Popular Music.*

That Phœbus' lute, the queen of music makes,
And I in deep delight am chiefly drown'd,
Whenas himself to singing he betakes;
One god is good to both, as poets feign,
One knight loves both, and both in thee remain."

—RICHARD BARNFIELD.

Middleton, Ben Jonson, Massinger, and Fletcher all allude to Dowland's "Lachrymæ" pavan, of which no perfect copy is known. Dowland died in the service of Charles I.

Puttenham, to whom we are indebted for descriptions of many kinds of ancient song, speaks of birthday pieces in the following terms:—"Others for magnificence at the nativities of Princes' children, or by custome used yearly upon the same days are called songs natall or Genethliaca. Others for secret recreation and pastime in chambers with company, or alone, were the ordinary Musickes amorous, such as might be song with voice or to the Lute, Citheron or Harpe, or daunced by measures, as the Italian Pavan and Galliard are at these days in Princes' courts and other places of honourable or civil assembly." He further distinguishes between the marriage-song and the ordinary ballad. The manner of celebrating weddings was "with great rejoicing due to such a matter and to so gladsome a time. This was done in ballade wise as the natal song, and was song very sweetely by Musicians at the chamber door of the bride and bridegroom at such times; and they were called Epithalamies as much as to say as Ballades; for such as were song at the borde, at dinner or supper, were other musickes, and not properly Epithalamies."

The morning serenade was sometimes called a "hunt's-up," as we see from *Romeo and Juliet*, in the verse—

> "Hunting thee hence, with hunt's-up to the day."

In 1591, when Queen Elizabeth visited the Earl of Hertford, at Elvetham (Hants.), she was awakened with such a song on the third day of her entertainment. It is thus recorded:—"On Wednesday morning about nine o'clock, as her Majesty opened a casement of her gallery window, there were three excellent musicians, who being disguised in ancient country attire, did greet her with a pleasant song of Corydon and Phillida, made in three parts of purpose. The song as well for the worth of the ditty, as the aptness of the note thereto applied, it pleased her Highness after it had been once sung to command it again, and highly to grace it with her cheerful acceptance and commendation." The verses, so charmingly introduced to her Majesty, were by Nicholas Breton, and are known and admired to this day. They begin—

> "In the merry month of May,
> On a morn by break of day,
> Forth I walkt the wood so wide,
> When as May was in her pride;
> There I spied all alone,
> Phillida and Corydon."

The music performed by those "three excellent musicians" was the composition of Michael Este; it appears in his *Madrigals* of 1604. Dr. John Wilson's setting is now better known. Another version by Dr. Benjamin Rogers became popular after its publication (in 1653) by Playford, but it cannot compare with Wilson's pretty melody.

It has already been seen that the minstrels unattached to the great houses (including the court) were leading for the most part an idle and vagabond life. Such legislation as was meted out to them was of a repressive kind. And no wonder. For in spite of preceding monarchs' statutes hundreds of able-bodied beggars roamed at will about the country committing all manner of robberies and violences, and of this number many were of the lowest class of minstrel, who picked up a fortuitous livelihood at the country weddings, Whitsun Ales, fairs, and May festivals; and, most commonly of all, at the taverns. In 1572 the Act declared that "all the parts of England and Wales be presently with rogues, vagabonds, and sturdy beggars exceedingly pestered." The description of the class whose suppression was aimed at included minstrels not belonging to any peer of the realm. The punishments allotted to the convicted were exceedingly severe. Whipping and branding with a hot iron came first, and, finally, death at the gallows without benefit of clergy. The severity of these punishments proved their own foil, and rendered the Act less effective than it might have been with reasonable lenience. Not until 1597, when new clauses were drawn, dealing with "rogues, vagabonds, and sturdy beggars," and distinguishing these from the real poor, did legislation effect any improvement in the state of affairs. Rates were levied for the maintenance of the indigent poor, while the rogues and vagabonds (including "minstrels wandering abroad") were to be sent to the House of Correction. Four years later (1600) the Act was extended and improved. It thus laid the foundation of our present poor laws. Ritson remarks that "it might not be long after the passing of the above Act against the minstrels that Dr. Bull wrote satirical verses upon them," of which part of the first stanza is as follows:—

> "When Jesus went to Jairus' house,
> He turn'd the minstrels out of doors,
> Among the rascal company;
> Beggars they are with one consent,
> And rogues by Act of Parliament."

CHAPTER X.

Stuart period—Gunpowder Plot—Catch for five voices—Musicians' Company—Masques and plays—Playford—Closing of the theatres—Cromwellian carols—Dorothy Osborne—"Loth to depart"—Restoration—Dr. Rogers—Four-and-twenty fiddlers—Mace—Jenkins—Purcell—Handel—Arne—Retrospect.

Stuart Period

ONE of the first acts of James I. was to grant an increase of stipend to the Gentlemen of the Chapel Royal. Dr. Bull was still organist, and among the musicians afterwards known to fame were William Lawes, who appears in the list of chaplains, and William Byrde. The king, though fond of poetry, did not take any special interest in music or painting. His children, however, were placed under Dr. John Coperario, who taught Prince Charles to play on the viol da gamba. Prince Henry in 1611 maintained a body of fifteen musicians, at the head of whom was Dr. Bull. Vocal music, so widely cultivated under Elizabeth, now gave way to instrumental. Among the publications of the time were Morley's *First Booke of Consorte Lessons*, arranged for treble lute, pandora, cittern, flute, and treble and bass viols. Even the madrigals were now issued for voices or viols. Masques and interludes were in great request at the chief houses, which still maintained a musical establishment. The Gunpowder Plot (1605) occasioned a ballad or two, such as that which appears in *Choice Drollery* (1656) beginning—

> "And will this wicked world never prove good?
> Will priests and catholiques never prove true?"[1]

Chappell mentions another ballad, to the tune of "The Barking Barber," but he does not quote the words. The most notable publication of old ballads and ancient songs occurred in Thomas Ravenscroft's three-fold work, *Pammelia* (1609), *Deuteromelia* (1609), and *Melismata* (1611). We quote an example of a round for five voices from the first-named work. It is remarkable for the fact that the first half-dozen bars are identical with William Byrde's Christmas Carol contained in *Songs of Sundry Natures* (1589).

The Musicians' Company, which claims to have been established in 1472 by Edward IV.'s Charter—though Stow in his *Survey* does not include it among the sixty companies existing in the twenty-third year of Henry VIII.—received a new charter from James I. in 1604. Members were limited to the City of London and within three miles of its boundaries. It also

[1] The witty editor of our modern reprint remarks—"With Charles Lamb, we have always regretted the failure of the Gunpowder Plot. It would have been a magnificent event, fully equal to Firmillian's blowing up of the Cathedral of St. Nicholas at Badajoz; and the loss of life of all the Parliament members would have been a cheap price, if paid, for such a remembrance."

practically granted a monopoly in outdoor performances, such as weddings, dances, serenades, etc., as all such performers required the Company's licence.

The number of people taking up music this while as a profession is said to have been very great. Some of these travelled abroad; like Dowland, who became

CATCH FOR FIVE VOICES. *Pammelia.*

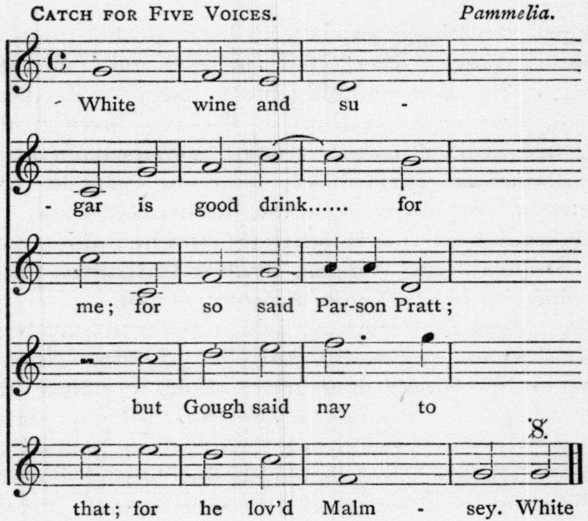
White wine and su -
- gar is good drink...... for
me; for so said Par-son Pratt;
but Gough said nay to
that; for he lov'd Malm - sey. White

lutenist to the King of Denmark; Peter Phillips, who obtained the appointment of organist to the Archduke of Austria; and Dr. Coperario, who spent so much of his time in Italy that his surname Cooper is to this day better known in the Italian form just given.

Masques and Plays

The masques[1] and plays produced in this reign were the following:—

Ferrabosco's *Volpone* (Ben Jonson), 1605.
Ferrabosco's *Masque of Blackness* (Ben Jonson), 1605.
Twelfth Night Revels (Ben Jonson), 1606.
Dr. Campion's Masque in honour of Lord Hayes and his bride (in conjunction with Thomas Lupo and Thomas Giles), 1607.
Ferrabosco's Masque for Lord Haddington's marriage (Ben Jonson), 1608.
Ferrabosco's *Masque of Beauty* (Ben Jonson), 1608.
Ferrabosco's *Masque of Queens* (Ben Jonson), 1610.[2]
Coperario's *Masque of the Inner Temple and Gray's Inn* (Beaumont), 1613.
Robert Johnson's *Tempest* (Shakespeare), 1612 *circa*.
Coperario and Lanier's Masque at the marriage of the Earl of Somerset and Lady Frances Howard, 1614.
Coperario's *Masque of Flowers*, 1614.
R. Johnson's *Valentinian* (Beaumont and Fletcher), 1617.
R. Johnson's *Masque of the Gypsies* (Ben Jonson), 1621.

Although the musicians' names are placed first, their share in the production of these masques was the least, and sometimes meant no more than a few songs and dances. Vast sums were spent on preparing the performances. For example, the *Gray's Inn Masque* cost £1,086 8s. 11d., which represented ten times our

[1] So early as 1431 the Lincoln's Inn Society celebrated four annual festivals, which for the most part consisted of the representation of masques.

[2] Reprinted by the Shakespeare Society in Cunningham's *Life of Inigo Jones*.

money value. The machinery and costumes were devised by Inigo Jones, while Lanier was responsible for much of the scenery. Coperario's celebrated air of "Mad Tom" was introduced in the *Gray's Inn Masque.* A few songs from Robert Johnson's *Tempest* also survive.

It may prove not uninteresting to note the rewards to the persons employed in the Masque. An example is seen in the Pell Records, where the payments for producing Ben Jonson and Ferrabosco's *Masque of Queens* are as follows:—

To 12 Musicions that were Preestes, that songe and played	£24
,, 12 other Lutes that suplied and with Flutes - -	12
,, 10 Violencas that continually practized to the Queen -	20
,, 4 more that were added at the Maske - - -	4
,, 15 Musitions that played the pages and fooles - -	20
,, 13 Hoboyes and Sackbutts - - - - -	10

Ferrabosco, "for making the songs," received £20; Mr. Johnson, for setting the same to the lutes, received £5. In addition to the players mentioned, there were the members of the royal band—stringed instruments almost entirely; thus there would be a full orchestra of not less than eighty performers.

In the *Survey of Cornwall* (1602), Carew gives a glimpse of the wandering minstrel, in speaking of "Tregarrick," then the residence of the Sheriff (Buller). "It was some time," says he, "the Widelade's inheritance, until the father's rebellion forfeited it, when the son led a walking life with his harp to gentlemen's houses, where-through, and by his other active qualities, he was entitled Sir Tristram; neither wanted he (as some say) a 'belle Isound,' the more aptly to resemble his pattern."

A deed dated 1612 bearing Shakespeare's autograph, shows that the poet purchased his house in Blackfriars from Henry Walker, "citizen and minstrel of London," who received the sum of £140, equal to about £700 in current value. This Walker was a member of the Musicians' Company; and it is believed that the roll of Freemen's names—unfortunately, lost—may also have included Shakespeare's. (See Grove's *Dictionary,* iii. 340, new ed.)

Opera

Opera had been successfully launched in 1600, when Peri's *Euridice* came to light. Several earlier composers had been instrumental in developing the movement, which came to a climax during the Renaissance through the efforts of that little band of Florentines—Galileo,[1] Peri, and Caccini, who met together towards the close of the sixteenth century. The first history of Opera is contained in the history of ancient Greece. But just as our drama came through the channel of miracle-play and mystery, designed often enough by men conversant with the plays of Plautus and Terence, if not those of Æschylus and Sophocles, so, too, may opera with no little degree of probability be traced to precisely the same source. The first English opera was Nicholas Lanier's[2] setting of

[1] Father of the astronomer.

[2] Born 1588, died 1665 or 1666.

Ben Jonson's Masque at Lord Hay's, for the entertainment of Baron de Tour, French Ambassador, in 1617. Lanier was long thought to have been an Italian, but it is now known that he came of English parentage: his father and maternal grandfather being English court musicians. We have no space to trace the progress of opera in this country; it must suffice to note the early landmarks. Such were Monteverde's *Orfeo* of 1608, and *The Siege of Rhodes* (1656)—the first opera *sung* in England—in which the composers collaborating were Charles Colman, Henry Cooke, Henry Lawes, and George Hudson. Matthew Locke's music to Shirley's *Masque of Cupid and Death* (1653) merits the title of opera no less than those previously named. Arrived at 1677, the reputed date of Purcell's *Dido and Æneas*,[1] we touch an epoch which may justly be claimed as one of supreme importance to English music. The foundations of dramatic music, then well and truly laid, will doubtless, as time goes on, lead to a superstructure being raised worthy of Purcell and of his country.

Charles I., himself an accomplished musician and patron of music, possessed in his Gentlemen of the Chapel Royal, several excellent musicians, such as William and Henry Lawes, Dr. Coperario, Lanier, and Dr. Charles Colman. An important publication early in the reign, was *Barnard's Church Music*, collected out of "divers approved authors." Church music temporarily passed

[1] Mr. Barclay Squire fixes the date as 1688 or 1690. ("Sammelbände" of the *Int. Mus. Ges.* v. 506.)

out of favour, and in 1644 the Book of Common Prayer was abolished. Instrumental music as regards the Church was now under ban. Sir Edward Deering, who introduced the bill for the abolition of Episcopacy, declared that "one single groan in the spirit is worth the diapason of all the church music in the world." With such views in favour, the next sixteen years was a blank in the history of ecclesiastical music. Not so the secular; for as lyric poetry began to be cultivated by Ben Jonson and others, including the court poets Carew, Waller, Suckling, Lovelace, and Herrick, music kept pace with her. Playford's *Select Musical Airs* (1653) contains excellent specimens of the songs of this period, many of which still continue to be reprinted. Hawkins gives a copy of Lord Commissioner Whitelocke's "Coranto"—a singular memorial of the Puritan stalwart. In his memoirs, Whitelocke explains that Simon Ives (a decidedly second-rate composer, who wrote nothing so interesting himself) assisted in the composition of this bright and melodious little dance-tune. The air caught the queen's fancy, and from first being played whenever lawyer Whitelocke entered a play-house, it afterwards travelled the length of the kingdom, and for half a century enjoyed great popularity. Having said so much, a copy might be expected. It is too long, however, for reproduction; the curious reader is therefore referred to *Hawkins' History* (bk. xiii. chap. cxxi.).

Of the Masques and Triumphs given during Charles' unfortunate reign, it will be observed that all were

English, Ferrabosco having disappeared from the stage. Milton's *Comus*, produced in 1634, originated through Henry Lawes' intimacy with the poet. The young people of the noble family of Egerton were the performers, one of whom—Lady Alice Egerton—was a pupil of Lawes. The two men had previously collaborated in a short pastoral entitled *Arcades*, given at Harefield, near Uxbridge, in 1633. Our list is quoted from Rimbault:—

Thomas Brewer's *Love Tricks* (Shirley) . . 1631
Henry Lawes' *Rival Friends* (Peter Hausted) . 1632
Dr. Wilson's *Northern Lass* (Richard Brome) . . 1632
William Lawes and Simon Ives' *Triumph of Peace* (Shirley) 1633
Henry Lawes' *Cœlum Britannicum* (Carew) . . . 1634
Henry Lawes' *Masque of Comus* (Milton) . . . 1634
Dr. Charles Colman's *Royal Entertainment at Richmond* (Davenant) 1634
William and Henry Lawes' *Triumphs of the Prince d'Amour* (Davenant) 1635
Henry Lawes' *Masque of Vices* . . . *circa* 1635
Henry Lawes' *Royal Slave* (Cartwright) 1636
Lanier's *Luminalia; or, Festival of Light* . . . 1637
Lewis Richard's *Salmacida Spolia* (Davenant) . . 1639

Cromwell

With the closing of the theatres in 1642, and the rigorous ordinances of 1647 forbidding music and dancing under heavy fines and imprisonment, secular music came to a standstill. Cromwell, a secret lover of music, presents the singular spectacle of a statesman discouraging in public an art which he privately approved. The organ, removed from Magdalen College, Oxford, was conveyed to Hampton Court, where the Protector often enjoyed hearing it played by John Hingston, a pupil of Orlando Gibbons. Music was denounced from the pulpit, anathematized openly by eminent writers, and finally made penal by Parliament itself. Such persecution could but defeat its own ends. While the Puritans were singing psalms to hornpipes, and the Protector entertaining ambassadors with psalmody; others there were, among the cavaliers, who fostered the fallen muse until such time as she could once again exercise her humanizing influence. Whether suggested or not by William Slater's *Songs of Sion* (1642)—a volume of pious verse set to secular airs—it was gravely suggested in Parliament in this year that the deeds of Oliver Cromwell should be put into rhyme, with a view to replacing the carols so fondly sung at Christmastide. In the country, the milkmaids' voices were still to be heard. Old Izaac Walton wrote in 1653—"As I left this place and entered into the next field, a second pleasure entertained me; it was a handsome milkmaid, who cast away all care and sung like a nightingale; her voice was good, and the ditty fitted for it; it was that smooth song made by Kit Marlow, now at least fifty years ago; and the milkmaid's mother sung an answer to it, which was made by Sir Walter Raleigh in his younger days."[1] Dorothy Osborne, in a letter

[1] The song referred to is "Come, live with me and be my love."

of the same date, gives similar testimony:—"The heat of the day is spent in reading or working, and about six or seven o'clock I walk out into a common that lies hard by the house, where a great many young wenches keep sheep and cows, and sit in the shade singing of ballads. I go to them and compare their voices and beauties to some ancient shepherdesses that I have read of, and find a vast difference there; but trust me, I think these are as innocent as those could be. I talk to them and find they want nothing to make them the happiest people in the world but the knowledge that they are so."

Dorothy Osborn

As a specimen of the music of the Commonwealth—cultivated in secret—the following little song from Elizabeth Rogers' Virginal Book will recommend itself for grace and refinement. The words are credited to Dr. Donne. "Loth to depart" became a descriptive title for any farewell song. We have a modern instance in "The girl I left behind me," which is the soldiers' "loth to depart"; our sailors, too, on leaving a foreign port, sing their farewell song. In Ravenscroft's *Deuteromelia* (1609) the following lines refer to this sort of air:—

> "Sing with thy mouth, sing with thy heart,
> Like faithful friends, sing Loath to depart;
> Though friends together may not always remain,
> Yet Loath to depart sing once again."

The Fitzwilliam Virginal Book has an arrangement of such a song, by Giles Farnaby; Orlando Gibbons is also known to have written a "loth to depart." Our copy is anonymous, and we prefer not to speculate on its authorship.

ELIZABETH ROGERS, HIR VIRGINALL BOOKE. *Feb. 27th*, 1656.

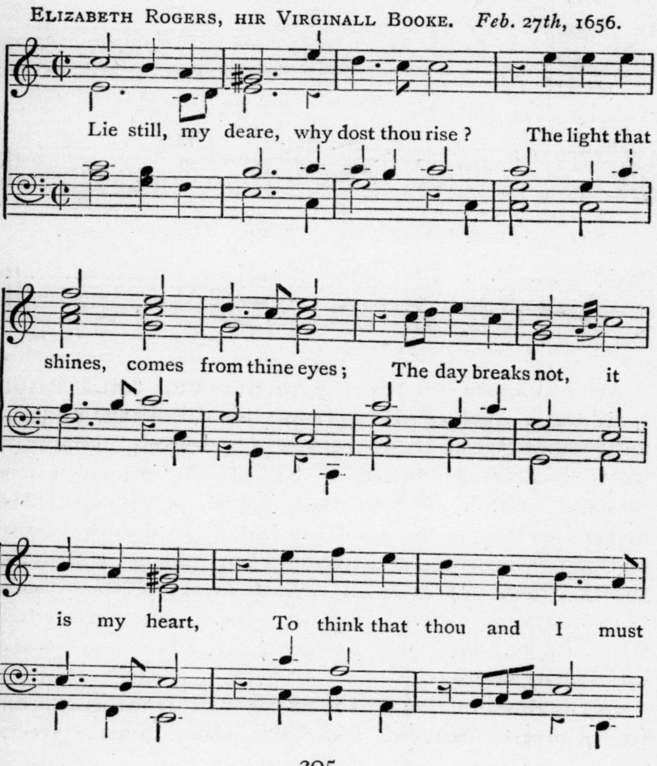

Lie still, my deare, why dost thou rise? The light that
shines, comes from thine eyes; The day breaks not, it
is my heart, To think that thou and I must

part: Oh, stay, oh, stay, oh, stay, or else
my joys must die, And pe-rish in their in - fancy.

An ordinance of the Commonwealth, dated 1656, reproduces much of the spirit of the Elizabethan edict, and enacts "that if any person or persons, commonly called Fidlers or Minstrels, shall at any time be taken playing, fidling, and making musick in any inn, ale-house, or tavern, or shall be taken proffering themselves, or desiring, or entreating any person or persons to hear them play or make musick in any of the places aforesaid, every such person or persons so taken shall be adjudged and declared to be rogues, vagabonds, and sturdy beggers."

At the Restoration, the forces of music were discovered to be much shattered and dissipated. Some sixteen years of enforced idleness had abolished the order of singing boys. Organs had been pulled down, destroyed, or mutilated, and organ-builders—with the exception of the Dallams—had disappeared from the land; and to crown all, books and music had perished in considerable quantities.

Dr. Rogers

One of the first events of musical importance was the entertainment given by the City of London, at the Guildhall, to the King and Parliament. A "Hymnus Eucharisticus," written by Dr. Ingelo, and set to music (in four parts) by Benjamin Rogers, served to honour the occasion. Hawkins, who confuses this hymn with a second composed by Rogers, remarks that he was "amply rewarded for his excellent composition." The other setting of words beginning "Te Deum Patrem colimus," sung as grace after meat, and annually from the college tower on the first of May, was written for Magdalen College, Oxford, where Rogers was organist for more than twenty years.

In restoring church music, Charles II. found himself in the singular dilemma of being unable to obtain choristers. Matthew Locke writing in 1673, remarks, "For above a year after the opening of his Majesty's chapel, the orderers of the music there, were necessitated to supply the superior parts of their music with cornets and men's feigned voices; there being not one lad for all that time capable of singing his part readily." The taste of the day now set towards instrumental music—especially that for strings. Tom Durfey's song of "Four-and-twenty Fiddlers, all in a row," satirized the actual state of things in regard to the court band. The fiddlers were not, however, as Hawkins imagined, all players of the treble violin; but were balanced as follows:—6 violins, 6 counter-tenors, 6 tenors, and 6 basses. Baltzar (one of the finest players of his day) was the first leader; after him came Bannister; and, finally, Monsieur Grabu, whom all the historians delight in picturing as an impudent impostor. Henry Purcell was now coming to the front, and the rivalry in stage-productions of the two men has tended to ridicule Grabu to all posterity. So fond was the king of this group of twenty-four fiddlers, that they were installed in the Chapel Royal, and the organ abandoned. While raising the salaries of his Gentlemen of the Chapel to £70 each, per annum, the king had no method in his payments. Pepys refers to this matter, under date December 19th, 1666:—"Talked of the king's family with Mr. Hingston, the organist. He says many of the musique are ready to starve, they being five years behind with their wages; nay, Evens, the famous man upon the harp, having not his equal in the world, did the other day die of mere want, and was fain to be buried at the almes of the parish, and carried to his grave in the dark at night without one linke, but that Mr. Hingston met it by chance, and did give 12d. to buy two or three links."

Purcell

We have Roger North's testimony that the French music did not entirely supplant our own. The old music, says he, was used in the country, and in meetings and societies in London. Mace, too, adds that "the common tunes are sung by the boys and common people in the streets, among them being many that are very excellent and well contrived." Mace, the great authority on the lute, mentions that Charles II. bought an old specimen of the kind, "a pitiful, battered, cracked thing," for £100.

Mace

This Thomas Mace (1619-1709), some time Clerk of Trinity College, Cambridge, has left in his *Musick's Monument* (1676), a good account of the art of his time. Though the larger part of his book treats of the lute, the author claims to have excelled more upon the viol. "We had for our grave musick," says he, "Fancies of 3, 4, 5, and 6 parts to the Organ; interpos'd (now and then) with some Pavins, Allmaines, solemn and sweet delightful ayres; all of which were (as it were) so many pathettical stories, rhetorical and sublime discourses; subtil and accute Argumentations; so suitable, and agreeing to the inward, secret, and intellectual faculties of the soul and mind; that to set them forth according to their true praise, there are no words sufficient in language; yet what I can best speak of them, shall be only to say, that they have been to myself (and many others) as divine raptures, powerfully captivating all our unruly faculties and affections (for the time), and disposing us to solidity, gravity, and a good temper; making us capable of heavenly and divine influences. 'Tis great pity few believe thus much; but far greater that so few know it." The authors he admires include Coperario, William Lawes, Simpson, and John Jenkins,[1] and "one Monteverde, a famous Italian." Mace has much to say on the balance of instrumental music, which he considers is left too much to the violins. He exclaims, "Six violins, nay ten, nay twenty or more, at a sumptuous meeting, and scarce half so many basses; which (as I said before) were more reasonable, sure, to be the greater number." His view of church music, with a few reservations, goes to show that sacred music was far behind the secular.

Henry Purcell

The most significant event of the period was the rise and popularity of Henry Purcell (1658-95). The list of his dramatic pieces, beginning with *Epsom Wells* (Shadwell), in 1676, includes some forty works, the last being *Don Quixote* (part iii.), produced in Purcell's last year. In some of the dramas music plays an exceedingly small part, as in the *Indian Queen;* others, like *King Arthur,* on the contrary, abound in songs, choruses, and instrumental pieces. No other music was tolerated until 1710, when Handel paid his first visit to England.

One of the remarkable song-collections of this reign, though not published in complete form until George I.'s time, is Tom Durfey's *Pills to Purge Melancholy*. The author states in his preface, "When I have perform'd

[1] John Jenkins (b. 1592) is remembered by the catch "A boat, a boat, haste to the ferry." Many of his MSS. are still in the Library of Christ Church College, Oxford. Stafford Smith asserts that "Henry Purcell *undoubtedly borrowed* from his works."

some of my own things before their Majesties King Charles II., King James, King William, Queen Mary, Queen Anne, and Prince George, I never went off without happy and commendable approbation." Some further notice is taken of this large song-collection in Appendix A.

During the period that Handel dominated music in England, there was at least one musician who could hold his own as a song-writer. "Arne," said the late Dr. Hullah, "was the most thoroughly national of all our song-writers. His fulness of melody, purity of harmony were equalled only by his sustaining power. No composer is more tuneful, and at the same time more spontaneously continuous than Arne."

A few further writers are briefly referred to, under our chapter on Songs. With the more modern development of song-writing, history, as yet, is scarcely concerned. Time, the only arbiter of Art, must be allowed to absorb and adjust new tendencies and new aims before a just appreciation can be pronounced. Briefly to sum up: it has been shown that music held an important place in the ancient Celtic scheme, and that with the Teutonic invasion of our shores, it became reconstructed with new ideas and added impetus. The Roman influence need not be taken into account, unless the ecclesiastical impulse of a later time is to be considered of weight. On this point, however, it must be borne in mind that most historians of music are agreed that the Church art was invariably behind the secular; or, to quote Burney,

Summary

"it seems as if ecclesiastical music was always inferior at any given period, and that the mutilated and imperfect scale of eight modes in Canto Fermo had not only injured Melody, but that bad harmony continued in the Church long after it ceased to be tolerated elsewhere."[1] With the Conquest, native art (such as it was) suffered a complete eclipse. But it cannot be supposed that a tenacious and hardy people, such as the survivors of Hastings undoubtedly were, completely abandoned the songs and musical diversions of their own land, and tamely surrendered all to the Norman. History is almost a complete blank on this point. The true storehouses where native art would be carefully (if secretly) treasured up, were the monasteries. With their decline, nearly all traces of English minstrel-art disappeared. Hence Ritson's retort that Dr. Percy's account of the Minstrels "might with more propriety have been entitled *An Essay on the Ancient French Minstrels.*"

Certainly the first glimpse of our English minstrel discovers a strolling musician, almost mendicant and vagabond in his tastes and proclivities. With the Welsh bards we have no concern. Their history is one apart, and when it is truly rendered, much of the glamour hitherto surrounding it will in all probability disappear, leaving a plain, unvarnished tale of trials and difficulties successfully overcome, with a small surviving record of work accomplished and preserved. It has been observed that "the first musicians were gods; the second, heroes; the third, bards; the fourth, beggars." Curiously

[1] Burney, ii. 166.

enough, the succession of the minstrels is only to be traced through the court records. It was so in the time of Canute and Alfred, and our accounts have invariably been intermingled with the annals of kings and queens—such scraps as we have been able to piece together. Here, also, is a link with the musicians who carried on art when the minstrel rogues and vagabonds ceased to occupy our attention.

A charter of Charles I. invested Nicholas Lanier and others with power as marshal, wardens, and cominality of the art and science of music, to suspend and take away the privilege of practising as minstrels from all those who were found short of ability, and to licence those who were found worthy. This link, slender as it might at first appear, joins in unbroken succession the minstrels of the Norman Conquest and the musicians of the Stuart period—Lanier, Lawes, and Wilson, until in due time we can add the name of Henry Purcell, the best court-musician England ever possessed. Such a continuation may be considered fanciful; it is at least illustrious.

A.D. 1636

CHAPTER XI.

"Sermons in stones"—Wells Cathedral—Worcester—Peterborough—Minstrels' Gallery, Exeter—Beverley Minster—St. Mary's—"Meynstyrls' Pillor."

"Sermons in Stones"

MINSTRELSY has left her mark not only in various manuscripts, missals, tapestry, and grave memorials, but also in the more visible witness of churches—such as the priory erected by Rahere (Smithfield, London), or the Church des Ménétriers, Paris. Turning to our ancient ecclesiastical edifices, the craft mark is traceable in several of the most famous. The west front of Wells Cathedral, though not strictly of this order, has been described as a reproduction in stone of the *Gloria in Excelsis*, which is the ideal song of all men in all ages; or as Fuller has said, "It is a masterpiece of art indeed, made of imagery in just proportion, so that we may call them *vera et spirantia signa*. England affordeth not the like." Worcester Cathedral preserves a bas-relief on the under portion of the choir seats, showing a twelfth-century player of the crwth or crowd, a rude form of violin with five strings. On one of the sculptures outside St. John's Church, Cirencester, the method of handling this ancient instrument is seen to be almost identical with that of the violin. The date of the sculpture is about 1522. A much earlier monumental brass erected to Robert Braunch of Lynne (Norfolk), in 1364, seems to show by its long neck and bent sides, that this ancient fiddle was originally intended to be held between the performers' knees.

Among the frescoes on the interior of the roof of Peterborough Cathedral (done between 1177-94,) are performers on instruments of the violin kind, dating from the twelfth century. In one of these representations, the incurvations on the sides of the body of the instrument and two sound-holes are to be seen. The restorations of 1835 are understood to leave the original designs intact.

Exeter Cathedral possesses a Minstrels' Gallery of the fourteenth century. Each of the twelve niches is occupied by a winged angel supporting an instrument. Viewing the group from left to right, the following descriptions of instruments are seen:—

1. Cittern.
2. Bagpipe.
3. Clarion.
4. Rebec.
5. Psaltery.
6. Syrinx (Pandean Pipe; rendered Organ in Bible).
7. Sackbut.
8. Regals.
9. Gittern (small guitar).
10. Shalm.
11. Timbrel.
12. Cymbals.

Beverley, in the East Riding of Yorkshire, has been especially favoured in regard to ancient memorials of

FIG. 9.—THE MINSTRELS' GALLERY, EXETER.

English minstrels. Not only at the Minster, but also at St. Mary's Church, numerous evidences remain to prove that the fraternity of minstrels was an ancient and honoured foundation. Under date 1555, orders of the ancient company (or fraternity) of minstrels at Beverley recite that it has been a very ancient custom for most of the minstrels attendant upon men or women of honour, between the Trent and Tweed, to annually visit Beverley on Rogation days, in order to choose an Alderman of the Minstrels, with stewards and deputies authorized to take names and receive "customable duties" of the brethren. A fair specimen of these orders is seen in that which (under the date mentioned) provides that no miller, shepherd, or husbandman playing on pipe or other instrument should perform without authority at any wedding or merry-making, outside his own parish. The columns of the Minster exhibit some curious figures of minstrels—though the date of its erection (*temp.* Henry VI.) was during the decadence of the craft. The lute-player, the singer, and the performer on pipe and tabor indicate types in the common minstrelsy of the age. The highest class is wanting.

Turning to St. Mary's Church, Beverley, we have an interesting proof that the common minstrels of the decadence were still able and willing to do their share in raising a worthy memorial to the religious zeal of the Middle Ages, for we find this inscription upon the easternmost pillar on the right side of the nave:—

Thys Pillor made the Meynstyrls.

It appears that in 1520 a portion of the nave was destroyed by the fall of the central tower. The restoration that followed was voluntarily undertaken by dwellers in and around Beverley. This circumstance accounts for the various inscriptions which appear on the corbels of the supporting columns of the nave. Thus we read, "Klay and his wife made these two pillars and a half"—on the two westernmost, "these two pillars made good wives," and further, "this pillar made the minstrels." The sculpture represents five dimly-coloured minstrels, with chains of office about their necks and goodly purses hanging from their waists, and with one exception, dressed in short coats reaching to the knees; while they are shown to be playing upon their instruments as follows, from left to right:—

1. Tabor and pipe.
2. Crwth (or violin).
3. Base flute.
4. Gittern (cittern or lute).
5. Treble flute à bec (or perhaps a wayght—a kind of early oboe).

In the sculpture the base-flute player is dressed in a longer coat than his comrades; and it is possible that he was of better degree.

Athelstan is credited with having conferred this ancient right. In 1610 the minster town was visited by the Plague, and none of the inhabitants were for a time permitted to leave Beverley without the Mayor's special permission.

[1] An illustration of the Minstrels' Pillar appears in the *Story of Notation* ("Music Story Series"), page 148. Much more musical-subject architecture abounds in Beverley Minster, pen-and-ink sketches of which are in our possession, and at the service of those interested.—ED.

CHAPTER XII.

Evolution of Harmony—Hucbald—Tenth century carol—Guido—Twelfth century example—Adam de la Hâle—A French chanson—Guillaume de Machault—Bodleian example.

HARMONY—its evolution and subsequent development—is without the purview of this little book. The subject is, however, too important to be entirely ignored. The following is an outline of the early attempts, which the labours of Coussemaker and others have made available for our purpose. Hucbald's examples (given by Burney) exhibit the first known specimens of harmony, or, to use the older expressions, diaphony or organum.

A great step was taken when the succeeding combination (in the example below) was conceived. Burney

Arundel MSS. 77, *fol.* 63*b.*
Tu Pa - tris sem - pi - ter - nus es fi - li - us.
&c.
Te hu - mi - les fa - mu - li

comments on it thus:—"Hucbald's idea that one voice might wander at pleasure through the scale, while the the other remains fixed, shows him to have been a man of genius and enlarged views, who, disregarding rules, could penetrate beyond the miserable practice of his time, into our *points d'orgue*, *pedale*, and multifarious harmony upon a holding note, or single base, and suggest the principle, at least, of the boldest modern harmony.

In a paper read before the Musical Association (May 7th, 1888), Dr. Mee brought to notice a two-part hymn, of which we give a translation. This venerable relic is understood to have been written in a Benedictine Monastery, in Cornwall, during the latter part of the tenth, or early in the eleventh century. The editor of *Early English Harmony* accepts the former approximate date. It is, of course, the earliest example of English harmony so far discovered. The notation is the old alphabetical; it is seen in double columns immediately above the Latin text, thus:—

Tenth Century

h	g	f
h	h	h
Ut	t u	o

A Cornish Carol. *MS. Bodleian*, 572, *fol.* 50.

Cornish Carol

- - - - tus, in - ter - ven - - tu Do - mi -
- - nus nos pur - ga - - tos a
pec - ca - - tis jun - gat cœ - - - -
- li ci - vi - bus.

The commas above the notes indicate a prolongation of the sounds so distinguished.

The next example is quoted from Guido (*circa* 1030). It will be observed that the bare fourths of Hucbald are now combined with the holding-note, giving a wider scope, and employing a greater variety of intervals. But compared with the Cornish Carol just cited, it scarcely shows any real advance. A chronological list of pieces does not, however, necessarily show progress in each specimen. Just as the poetry written soon after

Eleventh Century

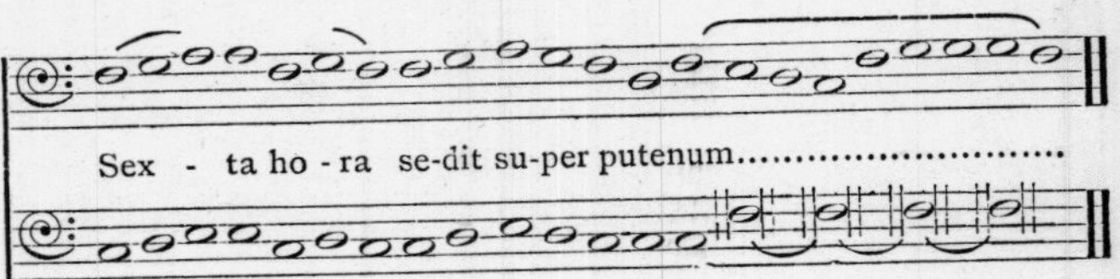
Sex - ta ho - ra se-dit su-per putenum.........................

Chaucer's day is full of retrograde tendencies, so music will be found sometimes returning for a brief spell to her recently discarded methods.

During the succeeding century it is by no means easy to show any striking progress; but the scanty material which has come down to us would alone account for this. Perhaps a little more ease and sonority may be traced in such a fragment as we quote beneath:—

Twelfth Century

12th Century MS., Ambrose Collection (Milan).

There is more musical interest in the little rondeau by Adam de la Hâle (le Bossu d'Arras), born in 1240.

Rondeau

This Adam de la Hâle was a late Trouvère, writing both words and music, and probably employing a minstrel to render them. Such a piece as the rondeau, ill adapted as it is for performance on harp or vielle, obviously could not have been designed for any such purpose, unless three minstrels joined in the performance. It is, therefore, not unreasonable to see in such early attempts the origin of musical composition of an undoubted artistic design having no connection with the two popular channels of musical invention—namely, the secular song or dance and the ecclesiastical chant.

RONDEAU.
Adam de la Hâle 1240–1285.
Tant com je vi - - vrai,
N'a - me - - rai au - - - -

- trui
que
vous
Ja

n'en
par
-
ti
-
-
rai.

As the monumental round which England brought forth during this period (thirteenth century) has already been quoted (p. 68), nothing need here be added, unless it be the observation that this remarkable four-part piece appears to have been in advance of any other known music the world had so far produced.

True progress may be traced, if we leave out of view the round, in the following little French *Chanson à deux parties*:—

Venés à neusches

Coussemaker, whose translation is quoted, gives a facsimile of the fourteenth century MS. in the Cambrai Library. Like many songs of the period, each voice had an independent set of words; so that in the above piece the upper voice sang "Venés à neusches sans detri," etc., while the lower had these, "Vechi l'hermite," etc. In the second bar it will not fail to be seen that the dominant seventh is suggested, if not actually employed.

FIG. 10.—FOURTEENTH CENTURY MINSTREL.

That it was no chance combination the following little passage from Guillaume de Machault (1364) serves to illustrate[1]:—

[1] The whole passage is given in Grove's *Dictionary of Music*, iii. p. 12 (new ed., p. 787).

Dominant Seventh

Our last illustration in this rapid sketch is chosen from an Oxford MS. of the same century (fourteenth). On the first syllable of the word "munditiæ" will be seen another (incomplete) dominant seventh. It lacks the major third, but no other interval could be added. The curious gravitation from tonic to dominant is pregnant of the idea which some two centuries later Monteverde developed to such an extent as to revolutionize by its aid the whole scheme of harmonic music.

From an English Gradual (357 *Bodleian*, 14*th Century*).

Vir - go pu - di - ci - ti - ae fe - rens ti - tu - lum
Ma - ri - a mun - di - ti - ae pro-mens spe - cu - lum
Cas - ti - ta - tis re - gi - a pa - ris par - vu - lum
Cu - jus est per om - ni - a mi - na - re sae - cu - lum.

Illustration has already been given in these pages of the Dunstable period—the fifteenth century (see p. 93). We add a short example by one of his contemporaries.

The rise and decline of the great contrapuntal schools which closed partially with Palestrina in 1594, and

finally with Bach in 1750, need no more than a passing reference. Enough has been brought forward to show that the progress of harmony was aided in the highest degree by secular musicians, whether minstrels or their successors.

CHAPTER XIII.

Chaucer and music—"Angelus ad Virginem"—Glasgerion—The Raye—Symphonie—Hornpipes of Cornewaile—Shakespeare and music—"Hold thy peace, knave"—"Hey, Robin!"—Autolycus' songs—"Heart's-ease."

It has been well said that "Before Chaucer wrote, there were two tongues in England, keeping alive the feuds and resentments of cruel centuries; when he

1328-1400 laid down his pen, there was practically but one speech; there was, and ever since has been, but one people." We shall not pretend that the poet was a minstrel in any other than a poetic sense of the word. It has already been seen that minstrelsy was on the decline, and so could offer but few attractions as a career. Chaucer's references to music are too valuable, however, to be passed over; so we proceed to a consideration of some of the most remarkable.

We have not to search far. In the prologue of the *Canterbury Tales,* we read of the "yonge Squier"—

> "Singing he was, or floyting alle the day,
> He was as fresshe as is the moneth of May.
> . . . . .
> He coude songes make, and wel endite,
> Juste and eke dance, and wel pourtraie and write."

The Squire's musical education had evidently not been neglected. Later the Frere's abilities are thus set down :—

"And certainly he hadde a mery note.
Wel coude he singe and plaien on a rote.
Of yeddinges[1] he bare utterly the pris."

The rote was in all likelihood a form of hurdy-gurdy, or vielle. A reference to this instrument is contained in the lines from "Midas"—

"Whom have we here? a sightly swain and sturdy,
Hum! plays, I see, upon the hurdy-gurdy."

Chaucer speaks of harmony, heard in the vision of "The House of Fame":—

"And the heavenly melodie
Of songes full of armonie,
I heard about her throne ysong
That all the palais walles rung."

Again, in "Troilus and Cresseide":—

"And there he saw, with full advisement,
Th' erratic starres heark'ning harmony,
With soundes full of heav'nly melody."

Among the few instances where the poet has named a particular song, quotation may be made of the following verses from "The Miller's Tale":—

---

[1] "Yeddinges," derived from the Saxon "geddian," to sing, stands for *songs*.

"And all above there lay a gay psalt'ry
On which he made at nightes melody,
So sweetely that all the chamber rang;
And *Angelus ad Virginem* he sang.
And after that he sung the *kinge's note;*
Full often blessed was his merry throat,
And thus this sweete clerk his time spent
After his friendes finding and his rent."

The melody of the *Angelus ad Virginem* is preserved in a manuscript written before the birth of Chaucer, which we quote. That this was the only air cannot now be determined, but its popularity is somewhat confirmed by at least one other version of about the same period—early fourteenth century.

FIG. II.—"ANGELUS AD VIRGINEM."

"Angelus ad Virginem"

An-ge-lus ad Vir-gin-em, Sub in-trans in con - cla - ve
Vir-gin-is for - mi - di - nem De mulcens in - quit A - ve.
A - ve Re - gi - na Vir - gin - num, Cœ - li ter -
rae-que Do - mi - num Con - ci - pi - es, et pa - ri - es in -
- tac - ta Sa - lu - tem, ho - mi - num tu por - ta
cœ - li fac - ta, Me - de - la cri - mi - num.

Perhaps the following were songs of Chaucer's day, though there seems no means of identifying them; indeed, the older poets and writers rarely distinguished between a quoted or original song, the necessity for such distinction only arising with the lapse of time:—

> "Now, dear lady, if thy will be,
> I pray that ye will rue on me."
>
> —"Miller's Tale."

> "Come hither, lovë, to me."
>
> —Prologue, *Canterbury Tales.*

"O May, with all thy flowers and thy green,
Right welcome be thou, fairë freshe May,
I hope that I some green here getten may."
—"Knight's Tale."

"Farewell, have good day."
—"Knight's Tale."

"Heried be thou and thy name,
Goddess of renown and fame."
—"House of Fame."

Chaucer's picture of the gentle Pardoner singing an offertory, and afterwards preaching a sermon to "winne silver," may be taken as a satire on the rapacity of unscrupulous churchmen:—

"But truely to tellen at the last,
He was in church a noble ecclesiast.
Well could he read a lesson or a story,
But alderbest he sang an offertory;
For well he wiste, when that song was sung,
He muste preach, and well afile his tongue,
To winne silver, as he right well could;
Therefore he sang full merrily and loud."
—Prologue, *Canterbury Tales.*

In another passage in "The House of Fame" there is mention of the "great Glasgerion":—

"There heard I play upon a harp,
That sounded bothe well and sharp,
Him, Orpheus, full craftily;
And on his side faste by
Satte the harper Arion,
And eke Æacides Chiron;

And other harpers many a one
And the great Glasgerion;
And smalle harpers, with their glees,
Satte under them in sees.
. . . . . .
Then saw I standing them behind,
Afar from them, all by themselve,
Many thousand times twelve,
That made loude minstrelsies
In cornmuse [bagpipe] and eke in shawmies,
And in many another pipe,
That craftily began to pipe,
Both in dulcet and in reed,
That be at feastes with the bride.
And many a flute and lilting horn,
And pipes made of greene corn,
As have these little herde-grooms,
That keepe beastes in the brooms."

This Glasgerion, according to the ballad of the same name,[1] was a king's son, and a harper withal; he wears a collar or gold chain, showing his rank, rides on horseback, and courts a king's daughter. The verses thus speak of a period when minstrelsy was in its prime.

Many of the instruments of which Chaucer wrote, it may be reasonably assumed, were extant in his own day:—

"Of all manner of minstrales
And gestiours that telle tales,
Both of weeping and of game,
Of all that longeth unto Fame."

---

[1] It is given in *Percy's Reliques*.

The picture is not always a flattering one, for in "The Pardoner's Tale" we read of—

"A company
Of younge folkes, that haunted folly,
As riot, hazard, stewes, and taverns;
Whereas with lutes, harpes, and giterns,
They dance and play at dice both day and night,
And eat also, and drink over their might."

Further in the same poem we read of—

"Singers with harpes, baudes, waferers,
Which be the very devil's officers."

A serenade is given in "The Miller's Tale," though it does not appear that the song which Absolon sings is one now known:—

"The moon at night full clear and brighte shone,
And Absolon his gitern y-taken.
He singeth in his voice gentle and small;
Now, dear lady, if thy will be,
I pray that ye will rue on me;
Full well accordant to his giterning."

Dancing is often alluded to by Chaucer, as in the same poem—

"But of her song, it was as loud and yern [shrill]
As any swallow chittering on a bern.
Thereto she coulde skip, and make a game,
As any kid or calf following his dame."

Further in the same piece, Hendy Nicholas

> "Taketh his psalt'ry
> And playeth fast, and maketh melody."

He had learned his dancing at Oxford:—

> "In twenty manners could he trip and dance,
> After the school of Oxenforde tho [then],
> And with his legges caste to and fro;
> And playen songes on a small ribible;
> Thereto he sung sometimes a loud quinible,
> And as well could he play on a gitern.
> In all the town was brewhouse nor tavern,
> That he not visited with his solas,
> There as that any gaillard tapstere was."

The ribible, or rebeck, was an early class of fiddle; quinible stands for treble. In another place, an old woman is described as "an old ribibe"; from an analogy of shrillness, "an old rebeck" is used in the same sense.[1]

The Raye (spelt also Hay and Hey) was an old country-dance, in which the performers first stood in a ring and proceeded winding round, joining hands in passing. Chaucer, in "The House of Fame," refers to the dance in the following verse:—

> "There saw I famous, old and young,
> Pipers of allë Dutchë tongue,
> To learnë love-dances and springs,
> Reyës, and these strangë things."

---

[1] "Friar's Tale."

The tune is copied from *Musick's Handmaid*, Part I. (1678):—

The Symphonie

In *Love's Labour's Lost* there is the following:—

> "*Dull.* I'll make one in a dance, or so; or I will play
> On the tabor to the worthies, and let them dance
> the Hay.
> *Hol.* Most dull, honest Dull."

Hackluyt also mentions this ancient dance in the *Voyages* (iii. 200):—"Some of the mariners thought we were in the Bristow Channell, and other in Silly Channell; so that, through variety of judgements and evill marinership, we were faine to dance the Hay foure dayes together, sometimes running to the north-east, sometimes to the south-east, and again to the east and east-north-east."

The symphonie[1]—described as "an instrument of music made of a hollow tree, closed in leather on either side, and minstrels beat it with sticks"—is mentioned in "Sir Topaz":—

> "Here is the queen of Faerie,
> With hap and pipe and symphonie,
> Dwelling in this place."

Martial music is thus indicated in "The Knight's Tale":—

> "Pipes, trompes, nakers, and clariounes,
> That in the bataille blowen blody sounes."

The music of the organ is commonly referred to in such passages as these:—

[1] "Nevertheless the accord of all sounds hight *symphonia*, is likewise as the accord of diverse voices hight *chorus*."—BÄRTHOLOMÆUS.

> "His voice was merrier than the merry orgon
> On Masse days that in the churches gon."
> —"Nun's Priest's Tale."

> "And while the organs playen melody
> Thus in her heart to God alone sang she."

If to the instruments mentioned we add the sackbut, fiddle, crouth, cittole, and hautboy, Chaucer's orchestra is complete. In the "Romant of the Rose" Chaucer has mentioned "hornpipes of Cornewaile," which is understood to refer to an instrument like the Welsh pib-corn—"a reed or whistle, with a horn fixed to it by the smaller end"—which afterwards gave its name to the dance. The Cornewaile referred to is in Bretagne. In the "Franklin's Tale" we read that—

> "These olde gentle Bretons, in their days,
> Of divers aventures made lays,
> Rhymeden in their firste Breton tongue;
> Which layes with their instruments they sung,
> Or elles reade them for their pleasance."

Roundelets, complaints, virelayes are often met with in Chaucer, whose ditees, rondils, balades, and songs also distinguish to a nicety the class of lyric intended. Some of these are referred to in Appendix B (p. 324).

Shakespeare

Everything associated with the memory of our greatest poet is fitly held in veneration by the English-speaking races; indeed, this sentiment has led to an attempt to stay the hand of Time as affecting the material monuments and edifices of his day. Music, owing to its inherent vitality, can never decay. It is, therefore, the more remarkable that so little attempt has hitherto been made to cast the light of its pages on those old times from which every scrap of poetry and snatch of song come to us as of priceless value. The best collection of harmonized airs of Shakespeare's period is seen in the Fitzwilliam Virginal Book. (See Appendix A, p. 312.) In studying such early harmonizations the modern musician will need to make some allowance for their comparative antiquity. He may, however, be assured quite confidently that if he will lend a patient ear to these old ditties and allow their quaint expressiveness full play, something of their old-world charm, exquisite grace, and antique humour will creep into his mind and soul. They will remain for him an abiding possession —the supreme test of all true song.

Shakespeare, of all the poets, makes the most consistent use of fragments and snatches of old traditional ballads. *Twelfth Night* is especially fruitful of these:—

> "If music be the food of love, play on;
> Give me excess of it, that, surfeiting,
> The appetite may sicken, and so die.
> That strain again! it had a dying fall."

Having introduced the play with the above words, there follows (in Act ii. Sc. 3) the song, "O mistress mine," the music of which is given in Morley's *Consort Lessons* (1599) and in almost every collection of our own day. "Hold thy peace," the catch which immediately follows, is thus given by Hawkins:—

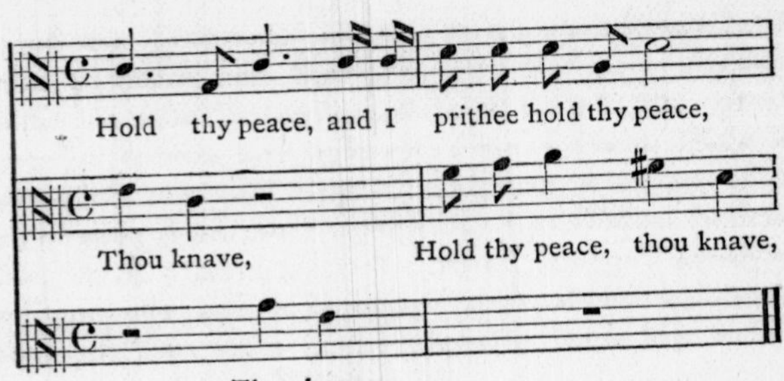

Hold thy peace, and I prithee hold thy peace,
Thou knave, Hold thy peace, thou knave,
Thou knave.

The humour of the catch lies in each singer being called in turn a knave. When the Clown is asked to begin, he exclaims—

"I shall be constrained in't to call thee knave, knight.
Sir And. 'Tis not the first time I have constrained one to call me knave.
Begin, fool; it begins, Hold thy peace.
Clo. I shall never begin if I hold my peace."

When this "caterwauling" is suddenly interrupted, Sir Toby utters the names of several old songs. Such are "Peg-a-Ramsey," to which there are two tunes remaining; the more popular being associated with Durfey's words, "Oh, London is a fine town!" and "Three merry men be we," for which Playford has an air (MS. Commonplace Book). "Tillyvally, Lady," is a mere scrap, as it comes to us, and "There dwelt a man in Babylon" is traditionally sung to a queer version of "Greensleeves." To "Farewell, dear heart," allusion is made on page 284. Another traditional tune to the same words is quoted by Dr. Naylor (*Shakespeare and Music*, p. 190). The air to "O, the twelfth day of December!" is lost. The Duke's preface (Act ii. Sc. 4) to the Clown's song is music in itself:—

"*Duke*. O, fellow, come, the song we had last night,
Mark it, Cesario, it is old and plain;
The spinsters and the knitters in the sun
And the free maids that weave their thread with bones
Do use to chant it; it is silly sooth,
And dallies with the innocence of love,
Like the old age.
Song. Come away, come away, death,
And in sad cypress let me be laid."

The original air is not known. In Act iv. the Clown sings—

"Hey! Robin, jolly Robin,
Tell me how thy lady does," etc.

Sir Thomas Wyat has commonly been credited with the words of this song, but Percy observes that "the discerning reader will probably judge it to belong to a more obsolete writer." The traditional tune runs thus—

Hey! Ro-bin, jol-ly Ro-bin, Tell me how thy la-dy does;

Hey! Ro-bin, jol-ly Ro-bin, Tell me how thy la-dy does.

Of the other clown's song in this act the music remaining is only fragmentary. The play ends with a song, viz.:—

"When that I was a little tiny boy,"[1]

and the traditional air is still in popular use.

The songs in *As You Like It* are six. Amiens' song of "Under the greenwood tree" (Act ii. Sc. 5), of which the air is preserved in the *Dancing Master* (1686), and "Pills to purge melancholy" (iv. 122; 1719). Arne's later setting has secured a greater popularity, both in this and the succeeding song—viz., "Blow, blow, thou winter wind" (Act ii. Sc. 7), of which the traditional air is lost. Hilton has set the song, "What shall he have that kill'd the deer" (Act iv. Sc. 2), and it appears likely that his late sixteenth-century setting is the original. The Page's song in Act v. Sc. 3, "It was a lover and his lass," was set to music by Thomas Morley, and is found in Morley's *Little Short Airs* (1600), and in manuscript in the Advocates' Library, Edinburgh. No other music is tolerated in connection with these words. There is no known *original* setting to the two final songs given to Hymen in the last scene—viz., "Then is there mirth in heaven," and "Wedding is great Juno's crown."

Dr. Burney, in pronouncing Autolycus' ditties as "two nonsensical songs," roused the anger of Steevens. Burney subsequently observed that "this rogue Autolycus is the true ancient minstrel in the old *Fabliaux;*"

[1] Compare, also, "He that has a little tiny wit."—*Lear*, Act iii. Sc. 2.

to which Steevens replied, "Many will push the comparison a little further, and concur with me in thinking that our *modern minstrels*, like their predecessor Autolycus, are pickpockets as well as singers of 'nonsensical ballads.'" *The Winter's Tale* contains three songs, and mentions the names of others once popular. "When daffodils begin to peer"—the music of which was obtained by Ritson for his *English Songs* "not without some difficulty"—comes at the beginning of Scene 3, Act iv. The Pedlar's second song, "Jog on, jog on the footpath way," is possibly a quotation of an older ballad. The air is the very last piece in the Fitzwilliam Virginal Book arranged by Richard Farnaby under the title "Hanskin." The words are in *An Antidote against Melancholy* (1661), with eight additional verses, usually printed in the modern copies. How excellent is the servant's recommendation of the Pedlar and his wares in Sc. 4:—

"*Servant.* O master, if you did but hear the pedlar at the door, you would never dance again after a tabor and pipe; no, the bagpipe could not move you; he sings several tunes faster than you'll tell money; he utters them as he had eaten ballads and all men's ears grew to his tunes."

"I love a ballad but even too well," says the Clown in reply. "Whoop do me no harm, good man" is a fragmentary line, of which the rest of the ballad is lost. An air—a somewhat poor one—has been preserved by Corkine. Other songs in *The Winter's Tale* are "Lawn as white as driven snow," "Get you hence for I must go," and "Will you buy any tape?"—the last-named being set as a round by John Jenkins, the composer of "A boat, a boat, haste o'er the ferry." Under the spell of the ballad, Mopsa becomes loquacious:—"I love a ballad," says she, "in print o' life, for then we are sure they are true." Out of his wonderful store, the Pedlar produces "The Usurer's Wife," "Of a Fish," and "Two Maids wooing a Man."

How strangely the text reads nowadays. As the last-named ballad is produced, Mopsa exclaims, "We can both sing it; if thou'lt bear a part, thou shalt hear; 'tis in three parts." So the two shepherdesses and the pedlar have at it without more ado.

The third act of *Love's Labour's Lost* opens thus—

"*Armado.* Warble, child; make passionate my sense of hearing.

Moth. Concolinel. [*Singing.*]"

Burney remarks on this—"This is a most beautiful and comprehensive request; none of the fine arts can subsist, or give rapture, without passion. Hence, mediocrity is more intolerable in them than in other inventions. Music without passion is as monotonous as the tolling of a bell. But," he continues, "no song is printed; though the author tells us there is singing." Dr. Johnson says—"Here is apparently a song lost." The ballad of "The King and the Beggar" is mentioned thus in Act. i. Sc. 2:—

"*Armado.* Is there not a ballad, boy, of 'The King and the Beggar?'

Moth. The world was very guilty of such a ballad some three ages since, but I think now 'tis not to be found; or, if it were, it would neither serve for the writing nor the tune."

The ballad, "King Cophetua and the Beggar-maid," is given in Percy's *Reliques*. Shakespeare alludes to it in *Romeo and Juliet* and in *Henry IV.* (Part II). An unattractive air is quoted by Chappell, entitled, "I often with my Jenny strove," which may be the original. For the fragment, "Thou canst not hit it, my good man," a tune is preserved in Dr. Fell's MS. (1620), Music School, Oxford. Lastly, come the best songs in the play—viz., "When daisies pied and violets blue," and "When icicles hang by the wall," both of which (in the absence of traditional settings) Dr. Arne has appropriated and dressed in tasteful melody.

Measure for Measure (Act. iv. Sc. 1) contains the well-known "Take, O take those lips away," with its single stanza. Beaumont and Fletcher's *Bloody Brother* offers two stanzas. Possibly the song is older than either drama. Dr. Wilson's air, printed in Playford's *Select Musical Ayres* (1653), is perhaps the original. There are many later settings. Commenting on the following passage :—

"'Tis good; though music oft hath such a charm
To make bad good, and good provoke to harm."

Burney objects—"This is a heavy charge which it would not have been easy for Shakespeare to substantiate, and does not agree with what he says in *The Tempest* of the innoxious efficacy of music—

'Sounds and sweet airs that give delight and hurt not.'" Burney adds, "Montesquieu's assertion is still in force; that 'Music is the only one of all the arts which does not corrupt the mind.'"

"Who is Sylvia?" the only song in *The Two Gentlemen of Verona* (Act iv. Sc. 2), must have had a good setting originally, for the Host says, "Hark! what fine change is in the music," which would be meaningless without a good melody to justify it. Leveridge's music (recently reprinted) is the best English version, which as a mere melody is scarcely inferior to Schubert's famous air. An old ballad of "Light of Love," alluded to in Act i. Scene 2, seems to have been a favourite with Shakespeare, who mentions it again in *Much Ado about Nothing* (Act iii. Sc. 4) as a dancing tune. "Clap us into Light o' Love, that goes without a burden; do you sing it and I'll dance it." The air is preserved in William Ballet's MS. Lute Book and *Musick's Delight on the Cithren* (1666); it has also been many times reprinted.

Portia asks for a song, in *The Merchant of Venice* (Act iii. Sc. 2), while Bassanio considers his choice of caskets, thus—

> "Let music sound while he doth make his choice;
> Then if he lose, he makes a swan-like end,
> Fading in music."

"Tell me where is fancy bred?" is then given.

In *The Tempest* (Act ii. Sc. 1), Ariel's song, "While you here do snoring lie" seems to have no ancient setting. Of the "scurvy tunes" which follow, "I shall no more to Sea" was sung to "The Children in the Wood" (see Chappell); the air to "The Master, the Swabber, the Boatswain and I" is quoted by Dr. Naylor (*Shakespeare and Music*, p. 191). The music of the catch, "Flout 'em and Scout 'em," has not been preserved. Similarly, Juno's song, "Honour, Riches, Marriage-blessing," with its pendent reply of Ceres' "Earth's increase," need not detain us. The first musical settings of Ariel's, "Where the Bee sucks" and "Full Fathom Five," were by Robert Johnson—Shakespeare's contemporary. These are now reprinted in Sir Frederick Bridge's *Shakespeare Songs*, which further contain "Come unto these Yellow Sands," by Banister; an early version of "Full Fathom Five" (by the same) and Humfreys' music to "Where the Bee sucks." It is no wonder that verse so singable should have attracted many composers—Purcell foremost of them all, with Arne not far behind.

The Midsummer Night's Dream, suggestive though it is of music, owing largely to Mendelssohn's treatment of it, nevertheless contains but two songs calling for music—viz., "Ye Spotted Snakes" (well set as a glee by Stevens) and "Now until the Break of Day"—a song and dance. No ancient settings are known.

To close this short notice of some of Shakespeare's ballads and ditties, a summary only is added of the most prominent songs not hitherto mentioned. Ophelia's songs in *Hamlet*, "How should I your True Love know?" "Good Morrow, 'tis St. Valentine's Day,"

"They bore him barefaste" (a fragment only), "Bonny Sweet Robin," and "And will he not Come Again?" are all well known through the traditional airs. The Fitzwilliam Virginal Book preserves "Bonny Sweet Robin" (No. 15 by John Munday, and No. 128 by Giles Farnaby), but only one line of the ballad is extant. For Desdemona's song, "Willow, willow," besides the traditional air, there is a setting by Pelham Humfreys (reprinted by Sir F. Bridge). Greene has left an excellent version of "Orpheus with his Lute" (*Henry VIII.*, Act iii. Sc. 1), which ought to be more widely known than it is. The words of "Heart's Ease" are not known; the tune—not later than 1560—is as follows:—

"*Peter.* Musicians, O musicians, Heart's ease, Heart's ease!
O, an you will have me live, play Heart's ease."

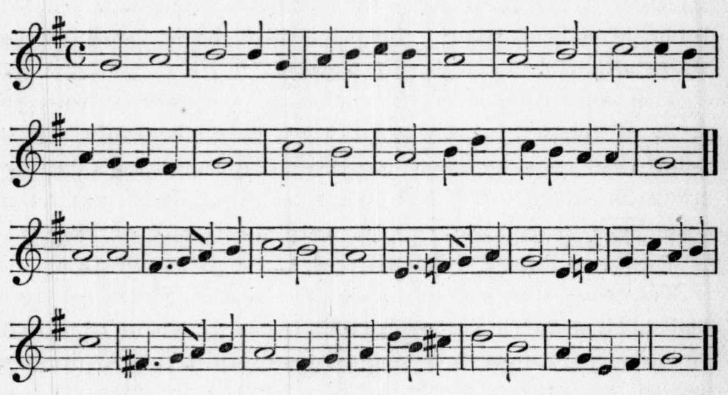

CHAPTER XIV.

OF BALLADS.

Ballads—Dance-tunes—*Nobilitas Ornata*—Thirteenth-century dance-tune—"Sellenger's Round"—Cushion dance—Trenchmore—Earliest printed ballad—Walsingham—Robin Hood Ballad—Hanging-tunes—"Come o'er the bourn, Bessy"—"Robin, lend to me thy bow"—Dorset's sea-song.

Any one coming straight from a consideration of the airs of his native country will no doubt be excused a reasonable enthusiasm and pride, partly justified, partly extravagant. Rashly or no, the present writer hazards the statement that the folk-song of England is the most wonderful in the world. Like our literature, it possesses a wider range than any other; in the same manner, it deals with the history of a people who, whatever their faults, have still maintained a leading place in the direction of the world's affairs for at least some several centuries. Therefore is it that we find the bulk of our songs of exceedingly practical import. There has been less time for the study of Nature, and an immensely pressing need to study the ways and habits of humanity. The Scots and the Irish, on the other hand, seem to excel in that beautiful communing with Nature that is possible only to the poetic mind in a situation, so to speak, of isolation. Our own Lake poets tried it; and, it appears, Wordsworth clearly succeeded. Such a couplet as—

> "To me the meanest flower that blows can give
> Thoughts that do often lie too deep for tears,"

would never occur to the townsman.

But while depriving the English singer, in general, of the gift of interpreting the mere moods of Dame Nature, we still leave him an immense scope and variety of song, which he has been ready enough to seize and stamp with his own form and feature.

"If a man were permitted to make all the ballads, he need not care who should make the laws of a nation," said Fletcher of Saltoun, and he bids fair to be remembered by the saying. He reinforces his argument by adding that "we find that most of the ancient legislators thought they could not well reform the manners of any city without the help of a lyric and sometimes of a dramatic poet." Not so long ago the German Emperor echoed something of the same enthusiasm. He would have a collection of the people's songs published in a handy form[1]: "Study that," said he, "and you will then be on the right path to show when next we meet, both to Germany and to foreigners, what a wealth of poetry and art is to be found in the people's songs." How true it is that there exists a rich vein of poetry and art in the people's songs, soon becomes plain to the student of our native ballads.

[1] Now published by Peters.

The art is of a primitive kind, and the poetry lacks the polish which the poets of a later day so easily commanded; but the minstrel art—such as it remains—has a sturdy music of its own which will carry it down the stream of time and delight and charm generations of English-speaking peoples yet unborn. In the old days we have been considering, every trade, and sometimes every branch of trade, had its song. Not only the trades, but each sport and amusement in such bygone times was identified with music and verse. The huntsman was roused with a merry stave; the milkmaid sang at her task; the vintner had an embarrassment of choice. Nor had the devil all the good tunes, as the parson of old so feared. Many of the best carols of the Nativity are true folk-song. Then there were the occupations of the sea, love, war, and the simple duties of the shepherd, or the risky livelihood of the poacher: each calling into existence melodies appropriate to their special purpose and use.

Ballads and dance-tunes are intimately associated, as the very words prove. The old French *baller*, to dance, no doubt drawn in turn from the late Latin *ballistea* (trivial songs) and the Italian *ballata*, indicates the source whence we have derived the word "ballad." Many of the old airs were real dance-tunes; indeed, the *Dancing Master* (of Playford) and other similar collections have been largely instrumental in preserving the old tunes to which the words of numerous ballads were composed. Warton says that about the year 1380, "in the place of the Provençal, a new species of poetry succeeded in France, consisting of Chants Royaux, Balades, Rondeaux, and Pastorales." This new poetry was cultivated by Froissart, who has consequently been described, though mistakenly, as its inventor. Chaucer acknowledges having written

> "Many a hymme for your holidaies
> That hightin balades, rondills, virelaies."

"Nobilitas Ornata"

We now proceed to an example of a dance-tune with Latin words, dating from the twelfth century, quoted from Coussemaker:—"Les compositions séculières étaient plus variées que les compositions religieuses sous le nom de 'rondeau, cantinelle, conduit et motet'; ils offraient un

"Nobilitas Ornata"

FIG. 12.—"NOBILITAS ORNATA."

AIR DE DANSE (12th Century). *Bibl. de Lille, MS.* 95.

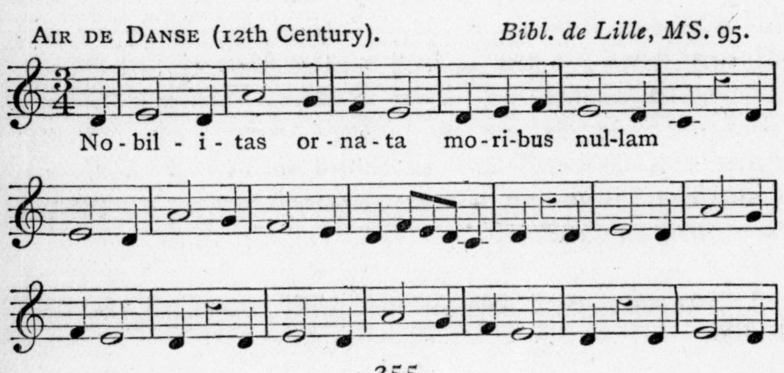

champ plus grand à l'imagination des artistes. Le motet surtout, qui était la composition favorite du temps, puisait une grande variété dans la diversité des paroles."[1]

The motet (perhaps from *mot* or *bon mot,* a jest) was a secular composition in the thirteenth century. Its characteristics were found in the melodious part-writing placed above a fixed and determined bass. In the Conductus (or Conduit) the melody was placed in the tenor. Our authority proceeds to state that there was no material difference, at the time of which we are writing, between the sacred and secular compositions. The next example is from Stafford Smith's *Musica Antiqua.* It is an undoubted dance-tune of the thirteenth century, and is found in MS. 139, Douce Collection, Bodleian Library, Oxford, where it appears in notation as follows :—

---

[1] *L'Art Harmonique aux XIIe et XIIIe siècles.* Paris, 1865, p. 134.

An Ancient Dance

FIG. 13.—THIRTEENTH-CENTURY DANCE.

Translation :—

S

Burney remarks that he had "never been so fortunate as to meet with a single tune to an English song or dance so ancient as the fourteenth century."[1] Our other famous historian of music, Hawkins, thought "Sellenger's Round" to be "the oldest country-dance tune now extant," an opinion in which he was doubtless mistaken. We give Byrde's version of this Round, which differs considerably from that printed in Hawkins' *History* (vol. 3, chap. ix., quarto ed.). "John Dory" was commonly used as a dance-tune. There is

[1] *History*, ii. p. 381.

"Sellenger's Round"

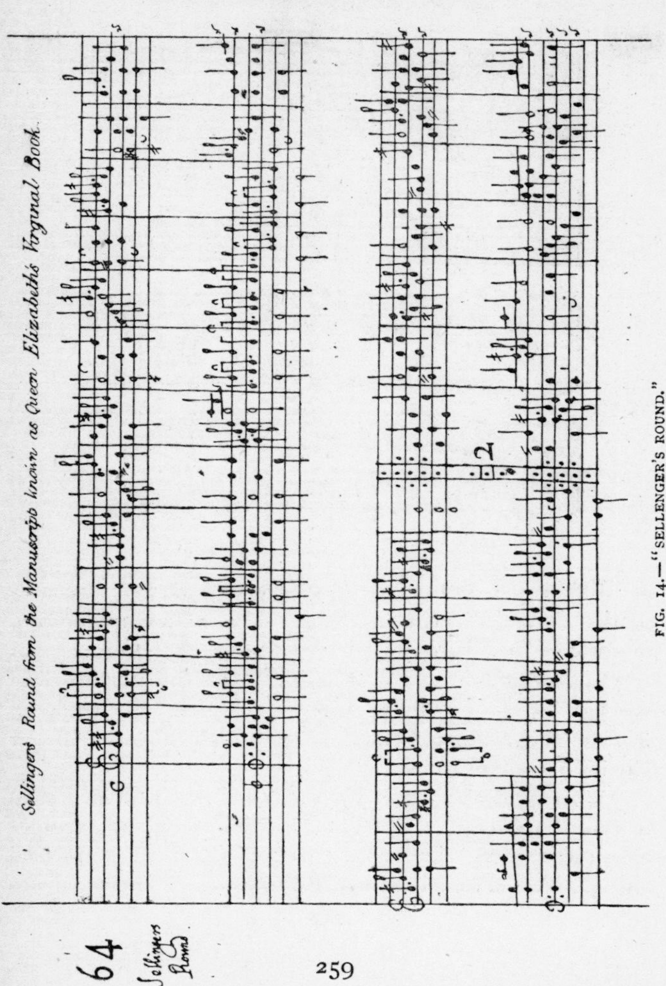

FIG. 14.—"SELLENGER'S ROUND."

(*Translation of "Sellenger's Round.*")

no difficulty in showing that singing actually accompanied dancing in the early days of these compositions, in spite of Dr. Burney's statement that "the movement of our country-dances is too rapid for the utterance of words." Even so late as 1686, we read in *The Dancing Master* the following description of the figures in the Cushion Dance:—

"This dance is begun by a single person (either man or woman), who, taking a cushion in hand, dances about the room, and at the end of the tune stops and sings, 'This dance it will no further go.' The musician answers, 'I pray you, good sir, why say you so?' *Man:* Because Joan Sanderson will not come too. *Musician:* She must come too, and she shall come too, and she must come whether she will or no.' Then he lays down the cushion before the woman, on which she kneels, and he kisses her, singing 'Welcome, Joan Sanderson, welcome, welcome.' Then she rises, takes up the cushion, and both dance, singing 'Prinkum-prankum is a fine dance.'"

A passage in Selden's *Table Talk* humorously refers to this dance:—"The court of England is much alter'd. At a solemn dancing, first you had the grave measures, then the Corantos and the Galliards, and this kept up with ceremony; and at length to Trenchmore, and the Cushion dance; then all the company dances, lord and groom, lady and kitchenmaid, no distinction. So in our court in Queen Elizabeth's time things were pretty well. But in King Charles' time there has been nothing but Trenchmore and the Cushion dance, omnium gatherum, tolly polly, hoite come toite."

Burton, in *The Anatomy of Melancholy* (1621), exclaims concerning this same Trenchmore, "Who can withstand it? be we young or old, though our teeth shake in our heads like virginal jacks, or stand parallel asunder like the arches of a bridge, there is no remedy; we must dance Trenchmore over tables, chairs, and stools." We quote Trenchmore in a ballad version, as it stands in Ravenscroft's "Freemen's Songs" (*Deuteromelia*, 1609). In this instance the ballad version is greatly superior to the mere dance. In the volume mentioned, Trenchmore is also adapted to the words "To-morrow, the fox will come to town, Keepe, keepe, keepe, keepe, keepe."

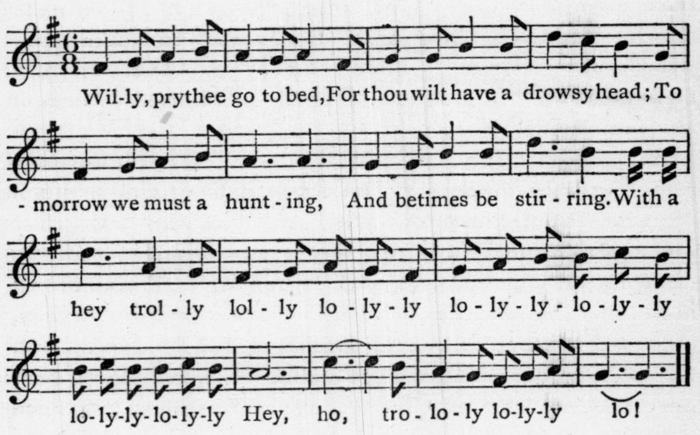

Wil-ly, prythee go to bed, For thou wilt have a drowsy head; To
- morrow we must a hunt - ing, And betimes be stir - ring. With a
hey trol - ly lol - ly lo - ly - ly lo - ly - ly - lo - ly - ly
lo-ly-ly-lo-ly-ly Hey, ho, tro - lo - ly lo-ly-ly lo!

It is like to be fair weather;
Couple all my hounds together,
Couple Jolly with little Jolly,
Couple Trolly with old Trolly.
With a hey, etc.

Couple Finch with black Trole,
Couple Chanter with Jumbole,
Let Beauty go at liberty,
For she doth know her duty.
With a hey, etc.

"Trenchmore"

Let May go loose, it makes no matter
For Cleanly sometimes she will clatter,
And yet I am sure she will not stray,
But keep with us still all the day.
With a hey, etc.

With "O masters and what you were,"
This other day I start a hare,
On what-call hill upon the knole,
And there she started before Trole.
With a hey, etc.

And down she went the common dale
With all the hounds at her tail,
Like yeaffe a yeaffe, yeaffe a yeaffe,
Hey Trole, hey Chanter, hey Jumbole.
With a hey, etc.

See how Clasper chops it in,
And so doth Gallant now begin;
Look how Trole begins to tattle,
Tarry awhile ye shall hear him prattle.
With a hey, etc.

For Beauty begins to wag her tail,
Of Cleanly's help we shall not fail,
And Chanter opens very well,
But Merry she doth bear the bell.
With a hey, etc.

So prick the path, and down the lane,
She uses still her old train,
She is gone to what-call wood
Where we are like to do no good.
With a hey, etc.

Returning for a moment to the point from which we have digressed, the following remarks of Sir Hubert Parry are worthy of consideration:—"The beating of some kind of noisy instrument as an accompaniment to gestures in the excitement of actual war or victory, or other such exciting cause, was the first type of rhythmic music, and the telling of national or tribal stories and deeds of heroes, in the indefinite chant consisting of a monotone slightly varied with occasional cadences, which is met with among so many barbarous peoples, was the first type of vocal music. This vague approach to musical recitation must have received its first rhythmic arrangement when it came to be accompanied by rhythmic gestures, and the two processes were thereby combined, while song and dance went on together, as in mediæval times in Europe." Old Thomas Morley mentions (in his *Easie Introduction to Practicall Musicke;* 1597) that "there is also another kind more light than this"—he has been discussing the Villanelle, a kind of dance part-song—"which they term Ballete or daunces, and are songs which being sung to a dittie may likewise be danced; these and all other kinds of light musick, saving the madrigal, are by a general name called aires. There be also another kind of ballets commonly called Fa la's; the first set of that kind which I have seen was made by Gastoldi; if others have laboured in the same field I know not; but a slight kind of musick it is, and as I take it devised to be danced to voices." In the beginnings of oratorio, dance-movements were not uncommonly sung; while on the stage, in our own times, the best writers scorn not so obvious an opportunity of pleasing the popular ear, as witness the dance sung by the Apprentices in Wagner's *Meistersinger* (Act. i.). Burney's unbelief might have been dispelled by the simple experiment of observing a party of children sing and dance "Here we go round the Mulberry bush," the original of which he could by no possibility escape.[1]

The earliest printed ballad is always said to be that on the downfall of Thomas Lord Cromwell in 1540, reprinted by Dr. Percy. It begins—

> "Both man and chylde is glad to here tell
> Of that false traytoure Thomas Crumwell,
> Now that he is set to learn to spell
> Synge trolle on away."

The contentious nature of the ballad brought forth a series on the opposite side, which in turn were answered. Eight of these remain. It is of interest to note the spelling *Crumwell.* The cavalier soldiers (in the time of Sir Thomas's great namesake) used to place a pellet of bread in their ale or wine, and drink to the toast "God send this crumb well down." Though ballads and songs were printed in great numbers long before Queen Elizabeth's time, few of these are now discover-

[1] The original was, of course, Nancy Dawson, a great dancer of George II.'s time. The hornpipe was introduced in "Love in a Village" (1762); but long before this, it had been danced by Nancy, who became "vastly celebrated, admired, imitated, and followed by everybody."

able. Captain Cox, a mason of Coventry, is said by Laneham[1] to have made a collection of such literary curiosities. He mentions the names of a few, in these words—"What shoold I rehearz heer, what a bunch of ballets and songs, all ancient—as 'Broom, Broom on Hil,' 'So wo iz me begon, troly lo!' 'Over a Whinny Weg,' 'Hey, ding a ding,' 'Bony Lass upon a Green,' 'My Bony on gave me a Bek,' 'By a Bank as I lay,' and a hundred more, he hath fair wrapt up in parchment, and bound with a whipcord." Of these, "By a Bank as I lay" is still extant. It has been reprinted as a Christmas carol.[2] "Hey, ding a ding" is probably none other than the well-known song of "Old Sir Simon the King." Nash (in two controversial tracts with Harvey, 1596 and 1599) gives us the names of a few further ballads, such as "In Sandon Soyle as late Befell," "Cutting Ball," "Have with you to Florida," "The Story of Axeres and the worthy Iphiis," "As I went to Walsingham," "In Crete," "Anne Askew," "All the Flowers of the Broom," "Pepper is Black," "John Careless," "Greensleeves," "Go from my Garden, go," "The Strife of Love in a Dreame," or "The Lamentable Burden of Teventon." The airs of a few of these are known, such as "Pepper is Black," and the famous "Greensleeves," sung and reprinted to this day. "Go from my Garden," is probably identical with "Go from my Window." The ballad "As I went to Walsingham" (given in Percy's *Reliques*) was sung to the following

[1] *Letter from Killingworth.* London, 1575.

[2] Under the title, "Welcome, Yule." (*Carols and Songs;* Augener.)

air, which is copied from the Fitzwilliam Virginal Book:—

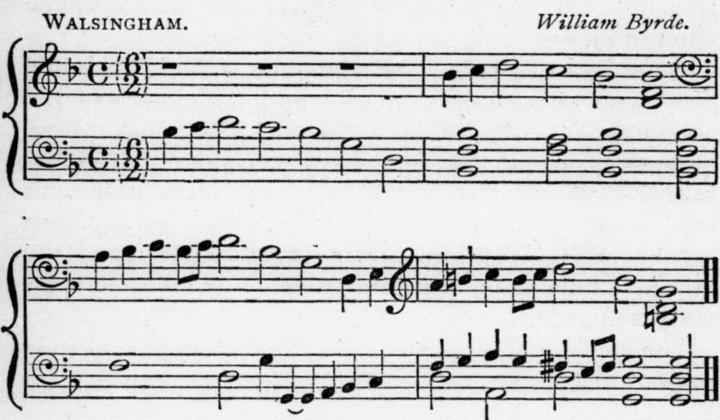

The form into which Byrde has cast the ballad-tune is, of course, one that would appeal to the skilled performer rather than the singer. We give it as a curiosity. These old ballads were hawked up and down the country in baskets. Ritson quotes from "a pleasant and stately morall of *Three Lordes and Three Ladies of London*" (1590), where Simplicity is asked what dainty fine ballad he has now to be sold. The answer is "Marie, child, I have 'Chipping Morton,' 'A Mile from Chappel o' the Heath,' 'A Lamentable Ballad of Burning the Pope's Dog,' 'The Sweet Balade of the Lincolnshire Bagpipes,' and 'Peggy and Willy,' 'But now he is Dead and Gone,' 'Mine own sweet Willy is laid in his grave, la, la, la, lan ti dan dan da dan, lan ti dan, dan tan derry do.'" The vendor of this singular parcel was dressed in "bare blacke, like a poore citizen," and was expected to bear his part, if called upon to do so.

It is natural that a large number of ballads should choose for their subject the romantic experiences of the popular hero of the greenwood. One such piece, treasured up in the Halliwell Collection (Chetham Library), shows the ballad to be in black-letter with two modest woodcuts, and of a class which Scott speaks of in *Ivanhoe* as once sold at the low and easy rate of a halfpenny, but now cheaply purchased at their weight in gold.

The air is found in the *Jovial Crew* (1731), and runs thus—

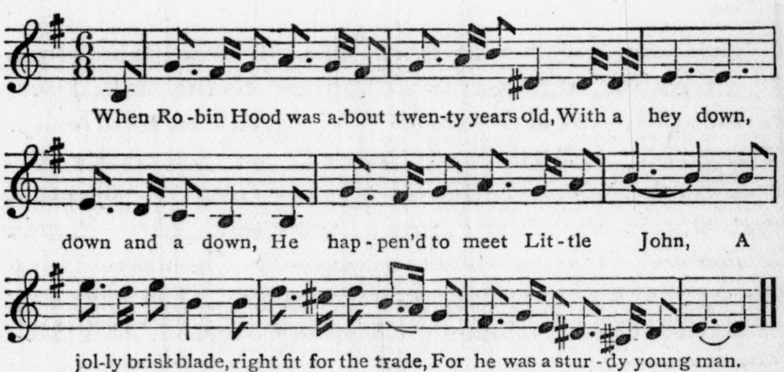

When Ro-bin Hood was a-bout twen-ty years old, With a hey down,
down and a down, He hap-pen'd to meet Lit-tle John, A
jol-ly brisk blade, right fit for the trade, For he was a stur-dy young man.

A remarkable use, to which melody was put in early times, may be traced in the "hanging-tunes"; for the executioner, despite his grim office, did his work accompanied with the voices of thousands, in such a chant as "Fortune my Foe, why dost thou frown on me?"[1] mentioned of both Shakespeare and Ben Jonson. The air, a fine old minor, must have been painfully impressive for the prisoner. There is no trace of the block or the gallows in it, but what poetic pageantry can be discovered in so serious a situation appears to have been touched upon with vividness, in the melody referred to. The value of the tune was perceived by William Byrde, who made it the text of a long improvisation. This appears in the Fitzwilliam Virginal Book, from which the following harmonization is borrowed:—

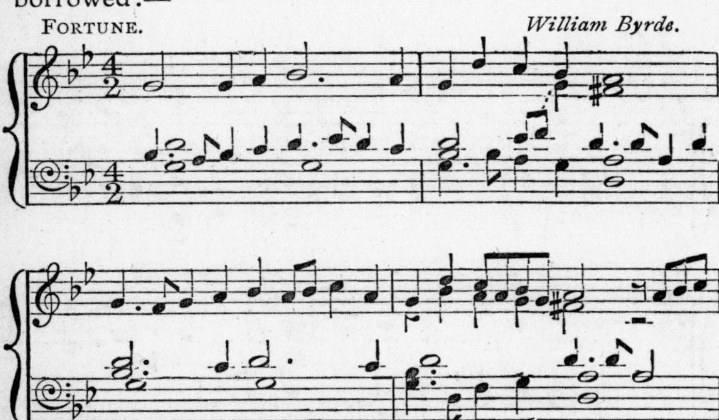

[1] "Titus Andronicus," the ballad from which Shakespeare drew his play, was sung to the tune of "Fortune my Foe." A moralization appears in Forbes' *Cantus* (1682), beginning "Satan my foe, full of iniquity."

Mention of this air is put into the mouth of Falstaff, in *The Merry Wives of Windsor* (Act iii., Sc. 3)—

"I see what thou wert, if Fortune thy foe were not, Nature thy friend. Come thou canst not hide it."

In Chappell's *Popular Music* there are two interesting quotations concerning this ballad. The first is from Rowley's *Noble Soldier* (1634)—

> "The King, shall I be bitter against the King?
> I shall have scurvy ballads made of me,
> Sung to the hanging tune."

The other reference is from "*The Penitent Traytor;* the humble petition of a Devonshire gentleman, who was condemned for treason, and executed for the same" (1641), as follows:—

> "How could I bless thee, couldst thou take away
> My life and infamy both in one day?
> But this in ballads will survive I know,
> Sung to that preaching tune, Fortune my Foe."

Another famous "hanging-tune" was "Welladay; or, Essex's last Good-night," the air of which is contained in Elizabeth Rogers' Virginal Book (Add. MSS. 10,337 fol. 7, British Museum). Better fortune has attended this graceful melody, which has acquired a new lease of life, and is now everywhere known by its being adapted as a Christmas carol. It figured in Wright's *Carols* (with the date 1661), to the words "All you that in this house be here," and also to those beginning "Christmas hath made an end." It was only the best class of ballad that confined itself to historical or sentimental subjects. The vast number (especially of the later times) fastened upon any trifling happening of the moment, and made it a peg upon which to hang indifferent verse.

We have already mentioned Henry VIII.'s repressive measures for dealing with this literature. In the reign of his successor, ballads increased and multiplied, though so few have come down to us. Such, it is said, are the following:—"Bring ye to me, and I to thee," "Hey noney, noney, houghe for money," and "Haye, haye, haie, haie, I will be merry while I maie"—preserved only in MS.

With the accession of Queen Mary, the legislative vehicle was again put in motion, and an edict against "books, ballads, rhymes, and treatises set out by printers and stationers, of an evil zeal for lucre, and covetous of vile gain," struck an effectual blow at the trade of the ballad-makers. This edict was apparently withdrawn when Elizabeth came to the throne, and ballads soon awoke to their liberty. We have already given Robert Laneham's list of pieces of this period. To these may now be added a few quoted in a "very mery and pythie commedie," bearing the title, *The longer thou Livest, the more Fool thou art,* described as a mirror very necessary for youth, and especially for such as are like to come to dignity and promotion. The character is thus introduced with his songs in a string:—

"Here entereth Moros, counterfaiting a vaine gesture and a foolish countenance, synging the foote of many songs, as fooles were wont:—

"Come o'er the boorne, Besse"

'Brome, brome on hill,
The gentle brome on hill hill ;
Brome, brome on hiue hill,
The gentle brome on hiue hill,
The brome stands on hiue hill, a !'

'Robin lende to me thy bowe, thy bowe,
Robin the bow, Robin lend to me thy bow, a !

'There was a mayde come out of Kent,
Deinte love, deinte love !
There was a mayde cam out of Kent,
Daungerous be.
There was a mayde cam out of Kent,
Fayre propre small and gent,
As ever upon the grounde went,
For so should it be.'

'By a banke as I lay, I lay,
Musing on things past, hey how !'

'Tom a Lin and his wife and his wive's mother
They went over a bridge all three together ;
The bridge was broken and they fell in ;
The Devill go with all, quoth Tom a Lin.'

'Martin Swart and his man, fodledum, fodledum ;
Martin Swart and his man, fodledum bell.'

'Come o'er the boorne, Besse,
My pretie Besse,
Come o'er the boorne, Besse, to me.'

> 'The white dove sat on the castell wall,
> I bend my bow, and shoote her I shall,
> I put her in my glove, both feathers and all;
> I lay my bridle upon the shelf,
> If you will any more, sing it yourself.'

A few of the above pieces are extant in one form or another. "Come o'er the Boorne, Bessie, to me" (to quote an example) has recently been reprinted[1] from Additional MSS. 5665 (fol. 140b), in the British Museum. The volume containing this ancient piece is of the end of the fifteenth century; it was once in the possession of Joseph Ritson, by whose gift it came to the Museum. Shakespeare's allusion to the song is as follows:—

> *Edg.* Look, where he stands and glares.
> Wantest thou eyes at trial, madam?
> Come o'er the bourn, Bessy to me—
> *Fool.* Her boat hath a leak,
> And she must not speak
> Why she dares not come over to thee.
> —*King Lear* (Act iii. Sc. 5).

Allusion has already been made to "By a Bank as I lay," one of Henry VIII.'s favourite songs. "Robin, lend to me thy Bow" is preserved by Ravenscroft in *Pammelia* (1609), "a mixed varietie of pleasant roundelayes and delightfull catches." The setting is for four voices; the first sings one line, the second voice immediately follows, and after completion of this same line the third voice enters, and so on. Like "John Dory,"

[1] By Messrs. Novello.

the arrangement in this form must have meant that the minstrel air had to be moulded to this special purpose; but in some cases there is no reason to doubt that the catch or round was an original invention. Here is the song itself:—

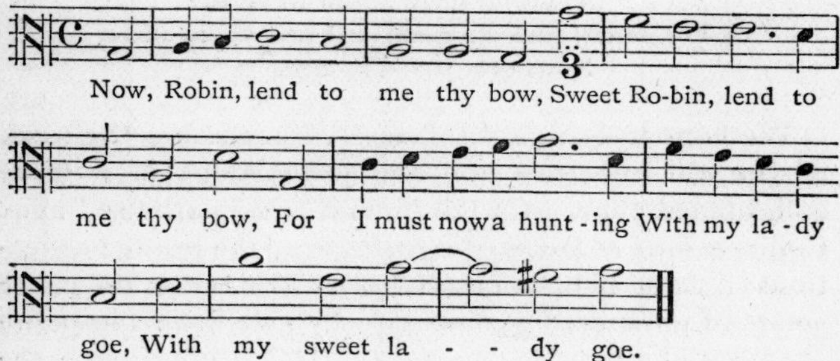
Now, Robin, lend to me thy bow, Sweet Ro-bin, lend to
me thy bow, For I must now a hunt - ing With my la - dy
goe, With my sweet la - - dy goe.

And whither will thy Lady goe?
Sweet Wilkin tell it unto mee;
And thou shalt have my hawke, my hound, and eke my bow,
To wait on thy Lady.

My Lady will to Uppingham,
To Uppingham forsooth will shee;
And I my selfe appointed for to be the man,
To wait on my Lady.

Adieu, good Wilkin, all beshrewde,
Thy hunting nothing pleaseth mee:
But yet beware thy babling hounds stray not abroad,
For angring of thy Lady.

My hounds shall be led in the line,
So well I can assure it thee;
Unlesse by view of straine some pursue I may finde,
To please my sweet Lady.

With that the Lady shee came in,
And wild them all for to agree;
For honest hunting never was accounted sinne,
Nor never shall for mee.

We hope to escape the charge of confusing the work of the old minstrels and the productions of a more enlightened time. Certainly, excepting perhaps Payne Collier's *Book of Roxburghe Ballads,* all the printed collections of these ballads offer without distinction the crude songs of unlettered genius side by side with the polite exercises of more refined poetry. This is notoriously the case with Percy's *Reliques,* concerning which Hazlitt has remarked: "It is fortunate for the lovers of early English literature that Bishop Percy had comparatively little to do with it." Ritson, in the section of *English Songs* (1783) headed "Ancient," somewhat strangely included a piece composed by his friend Scott—a mere imitation of old balladry. Then, again, in the same editor's *Ancient Songs* (1792) there are poems by Shakespeare, Raleigh, Wither, Suckling, and others. If, then, we sin in this respect, it is in good company. The reader will soon discover the secret, when he lights upon Lord Dorset's ballad, "never before printed." Such a treasure is worth all the classification in the world. So let us hasten onwards.

"Carman's Whistle"

We cannot afford to pass over Henry Chettle's pamphlet (of 1592) entitled *Kind Heart's Dream,* which gives a glimpse of "that idle, upstart generation of ballad-singers" who chant in every street—an evil which is said to have overspread Essex and the adjoining counties. Chettle continues: "There is many a tradesman, of a worshipful trade, yet no stationer, who, after a little, bringing up apprentices to singing brokery, takes into his shop some fresh men, and trusts his old servants of a two months' standing with a dozen groats-worth of ballads. In which, if they prove thrifty, he makes them pretty chapmen, able to spread more pamphlets by the State forbidden than all the booksellers in London." In the list of ballads mentioned we meet with "Watkins Ale," "The Carman's Whistle," "Chopping-knives," "The Friar and the Nun," and "Friar Fox-tail." The two first-named ballads are well known, the tunes being in the Fitzwilliam Virginal Book. Byrde's arrangement of "The Carman's Whistle," with its set of nine "divisions," is especially famous. "Friar Fox-tail" is not known, but "The Friar and the Nun" is contained in the *Dancing Master* (1650 and later editions). The words are lost of this last piece; and the two first, though preserved, are not suited to modern requirements.

The names of the best-known ballad-writers of the period under consideration include those of Thomas Elderton ("who did arm himself with ale, as old father Ennius did with wine, when he ballated")—the peerless Elderton—Thomas Deloney, Richard Johnson, and Anthony Munday.

In James I.'s time broadsides became common, with the ballads printed on one side of the sheet, giving the name of the (licensed) printer. "The Duke of Norfolk," "In Crete," and "My man Thomas did me promise," are well-known examples of this period. One of the most famous ballads ever written was Martin Parker's "When the King enjoys his own again," produced towards the end of the unfortunate Charles I.'s reign. This ballad, invented to support the declining interest of the Merry Monarch, served afterwards to maintain the spirits of the Cavaliers, and later to celebrate the Restoration in every corner of the kingdom. The doleful inventions of the Commonwealth period need not be dwelt upon. "Let Oliver now be Forgotten" (recently reprinted) is a fair example, which is more than counterbalanced by Milton's noble verses, "Cromwell, our chief of men."

We close this rapid sketch of some of the features of the ballad age by inserting Lord Dorset's fine poem, with its original music. The facsimile is reproduced from the Halliwell Collection, in the Chetham Library, Manchester.

Chappell quotes a later version of this air from *Watt's Miscellany* (vol. iii.; 1730), but mentions the original as "barbarously printed." Dr. Hullah came to much the same conclusion, and he dismisses it as "so absurdly barred that it is difficult to understand its rhythm." Nevertheless, the interest of an original must be allowed, and a correct copy, agreeing with

169

No. 1875

57

A Ballad by ye late Ld. Dorset when at Sea never before Printed.

2
But tho' ye Muses shou'd be kind,
& fill our empty Brain;
Yet if rough Neptune cause ye Wind,
To rouse ye Azure Main;
Our Paper Pens & Ink and we,
Rowl up & down our Ships at Sea.
with a fa la.

3
Then if we write not by each Post,
Think not ye we're unkind;
Nor yet conclude ye we are lost
By Dutch by French or Wind;
Our Greif will find a speedier way,
The Tide shall bring them twice a day.
with a fa la.

4
The King with wonder & surprize,
Will think ye Seas grown bold;
For that the Tide does higher rise,
Then ere it did of old;
But let him know ye tis our Tears,
Sends floods of Greif to White-hall Stairs.
with a fa la.

5
Shou'd Count Thoulouse but come to know,
Our sad & dismal story;
The French wd. Scorn so weak a Foe,
Where they can get no Glory;
For no resistance can they find,
From Men as left their hearts behind.
with a fa la.

6
To pass our tedious time away,
We throw the merry Main;
Or else at serious Ombra play.
But why shou'd we in vain
Each other's ruin thus pursue,
We were undone when we left you.
with a fa la.

7
When any mournfull tune ye hear,
That dyes in ery note;
As if it Sigh'd for each Mans care,
For being so remote;
Think ye how often Love we've made,
To ye while all those tunes were play'd.
with a fa la.

8
Let Wind & Weather do its worst,
Be you to us but kind;
Let French Men Vapour Dutch Men Curse,
No Sorrows we shall find;
Tis then no matter how things goe,
Nor who's our Freind or who our Foe.
with a fa la.

9
Thus haveing told you all our loves,
& likewise all our feares
In hopes this Declaration moves
Some pitty to our Tears;
Let's hear of no Inconstancy,
We have too much of that at Sea.
with a fa la.

Printed for J. Cullen at ye Buck without Temple-bar. T. Cross Sculp.

FIG. 15.—DORSET'S BALLAD.

the above, is found in Durfey's *Pills to Purge Melancholy* (vol. vi. p. 272, 1720). Readers may recall Pepys' allusion to this song, given in the *Diary*, under date January 2nd, 1665:—

"To my Lord Brounckner's, by appointment; where I occasion'd much mirth with a ballet I brought with me, made from the seamen at sea to their ladies in town; saying Sir W. Pen, Sir G. Ascue, and Sir G. Lawson made them. Here a most noble French dinner and banquet. The street full of footballs, it being a great frost."

It was claimed that the song was written at sea, in the first Dutch War, on the night before an engagement. In the controversy which this drew forth, Dr. Johnson expressed himself as follows:—"Seldom any splendid story is wholly true. I have heard from the late Earl Orrery, who was likely to have good hereditary intelligence, that Lord Dorset had been a week employed upon it, and only retouched or finished it on the memorable evening. But even this, whatever it may subtract from his facility, leaves him his courage."

It only remains to add that in 1648 the Provost-Marshal was empowered to seize upon all ballad-singers, sellers of malignant pamphlets, "and to send them to the several militias, and to suppress stage-plays." The Act which was passed for the purpose, served sufficiently for the stoppage of the theatres. Not so with the ballads or their singers. As an earlier writer had said, "these running stationers of London penetrate into every corner of cities and market-townes of the realme, singing and selling ballads."

CHAPTER XV.

OF SONGS.

Songs—What is a folk-song?—"Farewell, dear Love"—Weelkes—Coperario—"Wert thou much Fairer"—Purcell—"I attempt from Love's Sickness"—Cross, the engraver—"Lilliburlero"—Blow—Leveridge—Carey—Green—Young—Arne—Dibdin—Balfe—Madrigals and glees.

From Ballad to Song is but a step, but it is such a step as one takes from the bustling crowd of street-life to the dim quiet of a cloistered library.

No sharp delineation has been made in the foregoing pages between minstrel and musician, excepting in the mere incidental history proper to each. We cannot, however, evade the question: What is a folk-song? Is it possible within a reasonable compass of words to set down a definition which will give us insight to the particular qualities which music must possess to be so termed? With the literary explanation we are not concerned. William Chappell, who did more as a collector of old English airs than any one else, appears to have thought that the authorship of an air must be unknown to admit of its being regarded as folk-song.[1] In remarking this, it is not overlooked that songs by Coperario, Purcell, W. Lawes, Carey, Dibdin, and others crept into his great collections of 1838-40 and 1859; but these are sometimes accidental, as in the cases of the two composers first mentioned, and in others considerations of expediency (in all likelihood) compelled admission. In an excellent compilation of Hullah's,[2] songs such as "Cheer up, Sam," and "Wait for the Wagon," startle the eye, if not the ear. Made in America they certainly were, but a careful examination will probably show that the inclusion of such pieces was not altogether wrong in a volume of Folk-song. Ritson, the antiquary and indefatigable song-collector (it has already been pointed out), actually included a song by Sir Walter Scott in the portion of his *English Songs* devoted to ancient pieces.

Are we, then, to assume that age is not all? Can a short composition of inherent vitality jump the test of time, and range itself by the side of the melodies that have braved the remorseless tooth of the centuries? The unmusical mind can find a good equivalent for folk-song in the brief snatches of old verse so fondly reproduced by Shakespeare, in certain of Burns' inspirations, and, indeed, in any short poem which

[1] See first edition of *Popular Music*, under "Mad Tom," and "Ah! cruel, bloody fate." Among the old composers practically ignored are Robert Jones, Robert Johnson, Nicholas Laneir, Dr. Wilson, Dr. Colman, William Webb, Henry Lawes, and Dr. Blow.

[2] *English Song Book.* (Macmillan & Co.)

treats of life on a broad and common basis, in opposition to the narrow, personal, or particular. In such a sense, it is clear why people will accept "Home, sweet Home" as a folk-song, and, despite the quality of the words, no such piece as "Bid me discourse." Yet both—as regards the music—have a common origin, and neither, of course, can claim any antiquity. Our conclusion is that a folk-song could be made to-day, given the man to do it, and a nation to accept it. An instance of this having actually happened may be cited in A. von Lvoff's setting of the Russian National Anthem.

Among the oldest of the musicians' songs now known are the settings of Shakespeare. "Where griping Grief," by Richard Edwardes (1523-66), is an early instance, and of unique interest owing to the fact that Edwardes wrote both words and music. The song (in four parts) is given in Hawkins' *History of Music*. A reprint may also be seen in Dr. Naylor's *Shakespeare and Music*—unfortunately, in a transposed version:—

"Where griping grief the heart would wound
And doleful dumps the mind oppress,
There music with her silver sound
Is wont with speed to give redress
Of troubled minds, for ev'ry sore,
Sweet music hath a salve in store.

In joy it makes our mirth abound,
In grief it cheers our heavy sprites,
The careful head relief hath found,
By music's pleasant sweet delights;

“Music with her silver sound”

Our senses, what should I say more,
Are subject unto Music's lore [lure].

The gods by music have their praise,
The soul therein doth joy;
For as the Roman poets say,
In seas whom pirates would destroy,
A dolphin saved from death most sharp,
Arion playing on his harp.

O heavenly gift, that turns the mind,
Like as the stern doth rule the ship,
Of music whom the gods assigned,
To comfort man whom cares would nip,
Since thou both man and beast doth move,
What wise man then will thee reprove?”

The words are contained in *The Paradise of Dainty Devices* (1573), and the music in Thomas Mulliner's *Boke for ye Organ or Virginalls* (MS., sixteenth century). Shakespeare's use of the song is as follows:—

Pet. Answer me like men;

“When griping grief the heart doth wound,
And doleful dumps the mind oppress,
Then music with her silver sound——”

why “silver sound”? why “music with her silver sound”? What say you, Simon Catling?

1st. Mus. Marry, sir, because silver hath a sweet sound.

Pet. Pretty! What say you, Hugh Rebeck?

2nd Mus. I say “silver sound” because musicians sound for silver.

Pet. Pretty too! What say you, James Soundpost?

3rd Mus. Faith, I know not what to say.

Pet. O, I cry you mercy; you are the singer; I will say for you. It is "music with her silver sound," because musicians have no gold for the sounding—

"Then music with her silver sound
With speedy help doth lend redress." [*Exit.*]

1st Mus. What a pestilent knave is this same!

2nd Mus. Hang him, Jack! Come, we'll in here; tarry for the mourners, and stay dinner. [*Exeunt.*]

—*Romeo and Juliet*, Act iv. Sc. 5.

Another old setting, somewhat similar in character to the foregoing, is Robert Jones' "Farewell, Dear Love," the music and words of which are found in *The First Book of Ayres,* by Robert Jones, a folio printed by Este in 1601:—

"Farewell, dear love, since thou wilt needs be gone,
Mine eyes do show my life is almost done;
Yet I will never die, so long as I can spy
There be many mo. Though that she do go
There be many mo I fear not;
Why then let her go, I care not.

Farewell, farewell, since this I find is true,
I will not spend more time in wooing you;
But I will seek elsewhere, if I may find love there;
Shall I bid her go? what and if I do?
Shall I bid her go and spare not?
O no, no, no, I dare not.

"Farewell, dear heart"

Ten thousand times farewell;—yet stay awhile;—
Sweet, kiss me once; sweet kisses time beguile;
I have no power to move. How now, am I in love?
Wilt thou needs be gone? Go, then, all is one.
Wilt thou needs be gone? Oh, hie thee.
Nay, stay, and do no more deny me.

Once more adieu! I see loath to depart
Bids oft adieu to her, that holds my heart.
But seeing I must lose thy love, which I did choose,
Go thy ways for me, since it may not be.
Go thy ways for me. But whither?
Go, oh, but where I may come thither.

What shall I do? my love is now departed.
She is as fair as she is cruel-hearted.
She would not be entreated, with prayers oft repeated,
If she come no more, shall I die therefore?
If she come no more, what care I?
Faith, let her go, or come, or tarry."

The words of this song are to be found in *The Princely Garland of Golden Delights*. Shakespeare's allusion to the song is as follows:—

Sir Toby. We did keep time, sir, in our catches. Sneck up!

Malvolio. Sir Toby, I must be round with you. My lady bade me tell you that, though she harbours you as her kinsman, she's nothing allied to your disorders. If you can separate yourself and your misdemeanours, you are welcome to the house; if not, an it would please you to take leave of her, she is very willing to bid you farewell.

Sir Toby. "Farewell, dear heart, since I must needs be gone."

Maria. Nay, good Sir Toby.

Clown. "His eyes do show his days are almost done."
Malvolio. Is't even so?
Sir Toby. "But I will never die."
Clown. Sir Toby, there you lie.
Malvolio. This is much credit to you.
Sir Toby. "Shall I bid him go?"
Clown. "What an if you do?"
Sir Toby. "Shall I bid him go and spare not?"
Clown. "O no, no, no, you dare not."
—*Twelfth Night*, Act ii. Sc. 3.

Morley's finely expressive little air to "It was a Lover and his Lass" (1595) is widely known, and finds a place in all English song-collections that are representative. We have mentioned a song of Este's (of this period) in another part of the book (see p. 192). Passing reference may also be made to Thomas Weelkes' *First Set of Madrigals* (1597), which contains settings for three voices of the following Shakespeare songs:—"My Flocks feed not," "In Black mourn I," and "Clear Wells spring not." Settings by Robert Johnson of "Full Fathom Five" and "Where the Bee sucks" (1612) have been reprinted by Sir Frederick Bridge in his *Shakespeare Songs* (Novello). The same work includes "Take, O take those Lips away," by Dr. Wilson—thought by Rimbault to have been the "Jack Wilson" of Shakespeare's acquaintance. This song is contained in Playford's *Select Airs* (1653). Two of Banister's songs are also reprinted in the volume referred to—namely, "Full Fathom Five" and "Come unto these Yellow Sands." Henry Purcell afterwards set his seal on these two lyrics of Shakespeare; but we need not anticipate matters.

Coperario's famous song, "Mad Tom" ("Forth from this dark and dismal cell")—so long credited to Purcell, though printed before the latter was born—need only be named to be remembered. It is still not uncommonly sung in public. The publication of songs during the Commonwealth would scarcely be expected to have been productive of any very notable work; it is surprising, therefore, to discover such epoch-making collections as Lawe's *Ayres and Dialogues* (1653) and Playford's *Select Musical Ayres* (1653).

Henry Lawes (1595-1662), of whom Burney thought so little, was praised by all the famous poets of his day. These, with Milton at their head, were ambitious of having their verses set by this admirable artist. The reason was that then for the first time poetry was treated with proper consideration by the composer. Milton's words express Lawes' achievement with notable accuracy:—

> "Harry, whose tuneful and well-measured song
> First taught our English music how to span
> Words with just note and accent, not to scan
> With Midas' ears, committing short and long;
>
> . . . . . .
>
> To after age thou shalt be writ the man,
> That with smooth air couldst humour best our tongue.
> Thou honour'st verse, and verse must lend her wing
> To honour thee."

Burney is right when he remarks that the praise of the poets is durable fame. Songs of both Henry Lawes and his brother William are constantly reprinted to this day; so there is no need to specify the songs of these composers. The same copy often accommodated three singers. Two stood together; the third held the other end of the book facing the two, his part being printed the reverse way up.

Playford's publication of 1653 is remarkable in that it preserves some eighty songs by the most eminent writers of the early half of the seventeenth century, and that too through times of no ordinary political difficulty, with a Puritanical spirit abroad that condemned all secular song. A dozen composers are responsible for the settings, which are for one voice in Book I., for two in the second part, while the third is for three voices. A few of the pieces remain anonymous; others are ascribed to Dr. Charles Colman, Edward Colman, Henry Lawes, William Lawes, John Taylor, Jeremy Savile (whose "Here's a health unto His Majesty" is everywhere popular), Dr. Wilson, Nicholas Laneir, William Tomkins, William Webbe, William Cæsar (alias Smegergill), and Thomas Brewer. As a specimen of this class of song, though it does not differ greatly from Lawes' models, we transcribe Dr. Wilson's setting of "Wert thou much Fairer than thou art." The words are by Cotgrave, and afterwards appeared in *Wit's Interpreter* (1655). Henry Bold in his *Latine Songs* (1685) gave a version of this poem beginning "Si præsuisses formula."

"Si præsuisses formula"

Wert thou much fairer than thou art,
Which lies not in the power of art;
Or hadst thou in thy eyes more darts
Than ever Cupid shot at hearts;
  Yet if they were not shot at me,
  I should not cast a thought on thee.

I'd rather marry a disease,
Than court the thing I cannot please;
She that would cherish my desires,
Must court my flames with equal fires.
  What pleasure is there in a kiss,
  To him that doubts her heart not his?

I love thee not because th'art fair,
Softer than down, smoother than air;
Nor for the Cupids that do lie
In either corner of thine eye;[1]
  Would you then know what it might be?
  'Tis I love you, cause you love me.

Pelham Humfreys (1647-74) has left at least one song that is remembered with favour. This, the best known, is that beginning "I pass all my hours in a shady old grove," the words of which are by Charles II. Horace Walpole remarked that there was "nothing in this amatory song to contradict the report of its having been said in an old copy to be written by this witty prince." "He never said a foolish thing, nor ever did a wise one," said Rochester; the king, however, replied,

[1] The version in *Wit's Interpreter* reads "In every corner of thy eye," and in the next line "may" for "might."

3 — No. 1882.

A Song in the Indian Queen: as it is now Compos'd into an OPERA. By Mr. Henry Purcell, Sung by Mrs. Cross. and exactly engrav'd by Tho: Cross.

I attempt from Love's sickness to fly .... in vain, since I am my self my own

Feaver, since I am my self my own Feaver and Pain; No more now, no more now fond heart with

Pride, no more swell, thou can'st not raise Forces, thou can'st not raise Forces e-

nough to re bell; First strain again. First strain again. For Love has more pow'r and less mercy than fate, to

make us seek ru in, to make us seek ru in and love those that hate. End with the first strain. End with the first strain.

FIG. 16.—"I ATTEMPT FROM LOVE'S SICKNESS."

"his actions were his ministers, while his words were all his own." The song is printed in Playford's *Choice Ayres* (1676), and possibly earlier. Some of the copies are headed "The Phænix."

Perhaps the most extraordinary collection of songs ever issued under one authorship (with the single exception of Schubert's), is that known as *Orpheus Britannicus*, a work containing (in the first edition) no less than 71 compositions by Henry Purcell. It was put forward by the musician's wife in 1698, the year of his death. Such pieces as "I'll Sail upon the Dog-star," "I attempt from Love's Sickness" and "From Rosy Bowers"[1] (to mention only three of the best) are not likely to be forgotten. Though Purcell writes in a quaint and somewhat antiquated style, the inner spirit is instinct with fine feeling, and the melodies are glowing with true invention. Our facsimile of "I attempt from Love's Sickness" is reproduced from the Halliwell Collection, Chetham Library.

Burney's appreciation (written in 1789) supplies curious reading, in view of the great popularity the song now enjoys. "I attempt from Love's Sickness," says he, "is an elegant little ballad, which though it has been many years dead, would soon be recalled into existence and fashion, by the voice of some favourite singer, who should think it worth animation." The version above given agrees in all respects with that which afterwards was printed in the *Orpheus Britannicus*. It is perhaps worth pointing out that the

[1] Recently reprinted by Augener.

second melody-note of the last engraved line is D-natural—that is, a flat leading note; whereas all our modern copies sharpen the note. The engraver, Thomas Cross, was contemporary with Purcell, whom he outlived. He won much repute by engraving (with great accuracy) on copper-plates, when other printers were everywhere employing metal types. In a complimentary address (written by H. Hall, Organist of Hereford) to Henry Playford, prefixed to the *Orpheus Britannicus* (1706), there is the following curious reference to this Thomas Cross:—

"Duly each day, our young composers bait us,
With most insipid songs, and sad Sonatos.
Well were it, if the world would lay embargos
On such Allegros and such Poco Largos;
And would enact it, there presume not any
To teaze Corelli, or burlesque Bessani;
Nor with division, and ungainly graces,
Eclipse good sense, as weighty wigs do faces.
Then honest Cross might copper cut in vain,
And half our sonnet-sellers starve again."

The most popular tune, considered as a mere tune, that Purcell ever wrote, was the air which became associated with Lord Wharton's "Lilli Burlero." Dr. Percy (in the *Reliques*) remarks, "The following rhymes, slight and insignificant as they may now seem, had once a more powerful effect than either the Philippics of Demosthenes, or Cicero; and contributed not a little towards the great revolution in 1688. Burnet adds that "the whole army, and at last the people, both in city and country, were singing it perpetually. And perhaps never had so slight a thing so great an effect." The most remarkable thing, to our thinking, is the fact that the words are not worth copying out. Here is the first stanza (for the whole twelve, the reader is referred to Percy's *Reliques of Ancient English Poetry*):—

Ho, broder Teague, dost hear de decree?
Lilli burlero, bullen a-la.
Dat we shall have a new deputie,
Lilli burlero, bullen a-la.
  Lero lero, lilli burlero, lero lero, bullen a-la,
  Lero lero, lilli burlero, lero lero, bullen a-la.

Purcell's air, on the other hand, has a sprightliness and rhythmic grace that would easily account for its becoming a favourite in town and country. Uncle Toby, it has been observed, showed his discretion in *whistling* it. Here is the air, with Purcell's own harmony, copied from *Musicke's Handmaid* (Part I.; 1689), one year after it had figured with Wharton's astonishing verse:—

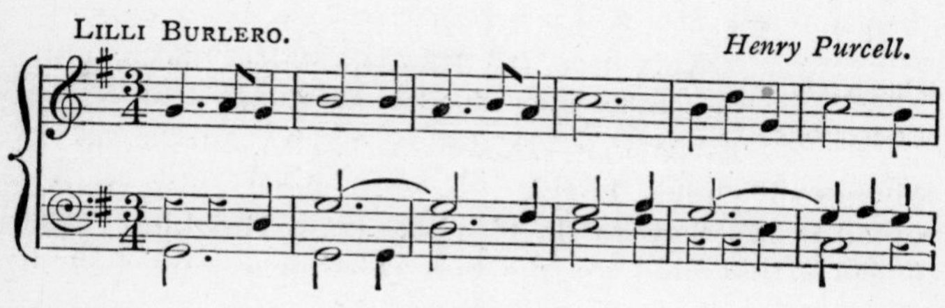

Looking backward for a moment, we have passed over his Majesty King Charles I., whose setting of "Mark how the Blushful Morn" is given in the Guise MS. (British Museum). In *Select Ayres and Dialogues* (1669), the song is given to Nicholas Laneir. A word should also be devoted to Matthew Lock, to whom (says Hawkins) "the world is indebted for the first rules ever published in

Charles I. (Acc. 1625)

this kingdom on the subject of continued or thorough-bass." The historian adds that the book is entitled *Melothesia* (1673). We are only concerned with Lock's songs. One of these, "My Lodging is on the Cold Ground"—the original setting—has recently been reprinted. Another air by Lock—an inferior one, however—became famous in its day. This was "The Delights of the Bottle," a never-failing source of inspiration in seventeenth-century vocalism.

Matthew Lock (1632-77)

A few songs by Dr. Blow have survived. Of these we may place first a charming little setting of Rochester's verses, "All my Past Life is mine Alone." Others by the same composer (still in our modern collections) are, "We all to Conquering Beauty bow," and "It is not that I Love you Less"—both good airs. Dr. Blow's publication of his collection entitled *Amphion* (in imitation of Purcell's *Orpheus Britannicus*) was a dire failure; it includes one good song—namely, the above-mentioned "It is not that I Love you Less." Burney wrote of Blow—his ballads "are in general more smooth and natural than his other productions, and, indeed, than any other ballads of his time; there is more melody than in those of Henry Lawes, or any composers of the preceding reign; yet it is not of that grateful kind in which the Italians were now advancing towards perfection, with great rapidity." If Burney were now living, would he consider perfection attained either in Italy or England? Echo answers—Neither in Italy *nor* England!

Dr. Blow (1648-1708)

Richard Leveridge (1670-1758) was an excellent bass singer, and took part in many of Purcell's compositions. His own songs are numerous, but of very unequal merit. One modern collection contains seven of Leveridge's pieces.[1] Perhaps the best song this musician has left is his setting of "Who is Sylvia?" a remarkably expressive and melodious air. His popularity must, of course, be ascribed to the well-known song, "The Roast Beef of Old England."

There is no difficulty in assigning a worthy place among song-writers to Henry Carey (1692-1743). His claim to "God save the King" is probably mistaken; and the tune usually sung to "Sally in our Alley" is merely an adaptation of an older tune.[2] Concerning "Sally in our Alley," a writer in Grove's *Dictionary* describes it as "one of the most striking and original melodies that ever emanated from the brain of a musician!" Two of Carey's best songs are "Saw ye the Nymph?" and "Brave Grenadiers rejoice," both recently reprinted.

A few of Dr. Greene's songs claim to rank with the best of their day. We shall content ourselves with quoting "The Merry Cuckoo, Messenger of Spring," a most spontaneous strain; and the once famous "Busy, Curious, Thirsty Fly," of which William Oldys wrote the words. The same composer's "Orpheus with his Lute" is well worth reprinting; though,

[1] *Minstrelsy of England* (A. Moffat).

[2] On the authority of Chappell and Hullah; but the words remain Carey's.

FIG. 17.—"THE VOCAL GROVE."

as far as the writer is aware, this has not lately been done.

Charles Young was organist of Allhallows, Barking, about the year 1720. His eldest daughter, Cecilia, became the wife of Dr. Arne. The songs of Young are mostly dead and gone, though it is of interest to note that his setting of Waller's "It is not that I Love you Less" has been recently reprinted.[1] We give a facsimile of another of Young's songs, from the Halliwell Collection, Chetham Library. The plate shows that the words of this song were written by Mr. William Monlass, concerning whom we can offer no information. The lyric has often been published (without music), as, for example, in *The Hive* (1732). Mr. Hullah included it, with a different air, in his excellent *Song Book* (Macmillan). In the fourth bar of the last line of our facsimile the note F is a mistake; it should be E, as is seen from the flute part. The third stanza mentions "Rosy Bowers"—an allusion to Purcell's great song of that name.

Dr. Arne (1710-78) is now known almost solely as a song-writer. His oratorios and dramatic pieces are silent and forgotten, and yet it is little over a century since these were in full favour. Fortunately, his songs, or the best of them, are not so perishable. "Rule Britannia," which Wagner found to sum up the English character, has taken its place with the few really national English tunes. The Shakespeare settings are highly popular, especially "Blow, blow,

[1] In Mr. Moffat's *Minstrelsy of England.*

thou Wintry Wind," "Under the Greenwood Tree," "When Daisies pied," "Where the Bee sucks," etc. Arne wrote a vast number of songs, some, if not most, of which appear childish to modern ears; nevertheless, the reprints scarcely offer all that is best of this great musician. *Lyric Harmony* alone would furnish several songs that should not be forgotten.

A contemporary of Arne, and a distinguished Church musician, Dr. Boyce (1710-79), has left us one song that will carry his name and fame to many succeeding generations of Englishmen. We, of course, refer to "Hearts of Oak"—a jolly sea-song, which owes some of its popularity to Garrick's sturdy words.

No song-writer of his period was more successful, within certain limits, than was Charles Dibdin (1745-1814). "Tom Bowling" and "Blow high, Blow low" appear to be his two finest songs. But among the three thousand works, in poetry and music, which this prolific composer bequeaths to us, there are many others which are still in vogue.

Perhaps, of Dibdin's contemporaries, the popularity of Shield most nearly approached his own. Such songs as "Old Towler" and "The Wolf" are Shield's surest appeals to fame, indeed, the first-named is the best hunting-song of its century.

Sir Henry Bishop (1786-1855) has enjoyed a large reputation, which, however, as time goes on, cannot be said to increase. The modern development of music, which has played such havoc with most of the English composers of his period, has dealt little less leniently with his own works. There is one quality traceable in his songs which will always assist their performance, and that is their extremely vocal practicability. Singers like singing them, and that is much. "Home, sweet Home," for sentimental reasons, is of world-wide fame. "Should he Upbraid" and "Bid me Discourse," and many others are still in demand.

Another song-composer of greater invention and no less musicianship was Balfe (1808-70). Our remark (hazarded in Bishop's case) is no less applicable to the brilliant Irish melodist. Most of Balfe's songs are still with us, but they are being performed less and less every day. "Come into the Garden, Maud," will probably not be so much heard in future; though the song is (of its class) an exceedingly effective one. "Good-night, Beloved" is undoubtedly among the best of Balfe's single songs. We shall be surprised if, in the compression which invariably overtakes the least voluminous writer—just as it does him who leaves whole archives—the "Good-night," and perhaps the "Arrow and the Song," together with the whole of the *Bohemian Girl*, do not stand as representative works, by which Balfe will be remembered.

Madrigals are not, strictly speaking, Minstrelsy, though many of the earliest examples, if we include "Sumer is icumen in," must have been sung by the minstrels or their successors. The fifteenth century certainly witnessed the more legitimate style of madrigal, an offspring of the so-called Flemish school. The first published book of madrigals appeared at

Venice in 1501, and some twenty-nine years later a collection of part-songs was issued in England from the press of Wynken de Worde, containing compositions by Taverner and others. Byrde's *Psalms and Sonnets*, issued in 1588, are somewhat in the spirit of the true madrigal style, which was further developed by Morley, Weelkes, Dowland, Benet, Hilton, and Este. The name of Orlando Gibbons must also be added to the list of those who carried the form to perfection. The author and composer of "Where griping Grief," Richard Edwardes (mentioned in another part of our book), was himself an excellent madrigal-writer. John Immyns, in 1741, founded a society which is said to be the oldest musical association in Europe, and styled it the Madrigal Society. From a humble meeting-place at the "Twelve Bells" in Bride Lane, with a membership of no more than sixteen, this little London music club successfully carried forward its founder's aims, gradually expanding its influence and enrolling many of the most prominent musicians from that day to this.

A long interval occurred between the decadence of the Madrigal and the rise of the English Glee. The former ceased to be much cultivated either at home or abroad after 1650, while the Glee did not come in until the latter part of the seventeenth century. The essential difference between Madrigal and Glee lay in the contrapuntal character of the former, which was altogether lacking in the latter. Madrigals, too, had modes; not so the Glee, which had a modern tonality. Both were unaccompanied. The spontaneity of the more modern form was its chief beauty. Many subjects could be introduced, touched upon lightly, and as lightly abandoned. On the other hand, development was a salient feature of the older form. Samuel Webbe (1740-1816) was perhaps the best glee-writer, though more eminent masters, such as Arne and Boyce, essayed the form. Stevens in his well-known "Ye spotted Snakes," reproduced the features of the instrumental first-movement form; in an elementary likeness, it is true, but nevertheless with success. To the names of the composers who excelled as glee-writers we may add those of Calcott, Horsley, Cooke, Danby, and Spofforth; and the list is then far from being exhausted.

It is not impossible that madrigals and glees may again come into popular use. Our system of musical education, at present almost exclusively tending in the direction of instrumental music, cannot be expected to permanently exclude the vocal forms, which necessitate for their true enjoyment an active participation in their performance. If, however, music is completely dominated by professionalism, so that instead of singing we prefer to pay to hear others sing, all this glee and madrigal music is for the time being, at all events, thrown utterly to waste, when it might have been turned to excellent profit.

CHAPTER XVI.

A word to the Folksong Society—Song-collecting—Author's experiment—"Come, all ye Foxhunters"—Adieu.

In taking leave of our subject, we venture to address a few words to the members of the Folksong Society, and to others who labour in the same field. Quite a rich harvest has been gathered in, since 1859, when Mr. William Chappell sounded the call to such pleasing duty. Many an interesting song is still awaiting the industrious collector, who should be encouraged to continue his self-imposed task, despite the uncertainty he can never escape, as to whether others have anticipated his efforts. The reason of this is not far to seek. Such labour is never entirely wasted. Even supposing traditional ballads be several times copied, so much the better, for the precise reason that singers and copyists are not infallible;[1] nor is it the best version of a song that necessarily first finds print.

[1] There is a reference to a somewhat risky method of collecting unwritten songs, which occurs in Hone's *Ancient Mysteries* (1823), as follows:—"This collection [viz., 89 Christmas carols] I have had little opportunity of increasing except when in the country I have heard an old woman singing an old carol, and brought back the carol in my pocket with less chance of its escape, than the tune in my head." Schubert trusted the same treacherous vehicle, the memory, and the

FIG. 18.—"TALLY-HO."

"Tally-ho!"

Not to be behindhand in the practice here referred to, the present writer has essayed a humble effort, the result of which he now offers to his readers. The ballad was taken down during a holiday in Patterdale (Ulleswater), where, thanks to the good offices of mine host of the "White Lion," an opportunity was afforded of investigating the traditional songs of the place. It will be seen that the ballad, which is full of local allusions, describes a fox-hunt in the immediate neighbourhood. Everybody in the district knew the song, but nobody had so far seen or heard of a printed copy. So with that it was jotted down, from the hearty strains of "Old Joe Hunt" (the Patterdale huntsman), while a friend secured the words in shorthand. The latter were composed by one Mark Steel, a shoemaker of some sixty or seventy years ago. The air should be much older. For convenience of performance a pianoforte accompaniment is added.

TALLY-HO, HARK AWAY!

Come all ye fox-hunters, where'er ye may dwell;
I pray give attention, to whom I will tell;
It's concerning a fox which we lately did kill,
By the hounds of Squire Head, which lived at Jenny Hill.
Tally-ho, hark away!
Tally-ho, hark away!
Tally-ho, tally-ho, hark away!

Hungarian air which he heard in a kitchen at Zélèsz (which afterwards appeared in the Divertissement), was kept in mind by his humming it over at intervals, until home was reached, with pen and paper available.

We rose from our beds on a fine winter's morn,
At the cry of the hounds and the sound of the horn;
Our sportsmen were few, but our skill for to try,
We thought in new planting bold Reynard to lie.
Tally-ho, etc.

Now, 'twas after we'd ranged it and found not a drag,
We thought we would try to the Colliers' Hag,
And after we'd ranged it all over the plain,
We came to his lair in Collier Hag stane.
Tally-ho, etc.

Now 'twas in at him our terriers did rush,
When they soon brought him out, hanging on at his brush;
But Joe being true sportsman, cries off let him go!
And away went the hounds in a view tally-ho.
Tally-ho, etc.

Now 'twas up Swinburn Park they made him to hie,
'Twas late on the day, and Helvellyn looked high,
When our gallant hounds him quickly pursue,
When they crossed Airey Bridge they came up in full view.
Tally-ho, etc.

Now 'tis up Glencoin Park like lightning they fly,
Resolved for the top of Brew Planting to try;
But our hounds being near him, which he didn't like,
He made for a bourne called Erring-green Pike.
Tally-ho, etc.

But our hounds having sworn him they'd end him his race,
They turned him down t'rake in a rallying pace;
Then right down the screes to Glenridding they went,
When he washed in the river to throw off his scent.
Tally-ho, etc.

"In Full Cry"

Now up Glamara Park he made a bold try,
But our hounds made him shuther and look very shy;
When Towler and Barmaid got close to his heels,
They forced him again to return down the fields.
Tally-ho, etc.

Now he passed the "King's Arms," but had no time to rest,
When a drop of good beer would have quenched his thirst,
When dash down the garden of Geldert he goes,
Expecting he there should escape from his foes.
Tally-ho, etc.

Next through the churchyard to the school-porch he went,
When finding the master on mischief was bent,
He called on our parson his sins to forgive:
He was afraid that he had not much longer to live.
Tally-ho, etc.

Now to Ulleswater he so slyly does creep,
To baffle our hounds he would wash in the deep:
But our hounds being good gamesters, maintained on their course,
They made him comply with our old ancient laws.
Tally-ho, etc.

Now, whilst he was creeping by Jenkin Wood side,
Up came little Ruby and soon him she spied,
With the rest of our hounds being up in full cry,
And they seize him and make his old jacket to fly.
Tally-ho, etc.

Then up rode Mr. Hutchinson, likewise Squire Head:
They knew by their hounds that bold reynard was dead,

When they leapt over paling and came up with a rush,
And took up bold reynard and cut off his brush.
Tally-ho, etc.

So now the sport's over, without more delay
To the village called Patterdale we bore him away,
When musical toast in bumpers goes round:
Long life and success to both Hunter and Hound!
Tally-ho, hark away!
Tally-ho, hark away!
Tally-ho, tally-ho, hark away!

Another Patterdale man gave the same song with a different burden. Thus:—

Tal-ly - ho! Tal-ly - ho! Tally - ho! Tally-ho! hark a-way!

A few further songs of the chase were readily forthcoming; but enough has been said for our present purpose.

Finally, in view of the descriptive list of modern collections of traditional airs and ballads given in Appendix A, the reader will be enabled to pursue the subject at will; and he will find that it is one which grows in interest the further he follows it. We bid adieu to the old Minstrels and their art with the one regret—vain though it be—that we have to part company so soon, and cannot travel further down the same road, which discovers so much delightful country on either hand, much of which remains still unexplored.

Appendices.

A.—I. Literature of Minstrelsy. II. Song Collections.

B.—Glossary and Definitions.

C.—Chronological Table.

Index.

Appendix A.

I. LITERATURE DEALING WITH MINSTRELSY.

THE literature dealing with minstrelsy is scattered broadcast in histories, dictionaries, and song collections. From a literary point of view, Percy's *Reliques of Ancient English Poetry* and Ritson's *Ancient Songs* are much the best, and almost the earliest. From a musical standpoint, Chappell's *Popular Music* and its forerunner, *Ancient Melodies*, offer the greatest amount of information, and may be regarded as the first systematic attempts to give a complete account of English minstrelsy.

Hawkins and Burney give a large amount of details concerning our subject, but neither historian thought it worth while to render any well-digested account of the minstrels as a class. Grove's *Dictionary*, though it also contains a mass of random details, notices only two distinct points in connection with minstrelsy. The first deals with the foundation of the Musicians' Company, the second occurs in the article on Song, where the troubadours, minnesingers, and English song-writers generally are considered in Mrs. Edmond Wodehouse's comprehensive article.

As all the histories of music, in addition to the encyclopædias, etc., of necessity treat of portions of our subject, it is unnecessary to mention them in detail.

History of Poetry, 1778; Thomas Warton.
A General History of Music, by Dr. Busby (2 vols.). London, 1819.
Bibliotheca Madrigaliana, 1847; E. F. Rimbault.
Histoire de l'Harmonie au Moyen Age, 1852; Les Harmonistes des 12e et 13e Siècles, 1864; L'Art Harmonique, 1865; Coussemaker.
History of the Opera, 2 vols., 1862; H. Sutherland Edwards.
Transition Period (a series of lectures), 1865-76; Hullah.

Introduction to the Study of National Music, 1866; Carl Engel.
Die Tansmusik, 1868; Herr Ungewitter.
Storia Universale del Canto, 2 vols., 1873; G. Fantoni.
The Troubadours: A History of Provençal Life and Literature of the Middle Ages, 1878; Francis Hueffer. One of the few English books on this interesting phase of music.
Literature of National Music, 1879; Carl Engel.
National Music of the World, 1880-82 (posthumous); H. F. Chorley.
Ouseley's Additions to Naumann's History, 1880-85; Cassell & Co.
Le Chant, ses Principes, et son Histoire, 1881; Lemaire & Lavoix.
History of Music (to the Time of the Troubadours), 1885-87; J. F. Rowbotham.
The Story of British Music, by Frederick J. Crowest (Richard Bentley & Son, 1896), covers more of the ground traversed in the present pages than any other volume in this list. It is well illustrated, and forms the best account of British Music from "the earliest times to the Tudor period" which the nineteenth century brought forth. The volume takes a much wider scope than does the *Story of Minstrelsy*, which by its very restrictions should tend to throw light on a phase of music admittedly obscure and hitherto almost ignored.
Notes on an Undescribed Collection of English Fifteenth-century Music issued in the *Sammelbände* (April-May 1901), by W. Barclay Squire.
Makers of Song, 1905, Anna Alice Chaplin. An excellent account of the troubadours, minnesingers, meistersingers, Purcell, etc.
The Morris Book: A History of Morris Dancing, by Cecil J. Sharp and Herbert C. Macilwaine. London, 1907; Novello & Co.

II. SONG COLLECTIONS.

Song collecting must be allowed to have all the prestige that antiquity can confer upon it. It has also been the diversion of kings. Charlemagne was an enthusiastic patron of ancient minstrelsy; so, too, was our own King Alfred. Many of the troubadours' songs are still extant, as are those of the minnesingers and meistersingers of later times. Of really ancient English songs there remain scarcely more than the scanty few scattered in these pages. Such are the Cornish Carol (on page 220), "Sumer is icumen in," the "Agincourt Song," and the carol on page 100. With the advent of the Tudor period we

Appendix A

touch surer ground. The extension of the art of printing to music characters (under Wynken de Worde) gave a new impetus to song collecting, which practically begins about that time. We add a short survey of the national song collections of England.

Early English Harmony, edited by Professor Wooldridge, for the Plainsong and Mediæval Music Society (1897), contains facsimile photographs of a few of the most ancient specimens of English music. The following extract from the index of the volume referred to mentions those pieces which most nearly concern our subject :—

Cornish Carol, in two parts, from the Bodley MS. 572, fol. 50; beginning at the words "Ut tuo propitiatus," written in alphabetic notation; tenth century.

"Sumer is icumen in," in Harley MS. 978, British Museum; thirteenth century.

"Worldis blis ne last no throwe," Bodley MS. (thirteenth century), and another copy in Arundel (fourteenth century).

Dance Tune, Bodley MS.; thirteenth century.

"Angelus ad Virginem," Arundel MS. 248; fourteenth century. Another copy in Cambridge Univ. Lib.

Several fifteenth-century Carols from Bodleian Library.

A group of three-part pieces by Dunstable and Benet; fifteenth century.

Among modern reprints of ancient songs, etc., may be mentioned the following :—

Carols of the Fifteenth Century; edited by J. A. Fuller-Maitland, M.A., F.S.A. (Leadenhall Press). This excellent print contains thirteen carols given in their original form from a manuscript roll in the Library of Trinity College, Cambridge. The editor conjectures that the whole set may be by Dunstable. The first lines of the carols are as follows :—

Hail! Mary, ful of grace, Modyr in virgynytee.
Nowel, nowel, nowel! To us is born owr god emanuel.
Alma redemptoris mater.
Now may we syngyn as it is.
Be mery, be mery, I prey zow every chon.
Nowel syng we now al and sum.
Deo gracias anglia (the "Agincourt Song").
Now make we merthe al and sum.
Abyde I hope it be the beste.
Qwat tydyngis bryngyst thou, massager?

Eya martir Stephane.
Prey for us the Prynce of Pees.
Ther is no rose of swych vertu.

The Appendix adds a copy of the Oxford version of the "Agincourt Song" (MS. Arch. B. Seld., 10, Bodleian Library).

Collection of Songs, printed by Wynken de Worde in 1530. Only the bass part is in the British Museum. It is not impossible that the other parts may yet be forthcoming from one of the great private libraries, where Wynken de Worde's name would secure preservation when the mere antiquity of the songs would fail. Compositions are herein contained by Cornysshe, Gwynneth, Jones, Cooper, and Fayrfax.

Christmas Carols (1521), printed by Wynken de Worde. One leaf only is preserved. From this, however, the famous "Boar's Head Carol" has come down to us.

Pammelia (1609), Deuteromelia (1609), and Melismata (1611). The three great song collections by Thomas Ravenscroft are unmatched in their variety, age, and excellence. Some of the songs come from the time of Henry VII., if not earlier. Many are given in the form of Catches and Rounds. See p. 196 of our text for an example.

Fitzwilliam Virginal Book. Edited by J. A. Fuller Maitland and W. Barclay Squire. 2 vols. Breitkopf & Haertel, 1899. This famous collection, so long erroneously known as "Queen Elizabeth's Virginal Book," is understood to have been made between 1550-1620. The MS. (preserved in the Fitzwilliam Museum, Cambridge) is a small folio of 220 leaves, written on six-line staves ruled by hand. Its importance to Minstrelsy arises from the number of old songs which find a place in its pages. Though these bear evidence of instrumental arrangement, the versions are remarkably pure. Byrde and Giles Farnaby may be named as the most masterly harmonizers of such traditional melodies as are employed. Among the airs, which were chosen as themes for movements designed for the virginals, are the following:—

Walsingham - - - -	Arranged by Dr. Bull
Go from my Window - - - -	Thomas Morley
Jhon, come kisse me now - - -	William Byrde
Robin - - - - - -	
Nancie - - - - - -	
Barafostus - - - - -	
Muscadin - - - - -	
St. Thomas' Wake - - - -	

Appendix A

The Woods so Wilde	Orlando Gibbons
Go from my Window	
King's Hunt	Giles Farnaby
The Carman's Whistle	William Byrde
The Hunt's up	William Byrde
Sellenger's Round	William Byrde
Fortune my Foe	William Byrde
O Mistris myne	William Byrde
The Woods so Wild (dated 1590)	
Walsingham	William Byrde
All in a Garden Green	William Byrde
Daphne	Giles Farnaby
Pawles Warfe	Giles Farnaby
Quodling's Delight	Giles Farnaby
Pavana Lachrymae (Dowland)	Set by William Byrde
Put up thy Dagger, Jemy	Giles Farnaby
Bonny, sweet Robin	
Tomkin's Ground	
Barafostus' Dreame	Thomas Tomkins
The King's Hunt	Dr. John Bull
The Spanish Pavan	Dr. John Bull
Woody-cock	Giles Farnaby
The New Sa-Hoo	Giles Farnaby
Nobodyes Gigge	Richard Farnaby
Malt's come down	William Byrde
Pavana (Lachrymae)	Thomas Morley
Galiarda (Lachrymae)	Thomas Morley
Wolsey's Wilde	William Byrde
Callino casturame	William Byrde
Rowland	William Byrde
Why aske you	
Packington's Pound	
Watkin's Ale	
Fayne would I wed	Richard Farnaby
Martin sayd to his man	
Gipseis Round	William Byrde
Loth to depart	Giles Farnaby
Up tails all	Giles Farnaby
Pescodd Time	William Byrde
Tell me, Daphne	Giles Farnaby
Mal Sims	Giles Farnaby
Why aske you?	Giles Farnaby
Hanskin (Jog on, jog on the footpath way)	Richard Farnaby

Playford's English Dancing Master (1651):—

1.* Upon a Summer's Day.
2.* Blew Cap.
3.* The Night-piece; or, the Shaking of the Sheets.
4. The Boate-man: a Bag-pipe tune, with drone.
5.* The Beggar Boy.
6. The Parson's Farewell.
7. Bobbing Joe (Joan?). "My dog and I" is sung to this
8. The New Exchange.
9. The Wish.
10.* Stingo; or, Oyle of Barley.
11. The Whirligig.
12. Picking of Sticks.
13. The Old Mole.
14. Grimstock.
15. Woodicock.
16.* Greenwood. This is "Shall I go walk the woods so wild?"
17. A Saraband.
18. Hit and Miss.
19.* Confesse; or, the Court Lady.
20. A Health to Betty.
21. Mage on a Tree.
22. Millison's (Millicent's) Jegge.
23.* The Spanish Jeepsie. This is "Come, follow, follow me."
24. Lady Spillor.
25. Kemp's Jegg (called after "Nine Days' Wonder," Kemp).
26.* If all the World were Paper.
27.* The Chirping of the Lark (Robin Hood and Guy of Gisborne).
28. Adson's Saraband.
29.* None Such; or, A la mode de France.
30.* The Merry, Merry Milkmaids.
31.* Daphne ("When Daphne did from Phœbus fly").
32.* Mill-field.
33. The Fine Companion.
34. Cast a Bell.
35. Shellamefago.
36. The Rose is Red, the Rose is White.
37. The Spanyard.
38.* Have at thy Coat, Old Woman.

---

* Indicates that the words have come down to us.

Appendix A

39.* To Drive the Cold Winter away; or, The Gun.
40. Pepper's Black.
41.* The Maid peept out at the Window; or, The Friar in the Well.
42. Halfe Hanniken.
43.* Once I Loved a Maiden Faire.
44.* Fain I Would; or, The King's Complaint.
45. The Irish Lady; or, Anniseed-water Robin.
46. My Lady Cullen.
47. The Bath.
48. Jog on, my Honey.
49.* Goddesses ("I would I were in my own country").
50.* The Health; or, the Merry Weasel.
51. Heart's Ease.
52. Jack Pudding.
53. Prince Rupert's March.
54. Dissembling Love; or, the Lost Heart.
55. Argeers.
56. Jack-a-Lent.
57.* Maiden Lane.
58. The Chirping of the Nightingale.
59.* A Soldier's Life.
60. Sweet Masters.
61.* Cuckolds all a-row; also the Cavaliers' song, "Hey, boys, up we go."
62. Petticoat Wag.
63.* Paul's Steeple; or, I'm the Duke of Norfolk.
64. Rufty Tufty.
65.* All in a Garden Green.
66.* Dargason (spelt Dagesson); or, Sedanny, "The Hawthorn Tree."
67. Aye Me.
68. The Punk's Delight.
69. The Milkmayde's Bobb.
70.* An Old Man is a Bed full of Bones.
71. Cheerily and Merrily.
72. The Country Coll.
73. Dull Sir John.
74. Saturday Night and Sunday Morning.
75.* New Boe-peep.
76. Hockley in the Hole.

---

* Indicates that the words have come down to us.

77. The Chestnut.
78. Staines Morriss
79. Paule's Wharfe.
80.* Tom Tinker's my True Love.
81. Kettle-drum; or, He that hath a Good Wife.
82. Hide Parke.
83. Mundesse.
84.* Ladye lie neare me.
85.* Lull me beyond thee.
86. Jenny pluck Pears.
87.* The Glory of the West.
88. Gathering Peascods.
89. Scotch Cap.
90. New Nothing.
91. Step Stately.
92. Shepherd's Holiday; or, Labour in Vaine.
93. Graie's Inn Maske ("Mad Tom").
94. The Slip.
95. The Tender Gentlewoman; or, The Hemp-dressers.

Select Musical Ayres, 1653; John Playford. This is a typical seventeenth-century song collection. The composers include Wilson, the two Colmans, H. and W. Lawes, Webb, Lanier, Jeremy Savile, and others. The verses are (as a rule) first-class poems, by Jonson, Suckling, Waller, Cotton, Dryden, and Shirley.

Ayres and Dialogues, three books, 1653; Henry Lawes. This is the first individual song-collection of any importance. Many of the airs are sung to this day.

Orpheus Britannicus, 1698 and 1706; Henry Purcell. The second edition of this posthumous collection is the more interesting of the two. It contains 105 well-selected songs by the first great song-writer of this country.

Pills to Purge Melancholy, 1719-1720. Set to music by Dr. John Blow, Mr. Henry Purcell, and other excellent masters of the town; written by Tom Durfey. From a musical point of view this queer old collection is a complete failure. As an authority, it is extremely unreliable. Its use is chiefly in confirming or rejecting other authorities. It has, however, secured a reprint, when many a better song-book lies obscured by the dust of centuries. No book has ever been oftener referred to, or less quoted. Durfey (1649-1723) issued three collections of songs written by himself and

---

* Indicates that the words have come down to us.

set to music by first-rate writers, between 1683 and 1685. He re-issued many of these in four small volumes in 1706, under the title *Wit and Mirth*, and in the second volume of the large work of 1719 the title appears as *Wit and Mirth; or, Pills to Purge Melancholy.*

The sixty-nine airs in *The Beggar's Opera* (1727-28):—

1. An Old Woman clothed in Gray.
2. The Bonny Gray-eyed Morn.
3. Cold and Raw.
4. Why is your Faithful Slave Disdained?
5. Of all the Simple Things ("The Mouse-trap")
6. What shall I do to Shew.
7. O! London is a Fine Town.
8. Grim King of Ghosts.
9. Jenny, where hast thou been?
10. Thomas, I cannot.
11. A Soldier and a Sailor.
12. Now, ponder well, ye parents dear.
13. Le Printemps (French air).
14. Pretty Parrot.
15. Pray, Fair One be Kind.
16. Over the Hills and Far Away.
17. Gin thou wert my ain Thing.
18. O! the Broom.
19. Fill every Glass.
20. March in Rinaldo.
21. Would you have a Young Virgin ("Poor Robin's Maggot").
22. Cotillon.
23. All in a Misty Morning.
24. When once I lay.
25. When first I laid Siege to my Chloris.
26. Courtiers, Courtiers, think it no harm.
27. A Lovely Lass to a Friar came.
28. 'Twas when the Sea was Roaring.
29. The Sun had Loos'd his Weary Team.
30. How Happy are we.
31. Of Noble Race was Shenkin.
32. Old air, the title forgotten by Gay.
33. London Ladies.
34. All in the Downs.
35. Have you heard of a Frolicsome Ditty.
36. Irish Trot.

37. Old air, name forgotten.
38. Gossip Joan.
39. Irish Howl.
40. The Lass of Patie's Mill.
41. If Love's a Sweet Passion.
42. South Sea Ballad.
43. Packington's Pound.
44. Lilliburlero.
45. Down in the North Countrie.
46. A Shepherd kept Sheep.
47. One Evening passing Lost my Way.
48. Now, Roger I'll tell thee.
49. O Betsy Bell.
50. Would Fate to me.
51. Come, Sweet Lass.
52. The Last Time I went o'er the Moor.
53. Tom Tinker's my True Love.
54. I am a Poor Shepherd undone.
55. Ianthe the Lovely.
56. A Cobbler there was.
57. Bonny Dundee.
58. Happy Groves.
59. Sally in our Alley.
60. Britons, Strike Home!
61. Chevy Chace.
62. Old Sir Simon the King.
63. Joy to Great Cæsar.
64. There was an Old Woman.
65. Did you ever Hear of a Gallant Soldier.
66. Why are Thine Eyes Still Glancing?
67. Green Sleeves.
68. All you that must take a Leap.
69. Lumps of Pudding.

I'm a Skiff (in Overture?)

The Beggar's Opera was written by John Gay in 1727, and produced by John Rich at Lincoln's Inn Fields Theatre not long after. Dr. Pepusch arranged and scored the sixty-nine airs, which contributed so much to the success of the work. Burney says that Pepusch "was very judiciously chosen by Gay, to help him to select the tunes for *The Beggar's Opera*, for which he composed an original overture upon the subject of one of the tunes ("I'm Like a Skiff"), and furnished the wild, rude, and often vulgar melodies with basses so excellent that no sound contrapuntist will ever attempt to alter them." Pepusch's basses have been long superseded. They were not, however, unskilful for their day; but collectors either write their own, or go further back to better sources.

The Minstrel: A Collection of English Songs and Cantatas. London, 1780.

English Songs, with their Original Airs, and a Historical Essay; Joseph Ritson. London, 1783. This excellent collection contains some hundreds of airs drawn from all sources. Its principal merit is its catholicity. When asked by a lady why he did not put a bass to the airs, Ritson replied, "What would you have a bass for? —to spoil the treble?"

Ancient Songs from the Time of King Henry III. to the Revolution; Joseph Ritson. London, 1792. Though not strictly a musical work, several important musical examples occur in this admirable volume. The very first piece is "Sumer is icumen in," with the notes. In commenting upon the observations of Wanley and Burney regarding this monumental work, Ritson fixed the date, without hesitation, as early at least as the year 1250, a judgment since universally accepted. The most notable additions which the compiler made in his *Ancient Songs* were drawn from an old MS. (Add. MSS. 5666) of the fifteenth century, which Ritson presented to the British Museum. Others of his choicest examples were taken from Ravenscroft.

Edward Jones' Popular Cheshire Melodies, 1798. This little collection preserves for us the well-known air of "The Cheshire Cheese."

Musica Antiqua, two volumes, 1812; Stafford Smith. Contains many early songs of the Troubadours, and a few by Coperario, Robert Jones, Johnson, Byrde, and others. Some are included in these pages.

Crotch's Specimens, three volumes, 1820 *circa;* includes a few good quotations of early English airs.

Some Ancient Christmas Carols, 1822; Davis Gilbert. A collection made in Cornwall.

The Sea Songs of England; selected from original MSS. and early printed copies in the library of William Kitchiner, M.D. London, 1823. A fine collection of its class, with old-fashioned accompaniments.

Loyal and National Songs; William Kitchiner, M.D. London, 1823. Dr. Bull's variations on "God save the Kinge" (a fugue subject, bearing no resemblance to the National Anthem) are reprinted in this excellent volume of part-pieces.

Ancient Songs and Old English Melodies, in two volumes, published 1838-39; by William Chappell. Form the first systematized attempt at a real song anthology. Volume I. contains the words and historical notes, while the music is confined to the second part. Crotch, G. A. Macfarren, and J. A. Wade, harmonized the airs, of which there are 245. The attention this excellent publication awakened led to a reprint with considerable additions. This is referred to below.

Minstrel Melodies. A collection of songs, 12mo. London, 1839.

The National Minstrel, or Songster's Companion. A collection of 400 popular songs. London, 1840.

Rev. J. Broadwood's privately-printed collection, drawn from Surrey and Sussex, 1840.

Musical Illustrations of Percy's Reliques, by E. F. Rimbault, 1850 (Cramer Beale & Co.). This useful collection contains several ballad-tunes not easily met with elsewhere.

Popular Music of the Olden Time, 1859; by William Chappell. In this work no less than 400 airs are included, with the whole of the harmonizations by G. A. Macfarren. Mr. Chappell's account of the songs is everywhere admitted to be authoritative. Without disparaging Macfarren's laborious share in the work, it may safely be said that Chappell would have done much better if he had copied the original harmonies where available. By a mistaken attempt to make the work suitable for practical performance, it is robbed of a lasting worth. The new edition of Professor Wooldridge has certainly restored and added weight to the whole work. In withdrawing the eighteen folksongs (of doubtful pedigree), Professor Wooldridge sensibly increases the value of the book.

English National Melodies, edited by Sir Henry Bishop and Charles Mackay.

Melodies of Various Nations; first volume arranged by Bishop.

Commonplaces of Music, 1871-73; John Curwen. Contains specimens of early English music, from the eleventh to the fourteenth centuries, etc.

Nursery Rhymes and Country Songs, 1877; Miss Mason.

English Songs (58), edited by John Hullah, 1880 *circa* (Augener & Co.). A capital collection of the seventeenth and eighteenth centuries.

Northumbrian Minstrelsy, 1882; Stokoe and Collingwood Bruce.

Fifty-four Folk-airs to Broadside Ballads (Novello), 1882; W. A. Barrett. These were collected, for the most part, from an old shepherd on the South Downs, near Shoreham, Sussex.

Songs of England. A collection of 274 English melodies of the last three centuries. Three volumes, Boosey & Co. The first two volumes are edited by J. L. Hatton, the last by Dr. Eaton Faning, 1886 *circa*, and more recent editions. The work has deservedly enjoyed a wide popularity.

Music of the Waters, 1888; Miss L. A. Smith.

Forty Sailors' Songs or Chanties, 1888; edited by Ferris Tozer Boosey.

The Besom Maker, 1888; H. Summer.

Songs of the West (Methuen & Co), four parts 1889-92, re-issued 1905, by Baring Gould. Contains chiefly traditional country songs.

English Songs, 1890 *circa* (Augener & Co.), W. A. Barrett. One hundred songs principally of the eighteenth century.

Sussex Songs, collected by Miss L. E. Broadwood, 1890.

Traditional Tunes (Yorkshire), 1891; Frank Kidson.

English County Songs, 1893; Miss L. E. Broadwood.

A Garland of Country Song, 1895; Baring Gould.

English Minstrelsie, 1895; S. Baring Gould, M.A. This eight-volume work—issued by Messrs. Jack, Edinburgh—contains 245 songs, many of which are genuine folk-lore. A few, such as "The Midsummer Carol" and "May-day Carol," are not easily met with elsewhere. Country songs are especially well represented. The annotations are always helpful and interesting, and a well-written essay appears in Volume VII.

The Minstrelsy of England: a collection of 200 English songs from the sixteenth to the middle of the eighteenth century; edited by Alfred Moffat (Bayley & Ferguson), 1901. This is a well-chosen selection of old songs, many of which were previously lost sight of. Useful annotations are included, from the pen of Mr. Frank Kidson, of Leeds.

Old Sea Chanties; J. Bradford and A. Fagge, 1904 (Metzler & Co.).

The Minstrelsy of England, edited by E. Duncan, 1905 (Augener & Co.). The collection numbers about 200 songs, the best of which are drawn from ancient sources. A few, such as "Westron Wynde," "Trenchmore," the "Agincourt Song," etc., possess the rare merit of being really ancient and at the same time practicable songs.

Journal of the Folk-song Society. Books 1-10 are issued. London, 1907. Many interesting little country airs may be found in these volumes, which form a useful record of surviving folk-song.

British Nursery Rhymes and Jingles; edited by Messrs. Moffat and Kidson. This collection of 75 simple melodies, arranged in an easy and attractive manner, boasts several airs of undoubted age. For instance, the song "To-morrow the Fox will come to Town" is a vocal version of the celebrated dance-tune "Trenchmore." Ravenscroft first printed it as a song, almost three centuries ago. "Old King Cole" is scarcely less ancient. "When good King Arthur ruled this Land," associated with several old airs (such as "Chevy Chase"), is set by Mr. Moffat to "one of our very early ballad tunes." "There was an Old Woman went up in a Basket," generally given to Purcell, but "probably erroneously" (if Mr. Kidson's note carries conviction), is none other than the far-famed air of "Lilliburlero." Most musicians will be inclined to believe that the music bears evidence that it could have been writ by no other hand. "Musick's Handmaid" (1689), issued one year after James II. was sung out of three kingdoms, bears the composer's name. Children, old and young, will welcome these fine old tunes. Hundreds more are in existence.

Children's Songs of Long Ago, also edited by Messrs. Moffat and Kidson (Augener), may be regarded as a continuation of the above-described volume. The airs are not, however, entirely English. Some few are old, such as "Sweet Summer is come," set to the tune of "The Winning of Cales" (Cadiz), possibly a relic of the Middle Ages.

Fifty Shakespeare Songs; edited by Charles Vincent, Mus. Doc., Oxon. (Oliver Ditson Co., Boston, U.S.A.). Folio, 1906. A handsome collection of Shakespearean airs, including most of the best traditional songs, and those associated with the poet's works. Part I. comprises the songs "Peg o' Ramsay," "Greensleeves," "Heigho for a Husband," "Heart's-ease," "Light o' Love," "Three Merry Men be we," and Robert Jones' "Farewell, dear Love." The second group includes an excellent arrangement of "The Willow Song," "O Mistress mine," "It was a Lover and his Lass" (Morley), "Where the Bee sucks" (Johnson), "Full Fathom Five" (Johnson), "Lawn as White as Driven Snow," and "Take, oh! take those Lips away" (Dr. Wilson). The interest is maintained in the third part, which offers some of the great settings by Purcell and Arne, and a few simple airs by Banister, Humfreys, and Leveridge. The English setting by the last-named composer of "Who is Sylvia?" deserves to be more widely known. Schubert, Schumann, Curshmann, and Rossini figure in the final division of the book, which gives some modern versions, a few of which are famous. Sir Hubert Parry's "Fear no more the Heat of the Sun," will be welcomed by many; it is thoughtful and expressive. Coleridge Taylor's music to "O, Mistress mine" is a clever piece of melodic work. The volume is a valuable one.

The Vocal Music of Shakespeare's Plays. Two vols. London: Samuel French.

The National Song Book (Boosey, 1906), edited by Charles Villiers Stanford. A fine collection of 50 English Songs, 6 Carols and 24 Rounds and Catches, supplemented with Irish, Scotch, and Welsh airs, suggested by the Board of Education (1905).

Twelve Old English Songs (Joseph Williams, 1907), edited by

Appendix A

E. Duncan. A choice selection of rare melodies by Purcell, Greene, Arne, etc.

English Music (1604-1904): being the Lectures given at the Music Loan Exhibition of the Worshipful Company of Musicians, held at Fishmongers' Hall, London Bridge, June-July, 1904 (The Walter Scott Publishing Co., Ltd., 1906). This interesting volume contains a valuable series of papers covering a period of three centuries of English music. The Musicians' Company has a history and association which belong to the Middle Ages; and though the actual charter dates only from 1604, Edward IV. granted a patent right to "his beloved minstrels" as early as 1469. The papers which deal most directly with Minstrelsy are the following: "English Songs," by Dr. W. H. Cummings; "Madrigals," Dr. Markham Lee; "Music in England in the year 1604," Sir J. F. Bridge; "Dances of Bygone Days," Algernon Rose; "Masques and Early Operas," A. H. D. Prendergast; "English Opera after Purcell," Dr. F. J. Sawyer; "Cathedral Music Composers," Dr. Huntley; "Music of the Country-side," Sir Ernest Clarke; "Early Music-printing," Alfred Littleton.

Jacobite Songs (Bayley & Ferguson); edited by Alfred Moffat. Though not of the finest period of native song, Jacobite productions are extremely numerous. Mr. Moffat's selection is a carefully-chosen one, and includes much of the best melody of the Stuart times.

Morris Dance Tunes; collected from traditional sources and arranged with pianoforte accompaniment by Cecil J. Sharp and Herbert Macilwaine (London: Messrs. Novello & Co., 1907). Mention has already been made of the history of Morris dancing; these two volumes offer twelve practical examples illustrating the several phases of this early and popular diversion. Pipe and tabor originally accompanied such pieces, and the very names, "Stick Dance," "Handkerchief Dance," and "Hand-clapping Dance," take us back to times when the village greens of old England witnessed the celebration of Robin Hood games and processions and pageants in honour of May-day.

The Oriana Collection of Early Madrigals (London: Novello & Co.). Although not confined to native productions, this fine edition of some of the best early vocal music deserves prominent mention in our anthology. It includes an issue of the famous *Triumphs of Oriana* (Thomas Morley, 1601), by Este, Benet, Hilton, Morley, Wilbye, and Weelkes, and maintains its high reputation by the addition of pieces by such writers as Byrde, Orlando Gibbons, and Thomas Bateson. The madrigals are for four, five, and six voices.

English Folk-song: Some Conclusions, by Cecil J. Sharp. Barnicott & Pearce, Taunton.

Appendix B.

Glossary and Definitions.

Bagpipe, a favourite instrument with the Celtic races. Known in Irish poetry in the tenth century. A form of the instrument appears on a coin of the time of Nero, who, according to Suetonius, was a performer on the instrument. In Henry IV.'s time the bagpipes were carried on the march, in order that when the barefoot pilgrim "striketh his too upon a stone, and hurteth him sore, and maketh him to blede, it is well done that he or his fellow begin then song, or else take out of his bosom a Baggepype for to drive away with soche mirth the hurte of his fellow."

Balades (Ballad), originally a dancing-song; afterwards a lyric tale in verse.

Bandores, *see* Pandora.

Burden (or Burthen), indicates the chorus, which was probably danced as well as sung. "Bourdon" (French for "drone") meant drone-bass, and bass. Chaucer uses it in the latter sense—"This sompnour bare to him a stiff burdoun."

Cantabanqui (Italian), Ballad-singers, singers on benches.

Carping, Reciting.

Chants Royaux. Pasquier describes the Chant Royal, or King's note, as "a song in honour of God, the Holy Virgin, or any other argument of dignity."

Cittern, or **Cithren,** like an old English guitar, with four double strings of wire. The gittern (or giterne) was somewhat similar, but strung with gut instead of wire. Both instruments, together with the lute and virginals, were common furniture of the barbers' shops of the sixteenth and seventeenth centuries.

Clarion, a small shrill trumpet.

Appendix B

Complaints, a short expostulatory poem of French origin, with seven-verse stanzas and few rhymes, with a *l'Envoy*. Chaucer has a "complaint" to his purse.

Coranto (Courante, Corrente), from *courir*, to run. A dance of French origin. The French and Italian dances of this name are both quick and in triple time. The Italian is usually in running passages, almost *moto perpetuo;* while the French is in 3-2 time, with more dignity and greater variety of rhythm.

Crwth (*i.e.*, Crooth), Crouth, or Crowd, the oldest stringed instrument played with a bow. In its oldest form there are but three strings, later forms have six. Known in the early seventh century, and in use in Wales at the beginning of the eighteenth century.

Ditees, Ditty (Lat. Dictum), a little poem for singing; a lay, a song of small and light design.

Drumslades, drummers.

Epithalmies, marriage songs.

Galliard (or Romanesca), a dance—in 3-4 and sometimes 4-4 time—of Roman origin. Every Pavan (a grave dance) had its Galliard (a lighter air made out of the former).

Harpe. This most ancient instrument was discovered by Bruce painted in fresco on the tomb of Rameses III., who reigned about 1250 B.C. The Anglo-Saxon harp was of triangular shape, with twelve strings; it was commonly used to accompany singing.

Lais (or Lays). The Breton Lays were originally in the Armorican tongue, being translated by a French poetess named Marie, about the middle of the thirteenth century.

Lute (Spanish "Laud," Arabic "Lud") is of oriental origin, and became westernized at the time of the Crusades. In shape it is modelled like the guitar, though the back of the former is pear-shaped, the latter flat. The early lutes had few strings, and even in Mace's time (1676) they varied from ten to twenty-four. The same writer's theorbo—a class of bass lute—had twenty-six. Matheson opined that a lutenist of eighty years must have spent sixty in "tuning," and that the cost of a horse or a lute was about the same in Paris.

Pandora, a large cither.

Pavan (Pavin, or Pavane), a solemn dance, of Spanish or Italian invention, in duple time, of four to eight measures. The dress suggested Pavo, a peacock. Masquerades, weddings, and religious ceremonies employed the dance, which originally was sung.

Psaltery (sautry in old English), a dulcimer played either with the fingers or with a plectrum. Chaucer chooses the sautry to accompany the angelus (see p. 232). The strings were trebled and sometimes quadrupled, in the manner of a pianoforte.

Quinible, an extemporized descant, or treble.

Rebec (see Ribible).

Regals indicate a small portable organ. Queen Elizabeth maintained an organ-maker at twenty pounds a year, and a "rigall-maker" at ten pounds per annum. The Tuner of the Regals, in the Chapel Royal, is now the organ-builder.

Ribible (rebec or fiddle). Diminutive form of Rebibe or Rebec, a small three-stringed fiddle.

Rote (Rota or Rotta), a kind of psaltery, dulcimer, or primitve zither with seven strings, in solid wooden frame. Used in church music during the middle ages.

Roundils (Roundel or Roundelay). An old form of poetical composition comprising thirteen verses, of which eight are in one rhyme and five in another. A rural dance.

Sackbut (or Sagbut), a bass trumpet or trombone.

Shalm (Chalumeau), a reed forming a shepherd's pipe. Also known as Bumbard (or Bombard). Chaucer uses the latter form.

Stillpipes, probably like Doucettes, a small soft pipe, in contrast to the "loud shallmys" (Lydgate).

Symphonie (or symphonia) seems to indicate a kind of bass drum, though the *tympanum* was employed concurrently.

Syrinx, Pan-pipes or mouth organ, also Pandean pipes, from the myth that they were the invention of the god Pan.

Tabor, or little drum, mentioned by Mersennus as commonly used in conjunction with a three-holed flute or pipe.

Tabret, diminutive form of tabor (*q.v.*).

Timbrel, a tambourine used for accompanying dancing and singing.

Viele (a softened form of fiddle, fithele, fiele, viele). It has been remarked that the Anglo-Saxon fithele survived the Norman

Conquest at least a century and a half. The French vielle, originally the large primitive violin of the troubadours, now indicates our English hurdy-gurdy (or organistrum).

Villanelle. A song in parts, used for dancing.

Viol, an early form of violin, with five or six strings, regulated by frets and played with a bow.

Virginals, a small oblong spinet, called Virginal possibly from being much used by the nuns and young girls. The compass was generally thirty-eight notes, with keys like the pianoforte. The strings were plucked, not struck as in the latter instrument.

Virlayes, an ancient French poetical form comprising short verses of seven or eight syllables, and in only two rhymes. Chaucer's "Alone Walking" is in this form.

Yeddings. From the Saxon Geddian to sing—a merry song.

Appendix C.

Chronological Table.

1013 B.C. Approximate date of foundation of Druids' orders in Britain.
753 B.C. Pytheas visited England.
54 and 55 B.C. Cæsar invades England.
194–211 A.D. St. Cæcilia (martyr) invented the organ.
397 Date of St. Ambrose's death.
449 Hengist and Horsa.
510 Boethius.
596 St. Augustine.
652 Anglo-Saxon youths study in France.
735 The Venerable Bede.
849–901 Alfred the Great.
923 The clergy turn minstrels.
925 St. Dunstan.
980 Cornish Carol (*q.v.*).
990 Guido d'Arezzo.
1036 Canute.
1066 Taillefer at Hastings.
1102 Minstrels found a priory, in Henry I.'s reign.
Beginning of 12th century. Rise of Provençal School.
1193 Richard I. and Blondel.
1212 Lacy and the Chester Minstrels.
1220 Court of Love.
1250 Sumer is icumen in. English language establishing itself.
1271 Minstrel Crusade.
1338 King of Minstrels.
1387 John of Gaunt's Minstrels' Court at Tutbury.
1403 Welsh bards prohibited.
1412 Caxton.
1415 Agincourt.

Appendix C

1416 Minstrels rewarded at Pentecost.

1456 Boys "impressed as minstrels" for Henry VI.'s chapel.

1469 Charter granted to minstrels by Edward IV.

1473 Music-printing.

1495 Date of Higden's "Polychronicon" containing first music printed in England.

1520 Minstrels' charter renewed by Henry VIII.

1539 Suppression of monasteries.

1597 Wanderings of minstrels cut short by Queen Elizabeth.

1636 Charles I. renewed the Musicians' Charter.

1637 Opera coming into vogue.

1650 Violins supersede viols, etc.

1653 Playford's "Select Ayres" issued.

1672 Macbeth music by M. Lock.

1675 Overture invented.

1676–95 Purcell's operas.

1683 Sonatas making their appearance.

1700 and onwards.—The Classical period.

1740 Arne's "Rule Britannia" produced.

1758 Symphonies appearing.

1759 Boyce's "Hearts of Oak" composed.

1760 English Glee period.

1781 Pianofortes coming into general use.

1800 Schubert's German *Lieder* bequest.

1809–47 Mendelssohn's influence on melody.

1810–56 Schumann's vocal individuality and bearing.

1813–1883 Wagner's influence on recitative and melody.

1814–1901 Verdi's melodic extravagance.

1900 Feeble sentiment and tune-unctuousness of songs.

Index.

Index

Index

Index

PRINTED BY THE WALTER SCOTT PUBLISHING CO., LTD., FELLING-ON-TYNE.